The Revolting French, 1787

This book investigates the impact of revolution on the French from the Revolution of 1789 to its centenary in 1889. It explores specific and linking factors in the main revolts and how historians have differed in their explanations.

Revolution has been explained in a multitude of ways from economic, social and philosophic, to a range of identities including religion, race and gender, contingency, emotions, and most recently global factors. The nineteenth-century French state was threatened by an unprecedented number of revolts. What impact did the 1789 Revolution have on nineteenth-century events? Why were there so many revolutions at the time? Were there common factors? Were non-revolutionary issues as significant or more significant in provoking change? Why was it that insurrection was rarer in the second half of the century when revolutionary rhetoric was more prolific? The book weighs political and philosophical differences, lack of trust and willingness to compromise, economic, social and cultural issues, urban geography, archaeology and contingency. The final section presents some contemporary explanations, written and visual.

This book will be essential reading for A-level and undergraduate historians of France and Europe and will be of interest to general readers keen to understand the impact of revolutions in the modern world.

Pamela Pilbeam is Professor Emeritus at Royal Holloway, University of London (1965–2012). Past roles include President of the Society for the Study of French History, a Leverhulme Emeritus Fellow, a Fulbright Fellow, and Visiting Professor at the Universities of Toronto, York, Ontario and British Columbia.

Introduction to the series

Series Editors

Mark Stoyle: mjs@soton.ac.uk
Gordon Martel: Gordon.Martel@unbc.ca

Each book in the Seminar Studies series provides a concise and reliable introduction to a wide range of complex historical events and debates, covering topics in British, European, US and world history from the medieval period to present day. Written by acknowledged experts and including supporting material such as extracts from historical documents, chronologies, glossaries, guides to key figures and further reading suggestions, Seminar Studies titles are essential reading for students of history.

Almost half a century after its launch, the series continues to introduce students to the problems involved in explaining the past, giving them the opportunity to grapple with historical documents and encouraging them to reach their own conclusions.

The Revolting French, 1787–1889
Pamela Pilbeam

For more information about this series, please visit: www.routledge.com/Routledge-Handbooks-in-Religion/book-series

The Revolting French, 1787–1889

Pamela Pilbeam

LONDON AND NEW YORK

Designed cover image: *A Barricade in 1830*, 1834 (gouache on paper), Manguin, P. (1815–1869)/Musee de la Ville de Paris, Musee Carnavalet, Paris, France/Bridgeman Images.

First published 2024
by Routledge
4 Park Square, Milton Park, Abingdon, Oxon OX14 4RN

and by Routledge
605 Third Avenue, New York, NY 10158

Routledge is an imprint of the Taylor & Francis Group, an informa business

British Library Cataloguing-in-Publication Data
A catalogue record for this book is available from the British Library

ISBN: 978-0-415-73441-7 (hbk)
ISBN: 978-1-408-20491-7 (pbk)
ISBN: 978-1-003-46059-6 (ebk)

DOI: 10.4324/9781003460596

Typeset in Sabon
by Apex CoVantage, LLC

To my daughter, Ashka, for her wise advice.

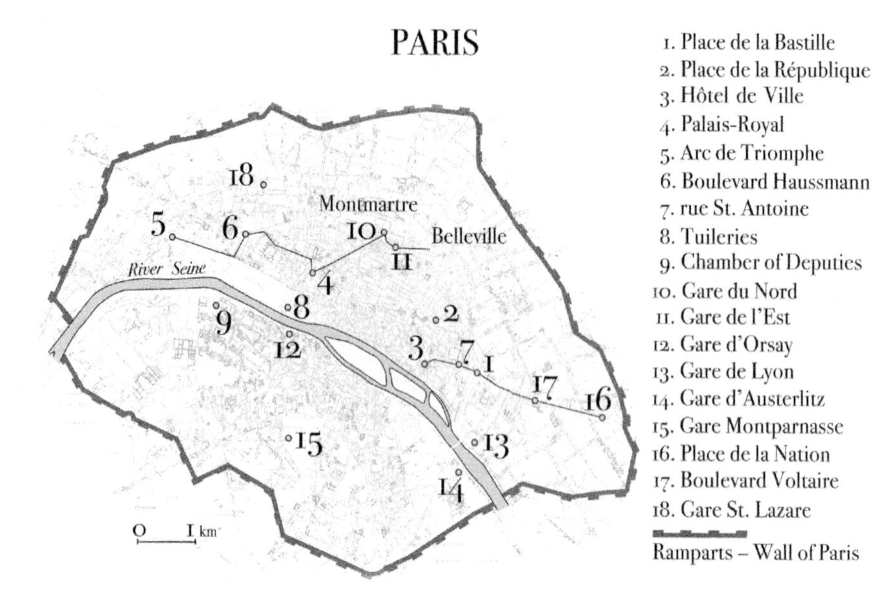

Frontispiece: Map of Paris.

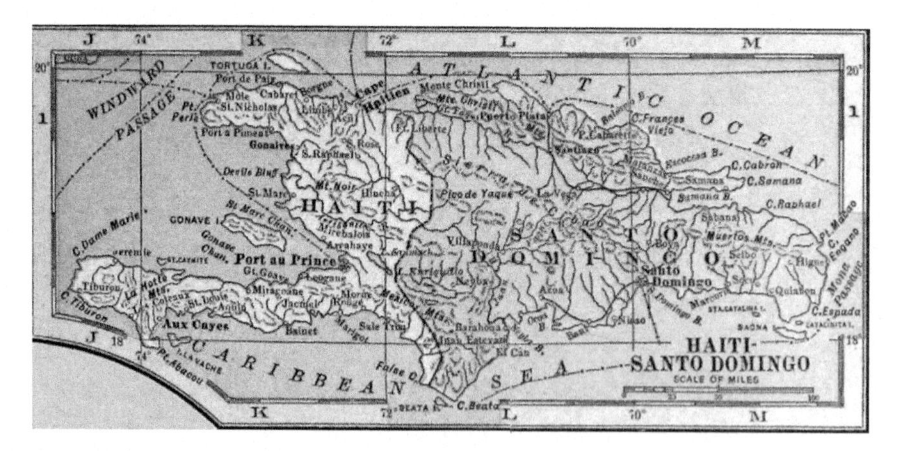

Frontispiece: Haiti 1844.

Contents

Figures

Chronology

1789	MAR.	Elections to Estates-General commence
	MAY	Estates-General meets at Versailles
	JUNE	Creation of National Assembly
		Royal session fails and all deputies join National Assembly
	JULY	Necker dismissed and Bastille is stormed on 14 July
		Municipal revolution in towns; Great Fear in countryside
	AUG.	Abolition of feudalism and privilege
		Declaration of the Rights of Man and the Citizen
	OCT.	Louis XVI and Assembly move to Paris following people's march to Versailles
	NOV.	Church property nationalised
	DEC.	Creation of departments
1790	MAY	Sections of Paris created
	JUNE	Titles of nobility abolished
	JULY	Civil Constitution of the Clergy passed by Assembly
		Feast of the Federation celebrated on 14 July
	NOV.	Oath to Civil Constitution imposed on the clergy
1791	MAR.	Dissolution of artisan guilds, later endorsed by Le Chapelier Law
	JUNE	King's attempted escape: the flight to Varennes
	JULY	Demonstration for Republic on Champs de Mars in Paris
	AUG.	Slave rebellion breaks out in Saint-Domingue
	SEPT.	Gouges, *The Declaration of the Rights of Woman*
		Inhabitants of Avignon and Comtat vote to join the French state
		Louis XVI accepts Constitution (of 1791); National Assembly dissolves
	OCT.	New Legislative Assembly convenes
	NOV.	Decrees against *émigrés* and refractory priests (vetoed by the King)
1792	APR.	Declaration of war against Austria
	JUNE	Prussia declares war on France

	JULY	Decree of 'Country in Danger' in response to threat of invasion
	AUG.	Paris sections demand dethronement of King Tuileries palace stormed; King overthrown
	SEPT.	Fall of Verdun produces panic September massacres in Paris Elections for a fresh assembly, the National Convention Victory at Valmy reduces military pressure Convention meets and proclaims Republic
	DEC.	Trial of the King begins in Convention
1793	JAN.	Condemnation and execution of Louis XVI
	FEB.	War declared on Britain and Dutch Republic Decree conscripting 300,000 men
	MAR.	War declared on Spain Revolutionary Tribunal established Revolt breaks out in the Vendée
	APR.	Creation of Committee of Public Safety
	MAY	Revolts in Marseille and Lyon Anti-Girondin uprising begins in Paris
	JUNE	Girondins purged from Convention 'Federalist' revolt spreads to Bordeaux New Constitution (of 1793) accepted by Convention
	JULY	Robespierre joins Committee of Public Safety Final abolition of feudal dues
	AUG.	Decree of *levée en masse* Rebel Toulon surrenders to the British fleet
	SEPT.	Law of Suspects introduced 'Maximum' on prices decreed
	OCT.	Girondins sent for trial Republican calendar introduced: beginning of Year II Government will be 'revolutionary until the return of peace'; new Constitution, accepted by popular vote, is suspended due to crisis
	DEC.	Law on Revolutionary Government Vendéans defeated and Toulon recaptured
1794	FEB.	Abolition of slavery
	APR.	Danton executed
	JUNE	Festival of Supreme Being at Paris Executions accelerate with Law of Prairial
	JULY	Fall and execution of Robespierre
	AUG.	Law of Prairial repealed; revolutionary government reorganised
	NOV.	Jacobin Club of Paris closed
	DEC.	Surviving Girondins reinstated to Convention and 'Maximum' is abolished

1798	FEB.	Pope overthrown: Roman Republic proclaimed
	MAR.	Parliamentary elections return left-wing deputies
	MAY	Coup d'état of Floréal: left-wingers excluded from parliament
		Bonaparte sets out for Egypt
	AUG.	French fleet destroyed in battle of the Nile
1799	OCT.	Bonaparte returns from Egypt
	NOV.	Coup d'état of Brumaire: Directory replaced by a Provisional Consulate
	DEC.	New Constitution (Year VIII) implemented and put to popular vote; Bonaparte becomes First Consul
1801	FEB.	Treaty of Lunéville between France and Austria
	MAR.	Deposition and murder of Paul I of Russia
		Alexander I Emperor of Russia
		Internal reforms in Russia
	JULY	Napoleon signs Concordat with Papacy
1802	MAR.	Peace of Amiens between France and Britain
	MAY	Napoleon Consul for life
1803		Abolition of territorial sovereignty of ecclesiastical princes in Holy Roman Empire
1804	MAR.	Civil Code
	MAY	Empire proclaimed
	AUG.	Proclamation of Austrian Empire
	DEC.	Napoleon crowned
1806	JULY	Confederation of Rhine formed by Napoleon
	AUG.	Abolition of Holy Roman Empire (founded AD 800)
	OCT.	Battle of Jena
1807		Treaty of Tilsit
		Baron Stein begins reform programme in Prussia
		Speranski reforms in Russia
1808	DEC.	Invasion of Spain
1809		Count Metternich Austrian foreign minister
1812		Invasion of Russia
1813		Wars of 'Liberation' against Napoleon
	OCT.	Battle of Leipzig, 'of the Nations'
1814	APR.	Napoleon abdicates; Restoration of Louis XVIII
	MAY	Treaty of Paris between France and allied powers
	JUNE	Constitutional Charter issued
	SEPT.	Congress of Vienna opens
1815	MAR.	Napoleon returns from Elba for the 'Hundred Days'
	JUNE	Battle of Waterloo. Napoleon's second abdication follows defeat
		Second Restoration and White Terror
	AUG.	Ultra-royalist *Chambre Introuvable* elected
	NOV.	Second Treaty of Paris reduces France to frontiers of 1790

1816		Dissolution of *Chambre Introuvable* and fresh Legislative elections
1820		Murder of Duc de Berry
		Law of Double Vote
1821		Death of Napoleon on Saint Helena
		Villèle government
1822		Four Sergeants of La Rochelle conspiracy
1823		French invasion of Spain to restore Bourbon monarchy
1824		Ultra-royalist election victory
		Death of Louis XVIII; accession of Charles X
1825		Sacrilege law and indemnification of *émigrés*
		Coronation of Charles X at Reims
1827		National Guard dissolved
		Passage of Forest Code
		Legislative elections
1828		Resignation of Villèle; Martignac forms government
1829		Balzac begins publishing *The Human Comedy*
		Polignac becomes chief minister of ultra-royalist government
1830	JUNE	Legislative elections produce huge Liberal gains
		Conquest of Algiers; beginning of French Empire in North Africa
	JULY	Four Ordinances; 'Three Glorious Days' of revolution in Paris
	AUG.	Charles X abdicates; Louis-Philippe becomes 'King of the French People'
	SEPT.	Riots in provinces
		Stendhal, *Scarlet and Black*
		Delacroix, *Liberty Leading the People*
1831		Casimir Périer becomes chief minister
		Laws on election of municipal councils and National Guard
		Legislative elections with wider franchise
		Revolt in Lyon
1832		Cholera outbreak in Paris
		Popular unrest at funeral of General Lamarque
1833		Guizot's Education Law
1834		Law against Associations
		Further revolt in Lyon
		Rue Transnonain massacre follows uprising in Paris
1835		Fieschi bomb plot to assassinate Louis-Philippe
		Press Laws restrict publications
1836		Louis-Napoleon attempts to raise the garrison in Strasbourg
1839		Society of Seasons' uprising, led by Blanqui
		Louis Blanc, *The Organisation of Work*
		Cabet, *Voyage in Icaria*
		Louis-Napoleon, *Napoleonic Ideas*

1840		Napoleon's body is returned from Saint Helena and interred at Les Invalides in Paris
		Louis-Napoleon tries to raise a rebellion at Boulogne
		Guizot forms a government
		Proudhon, *What Is Property?*
1842		Tahiti becomes a French protectorate
1843		France annexes Dahomey and the Ivory Coast
1846		Legislative Elections result in victory for Guizot
		Onset of economic crisis
1847		Banquet Campaign commences, aimed at franchise reform
1848	FEB.	Revolution in Paris. Guizot resigns
		Louis-Philippe abdicates
		Second Republic proclaimed
		Universal suffrage decreed
	MAR.	Radical demonstration in Paris
	APR.	Election of Constituent Assembly, with conservative majority
	JUNE	Popular uprising in Paris is crushed. General Cavaignac becomes head of government
	NOV.	Constitution of Second Republic
	DEC.	Election of Louis-Napoleon as President
1849		Elections to Legislative Assembly; good showing by left-wing democ-socs
		Unrest in Paris and Lyon
		French army restores papal power in Rome
1850		Falloux Law on Education, gives Catholics right to open schools
		Left-wing by-election victories
		Suffrage restrictions introduced briefly
1851		Coup d'état establishes dictatorship for Louis-Napoleon
		Republican insurrection in south and centre of France
		Plebiscite, approves coup
1852		Constitution creating Second Empire accepted in a plebiscite
		Legislative Elections return only three republicans
1853		Haussmann becomes Prefect of the Seine
1854		Outbreak of Crimean War against Russia
1856		Peace of Paris successfully concludes Crimean campaign
		Tocqueville, *The Old Régime and the French Revolution*
1857		Conquest of Algeria completed
1858		Bernadette Soubirous experiences a vision of the Virgin Mary at Lourdes
1859		France and Piedmont declare war on Austria
		French occupy Saigon
1860		Treaty of Turin cedes Nice and Savoy to France
		Constitutional reforms introduced

1862		Hugo, *Les Misérables*
1864		Industrial Relations law recognises right to strike
		French protectorate established over Cambodia
1867		Right to question ministers granted to Legislative Body
		World fair in Paris
1868		Greater freedom of press and legalisation of public meetings
1869		Flaubert, *Sentimental Education*
		Election of 30 republicans; Ollivier becomes head of government
		Opening of Suez Canal, French engineer de Lesseps
1870	MAY	Plebiscite on further constitutional reform, to create so-called 'Liberal Empire'
	JULY	Outbreak of Franco-Prussian war
	AUG.	Invasion of France; army besieged at Metz
	SEPT.	Louis-Napoleon surrenders at Sedan
		Republic declared at Paris: Government of National Defence established
	OCT.	Paris besieged and government withdraws to Tours
1871	JAN.	Parisians fail to lift siege; armistice signed with Prussians
	FEB.	Election of National Assembly; Monarchist majority elects Thiers as head of government
	MAR.	Peace of Frankfurt: France cedes Alsace-Lorraine to German Empire
		Uprising in Paris leads to proclamation of Paris Commune
		Revolts in provincial towns, including Lyon, Marseille and Toulouse
	MAY	Bloody Week and end of Commune
	AUG.	Thiers confirmed as head of state

Who's Who

Babeuf, Graccus Feudal lawyer before 1789; 1796, organised Conspiracy of Equals, executed.

Danton, Georges Lawyer, Cordelier Club, in 10 August 1792 Paris rising; Minister of Justice; from 1792 Montagnard deputy in Convention. Executed April 1794.

Barrot, Odilon Liberal lawyer, opponent of Guizot in Banquet Campaign, 1847.

Blanc, Louis Socialist journalist before 1848, ran Luxembourg Commission 1848, exiled to Britain, returned to France 1871.

Blanqui, Louis-Auguste Socialist revolutionary from 1830, spent half his life in jail.

Cabet, Étienne Republican in Chamber of Deputies, 1831–1834, journalist, socialist, exiled to Britain 1835, 1848 supported Republic, ran socialist community in the USA.

Considérant, Victor Fourierist journalist, supported Republic 1848.

Deroin, Jeanne Saint-Simonian, teacher, wrote for *Voix du Peuple* 1848, ran associations 1848, demanded votes for women, exiled to Britain 1849.

Enfantin, Prosper Self-declared leader of Saint-Simonians 1832, supported Algerian colonisation.

Fouché, Joseph Oratorian before 1789, elected to Convention 1792, deputy sent on missions; Napoleon's Minister of Police.

Fourier, Charles Socialist writer, female equality.

Guizot, François University professor and historian 1820s, dismissed, liberal leader in Chamber of Deputies, Minister of Education 1833, frequently minister, chief minister 1842–48, opposed franchise extension.

Lafayette, Marquis de Liberal noble, fought for Americans in War of Independence; commander of National Guard 1789; defected to Austrians August 1792; commander National Guard, July 1831–1832.

Ledru-Rollin, A.A. Left-wing journalist before 1848, editor of *La Réforme*, Minister of Interior after February Revolution, 1848.

Louis-Philippe, duc d'Orléans Cousin of Charles X, King of the French People, August 1830 – February 1848. Exiled in England.

Marat, Jean-Paul Doctor, editor extreme *Ami du Peuple*, involved in September Massacres, elected to Convention, assassinated July 1793.

Périer, Casimir Louis-Philippe's banker, chief minister March 1831, died of cholera 1832.

Proudhon, P.J. Socialist journalist in July Monarchy. Supported 1848 revolution, elected to Constituent Assembly, wanted *Bank of the People*.

Robespierre, Maximilien Lawyer, Montagnard elected to Convention, leader in Committee of Public Safety, arrested 27 July 1794, executed next day.

Saint-Just, Antoine, Marquis de elected to Convention, Committee of Public Safety, executed 28 July 1794.

Thiers, Adolphe 1820s historian, liberal journalist, Chamber of Deputies and minister July Monarchy, supported Louis-Napoleon for presidency 1848, elected to National Assembly February 1871, head of state.

Tocqueville, Alexis de 1830s liberal, wrote *Democracy in America*, critic of Guizot, supported Algerian colonisation, hostile to June Days, 1848.

Ultras, ultra-royalists Supporters of Charles X and clerical right 1820s.

1 Legacy of 1789

'When the government violates the rights of the people, insurrection is for the people and for each portion of the people the most sacred of rights and the most indispensable of duties'. The right of rebellion was a clause in the Jacobin constitution of 1793. The French still take to the streets at the drop of a hat in quarrels with the government. Are the French revolutionary? If so, why? Do they still remember 1789? Are they more revolutionary than other nations, and what impact have French ideas on revolution had on the rest of the world?

The nineteenth-century French state was threatened by an unprecedented number of revolts. What impact did the 1789 Revolution have on nineteenth century events? Why were there so many revolutions in the nineteenth century? Were there common factors? We will weigh political and philosophical differences, lack of trust and willingness to compromise, economic, social, cultural issues, urban geography, archaeology and contingency. Did the revolts change anything? If so, what? Were non-revolutionary issues as significant or more significant in provoking change? Why was it that insurrection was rarer in the second half of the century when revolutionary rhetoric was more prolific? Why have the views of historians differed over time? Why are past French revolutions remembered with so much passion when the British prefer to forget executing Charles I and dismissing James II?

Today revolution is used vaguely and can imply little more than some sort of change. It may describe political upheaval in the Middle East or a new song. In the nineteenth century it was invoked in contradictory senses, sometimes indicating a return to a starting point, sometimes a dramatic launch into the unknown. If a revolution failed the events might be referred to as an insurrection, a revolt, a riot, a rising, an episode of popular effervescence, a conspiracy, or a criminal event, depending on which side of the barricades the commentators visualised themselves to be. Historians have added further layers of imprecision by using the word 'revolution' to describe all manner of change, economic, social, cultural and political, and most recently civil war or 'trauma' to describe unrest.

There were three strands to nineteenth-century concepts of revolution, ranging from the vigorous rejection of right-wingers, to the tempered

DOI: 10.4324/9781003460596-1

acceptance of the moderate conservative/liberal *juste milieu* and the enthusiasm of some radicals. Thinkers and politicians on the extreme right, including ultra-royalists like Joseph de Maistre in 1796, believed that revolutions were part of social degeneration and collapse, a threat to the traditional authority of monarch, church and landed titled elites. For those on the right 1789 was the result of moral deterioration. Materialism, disregard of spiritual authority and community values underlay right-wing explanations of the revolution in the 1790s and in subsequent decades. De Maistre, indeed, was convinced that Satan had a role in bringing about the Revolution. The right did not see revolutions as mere accidents, but as manifestations of an Anti-Christ. More moderate liberal contemporaries, who gained power in the 1790s and held it in subsequent upheavals, did not look for long-term causes. For them revolution was the work of mankind (generally written up as the work of man, rather than the work of women), the result of error by political leaders, accident or ill-judged government policy. They were inclined to deplore the violence of revolution, but to appreciate its potential to rationalise, secularise and centralise the state, and, of course, maintain themselves, its rightful inheritors, at the helm. Going further left, republicans had the most positive view of revolution, anticipating democratic and egalitarian consequences but could not agree amongst themselves on what sort of republic they wanted or whether revolution was needed to achieve it.

In assessing the impact of the revolutionary years in this first chapter (which for the purposes of this book, we are defining to fall within the time span 1787 to 1814, though as you will have seen from the introductory words, revolutions and revolutionary times do not fold themselves neatly into precise chronological boxes), we will consider the journey from absolute kingdom to a modern nation state; political institutions and politics; social change; religion; individual rights from subject to citizen; and colonial and European empires.

The Journey from Absolute Kingdom to a Modern Centralised Nation State

Louis XVI (1754–1793), King of France from 1774, was absolute hereditary ruler, but a combination of personal, political, economic and financial problems forced him to share power which led to revolution in 1789. Louis was a passionate admirer of his great grandfather, Louis XIV, the 'Sun' King, who had emasculated his rebellious nobles, forcing them to spend their lives as powerless sycophantic admirers of their King at Versailles. Louis XVI was a well-meaning, indecisive man who shut himself in Versailles and knew nothing of his people. In 1770 he married Marie-Antoinette, daughter of the Holy Roman Emperor. He was unable to consummate his marriage until after surgery. His wife's exploration of other male and female partners was much publicised, as was her financial extravagance. The reputation of the royal family declined. Meanwhile enlightened writers, *philosophes*, including

Voltaire, Montesquieu and Rousseau, were debating how to improve government and were being listened to widely throughout Europe, by rulers and royal ministers as well as by other reformers. They wanted government to become more rational and efficient, but not necessarily representative. The *philosophes* based their thinking on contemporary developments in science in which they were often involved. They published an encyclopaedia to set out their ideas. They were anti-clerical, very critical of the political and social power of the Catholic Church (Cobban, 1960). The King's absolute power was also being questioned by the 13 high courts of appeal, the *parlements*, composed of senior *robe* nobles (they bought their noble titles), which had the right to register royal decrees. Since the mid-century they had claimed that they had the right of remonstrance, to question royal decrees, because no other body represented the French nation. They had repeated battles with royal ministers and began to work in conjunction with surviving provincial estates, such as Brittany. In 1771 Turgot, Louis XV's reforming minster, exiled the Paris *parlement*, but it was recalled on the accession of Louis XVI. The King lacked the power to tax his wealthiest subjects, the first estate, the clergy, and the second, the nobles. His fiscal problems had been exacerbated by France's involvement in repeated disastrous wars, most recently the American War of Independence from Britain. France helped the Americans to become an independent republic in 1773, but lost their main Canadian colony, Quebec. A nation-wide economic crisis developed following harvest failures in 1776. Government debt soared. By 1788 the accumulated debt was equal to eight year's income (Jones, 2003, 9). In 1787 an appeal for funds to an Assembly of Notables of the first two estates failed. The Paris *parlement* demanded the calling of the Estates-General, an assembly elected by all three estates, which had not met since 1614. Reformers were inclined to remember that the Americans had fought the British (with their help) with the slogan 'no taxation without representation'.

What Was Agreed by Revolutionaries 1789–1791

The Estates-General met in May 1789, complete with extensive lists (cahiers) of what electors expected them to reform. The assembly was composed of equal numbers of clergy, nobles and everyone else, in effect well-off non-nobles (the third estate). The third insisted on doubling its numbers to equal the other two and that the three estates should meet as one body. The King and his Chief Minister, the Swiss Protestant, Necker, expected the Assembly to agree to pay necessary taxes and go home. The third estate and a small number of nobles and clergy hoped to follow the precepts of the enlightened writers and create a constitutional, decentralised monarchy in which the rule of reason would replace traditional privilege – the Enlightenment writ small, but writ at least, on the political sphere. The reformers wanted a written constitution, a regularly elected national assembly which would vote on taxes and legislation, the introduction of rational uniform state institutions, an end to inherited privilege, including the abolition of the relics of feudal rights. These reformers began with demands that, looking back, were modest, though viewed from the King's perspective seemed dangerous indeed. Their first demand was that the newly elected Estates-General become a constituent Assembly.

On 14 July a revolutionary crowd sacked the Bastille fortress, in which individuals had been imprisoned by royal authority on the request of family members. The wrecking of the royal fortress became a key event of 1789, the first occasion determined by a violent crowd. During the spring and summer of 1789 popular insurrection in urban and rural France escalated, 'the Great Fear'. It was rumoured that 'brigands' were scouring the countryside. In reality the demonstrators were poorer country people, fearful of increasing food prices and shortages and keen to put pressure on the new Assembly to issue reforms to help them. The poor were suffering after several years of harvest failure, economic disaster and demands that they pay increasing amounts in feudal dues to their overlords. The right to collect feudal dues had become part of a market economy, separated from land ownership and exploited by wealthy urban non-nobles. The rural poor expected that these feudal dues would be abolished by the new Assembly. To put pressure on the Assembly they destroyed feudal and fiscal documents and set fire to chateaux. At first many of the members of the National Assembly were idealistic and dreamt of the triumph of liberty and equality, only for men of property of course. But they were far from comfortable as polite debate gave way to violence. At the beginning of August, the Assembly, now rebadged as a Constituent Assembly, published a well-intentioned Declaration of the Rights of Man and of the Citizen (Document 3), in part inspired by the 1776 American declaration of independence from British rule (Document 2).

Traditional privilege was abolished. Feudal levies and the tithe (one tenth of income paid directly to the Church) were to go, but owners were to be compensated by those who had paid the levies. The first problem the Assembly had to deal with was fiscal. A new 16% direct tax on land came into play in 1791. In the meantime the Assembly set a three year 'patriotic contribution' to be paid by all citizens, with an extra back-dated demand on the former privileged orders, nobles and clerics. The detested indirect taxes, particularly the salt tax, were abolished. The government decided that venal officer-holders had to be compensated and issued *assignats*, paper money, to cover the cost. Church property and land (c. 10% of France) and land confiscated from the heads of noble families who decided to emigrate was declared national land. Its sale, it was hoped, would fill the large fiscal gap.

The abolition of privilege meant a new administrative order was vital. The nine provinces through which France had been governed by royal appointed *intendants*, some of which partially ran their own affairs in provincial assemblies dominated by nobles, were replaced by 83 departments, each with sub-departments and communes. In December 1789 the Assembly decided to make all public offices in these elective. Judicial reform followed. The revolutionaries set up a unified legal system to replace a variety of earlier jurisdictions. They created a completely new office of justice of the peace to replace basic seigneurial jurisdiction, with courts in each district and an appeal court in each departmental capital. Laws were to be inscribed in written codes. The revolutionaries took over a decade to agree on the details of the codes. Next came laws restructuring the Church. In this anti-clerical legislation the revolutionaries showed their true colours as partisans of the Enlightenment. Their policy towards the Church stimulated a counter-revolution, the first serious opposition to the Revolution. A Civil Constitution of the Clergy was published by the Assembly in July 1790. Bishoprics were reduced from 136 to one in each department. The monastic orders and cathedral chapters were closed. Clergy were no longer allowed to hold more than one benefice and had to live in it. All the clergy, including bishops, were to be elected by their parishioners. The first anniversary of the Revolution was celebrated with a Festival of the Federation, 14 July 1790 (Jones, 2003, 29–37).

Thoroughly indoctrinated in enlightened ideas, revolutionaries, including leading scientists like Condorcet, eagerly built on earlier royal attempts to encourage higher education with outstanding results. In June 1793 the *Jardin du Roi* was converted into the Museum of Natural History. In September 1794 a college devoted to artisan crafts was established, the *Conservatoire des arts et metiers*. In October 1794 a college for teaching training, the *Ecole normale*, was opened. In October 1795 the former royal college *Ponts et Chaussées* which trained high-level army engineers was renamed the *École Polytechnique*. In October 1795 the *Institut National des Sciences et Arts*, a government-funded research institute, took over from the royal academies. From 1808 the Grand Master of the University in Paris was appointed by Napoleon. Primary education remained in the hands of the Church. In 1802 central-government-administered *lycées*, the successors to colleges, provided elite secondary education to a small minority of boys, with scholarships, half for sons of officials or army officers.

Reformers argued about the details of their projects and especially how to complete the written codes of law throughout the 1790s. What we have discussed so far was basically agreed and implemented, except for religious policy which we will examine later.

What Was Not Agreed by Revolutionaries: Political Institutions and Politics

A consensus was achieved in two novel political concepts: that a written constitution and elections to national assemblies were indispensable to political organisation. But there was no agreement on what was to be included in a constitution or who should qualify as electors. Electors were chosen by a variety of franchises ranging from an electorate of c. 60,000, based on the payment of three days' labour in direct taxes, which disqualified 39% of adult males (Legislative Assembly, September 1791), to indirect universal male suffrage, when all male citizens chose about 50,000 voters (Convention 1792). In 1799 Napoleon introduced the concept of a plebiscite, in which all adult males voted on questions posed by the central government. Written constitutions and some sort of voting for national assemblies remained in place through the nineteenth century but in all other respects the political legacy of the revolutionary years was divisive and sometimes brutally violent. Undoubtedly the memory contributed substantially to provoking repeated revolution in the following century. The French experimented with a constitutional monarchy (September 1791 to June 1792) which was terminated after the King's abortive attempt to flee the country on 20 June 1792 when the war was going badly. A counter-revolution was growing among exiles in the Holy Roman Empire. Many aristocratic army officers fled the country to join the King's brothers along with some members of the first and second estate. The country was threatened by invasion from the armies of the Holy Roman Empire and Prussia, which included French *émigrés*, and on the night of 9–10 August 1792 the 48 Sections in Paris who now helped govern the capital rose in rebellion against the municipality. In September rumours that opponents of revolution in Paris jails were about to launch a counter-revolution led to the summary trial and deaths of at least 1200, about a sixth of whom were non-juring priests. In October a new assembly, the Convention, was elected which tried the King and executed him in January 1793. Marie-Antoinette followed him to the guillotine in October 1793. The Convention was dominated first by the Girondins, then the Jacobins. There was not much difference between them. Both groups were bourgeois, though the Girondins were keener on war which they launched in April 1792. In the summer of 1793 they were replaced by Robespierre and the Jacobins. The subsequent mass killings of the Terror (1793–1794) were carried out in the name of republican virtue. (Sutherland, 2003; Document 4). The episode of the Terror did more than anything to make the memory of the republic detestable to the French in the nineteenth century (Greer, 1935). It used to be said 40,000 were summarily tried and executed or simply killed. It is now thought that the figure was far higher, perhaps 250,000. The Vendée suffered most. In the four departments south of the Loire up to one-third of the population was put to death. The main victims were ordinary folk: 6.5% clergy, 8% nobles, 31% workers, 28% peasants, the rest middle class. Two-thirds of the victims were workers or peasants, but proportionately more were nobles and clerics; 90% of the death sentences were carried out in 13 departments. In half of France there were fewer than 25 executions, none in six departments. To republicans the Vendéans were traitors in league with the British. There were not enough troops to fight or equipment to fight them. Most of the republican troops in the west were on the coast looking out for British invaders. Robespierre's leadership was crucial to the Terror. He became so ruthless and insistent on the need for a pure republic that no-one, even his close friends, felt safe. He was finally arrested in the Convention on a charge of dominating public opinion and guillotined the next day, having attempted suicide. Why did the

Terror happen? War going badly? Civil war? Economic disasters? Government not in control? Inevitable consequence of revolution? Robespierre and the Terror have been endlessly debated. Tackett explained the Terror as the build-up of institutional fears and violence, from fears of plots, of dearth and starvation in the summer of 1789 to the murder of suspects in the autumn of 1792 (Tackett, 2015). Colin Jones devoted an entire book to Robespierre's final day (2021).

The death of Robespierre was followed by prolonged disputes and the election of the Directory (1795–1799). The mechanism of the Terror was gradually unpicked with continuing executions and the law of the maximum was withdrawn. The economy worsened. In April 1795 assignats slumped to 10% of their original value, 1% by end of year. In 1797 two-thirds of the state debt was repudiated. The detested indirect taxes were brought back to try to raise more revenue. But the war began to go well and there was some success in containing the Vendéan rebellion. A new constitution was introduced with annual elections for the Legislative Council. France was run by an oligarchy, a five-man Directory elected by the Legislative Council. Between 1795 and 1799 the assembly seesawed between a majority of constitutional monarchists who hoped to appoint the young Louis XVII (he died in jail), then Louis XVI's brother, the *comte de* Provence, as Louis XVIII. The latter had been in self-imposed exile in Holyrood financed by the British government since 1789 and only wanted to return if the old regime system was restored. Neo-Jacobins clung to the other end of the political seesaw, but the memory of the Terror made their version of the republic unpalatable.

Consulate and Empire 1799–1814

Military triumphs juxtaposed with continuing political conflicts allowed the most successful and politically astute general, Bonaparte, to first take the role of First Consul in 1799, and in 1804, Emperor. Liberal political institutions, so desired by revolutionaries earlier, were eliminated. The Consulate was created by force, a coup, not by voting, on 9–10 Nov 1799 (18–19 Brumaire). Sieyès, an influential revolutionary theorist, planned the coup with Napoleon as the figurehead leader. He miscalculated. Lucien, Napoleon's brother, head of the Council of Five Hundred, helped Napoleon, a Corsican by birth and a mere 30 years of age, declare himself First Consul. Napoleon made a former regicide, Cambacérès, and a former royal official, Lebrun, his associates, which seemed a reasonable compromise.

Why was Napoleon able to take power? Undoubtedly military success and his judgment in choosing associates were significant. He was French but Corsican by origin and this might have counted against him. He was born in 1769, months after France bought Corsica. He came from a respected noble landowning family. His father, Charles, was a member of the Upper Council and represented Corsica in Versailles in 1778. Napoleon had seven brothers and sisters. His father died in 1785, leaving four children under ten.

Napoleon won a scholarship to the seminary in Aix, then college in Autun, and from 1779 to 1784 attended the Royal Military College Brienne for sons of nobles destined to the army. He passed 42nd out of 58 candidates and joined the French officer corps. He was a known republican, loyal to Corsica, hostile to the French 'corrupting our morals' and keen on some enlightened ideas. In 1789–1792 he was granted leave from the army and became involved in Corsican affairs supported by the Governor of Corsica. In 1793 with some difficulty because of his long absence, he returned to the French army as a captain. In 1794 he was briefly jailed because of his support for Robespierre. He turned to the revolutionary politician Barras. In 1795 he served in Italy and was promoted to general. The Italian offensive ended and Napoleon reluctantly moved to the Vendée where he became depressed and suicidal. He met and fell in love with Josephine, mistress of Barras and widow of a guillotined general, a lady past her best, but Napoleon hoped she'd get him promotion and in 1796 they wed. Napoleon conceived a plan to resume an attack in Italy, where he pursued decisive strategies and acquired most of the peninsula for France. The Directors were alarmed by his independent action. He stopped a second royalist attempt in Paris. Amid much pro-Napoleon publicity (he was a good self-publicist) the Directory feared a coup. In 1798 an attack on Britain was planned. Napoleon advised against it and proposed an expedition to Egypt to try to rebuild France's much reduced colonial empire. The Directors agreed, to get rid of him. Egypt was a failure and in 1799 the war also went badly in Italy and Belgium. Imprisoning Pius VI in France, where he died, was unpopular with French Catholics. The military setbacks in Europe were temporary, and the politicians were still fearful of a military takeover, most likely by Bonaparte, who returned to France before the details of Egypt were known.

As was now customary, a new regime meant a new constitution, the Constitution of Year VIII (1799). Three assemblies – none of which exercised any power – were invented with names drawn from ancient Rome. First the Legislative Body, which could vote but not debate, then the Tribunate, which could speak but not vote. Their members were not elected but chosen by the government from lists of candidates drawn up by the entire adult male population. The third assembly was an advisory Senate composed of the great and good. For the first time ever a plebiscite allowed all adult males to vote on the constitution. It was approved by 3 million votes to 1,500, with less than half of all electors bothering to vote.

France was still called a republic but the new regime was a sort of police state. Napoleon made all the decisions and appointed his own ministers, Talleyrand became Minister of Foreign Affairs and Fouché became Minister of General Police and Minister of Justice. He appointed general police commissioners to the main towns and employed 120 informers and spies. Joseph Fouché, 1st Duke of Otrante (1759–1820) was educated by Oratorians in Nantes and became an Oratorian teacher. He met Robespierre before 1789 in Arras. He joined the freemasons, became a democrat and anti-clerical. His formal break with religion came in 1792. He was elected to the Convention, first as a Girondin, then a Jacobin. He was an enthusiast for the guillotining of the King. He was sent to repress the royalist rising in the west and proved an ardent de-Christianiser: 'Death is an eternal sleep'. In November 1793 he was shipped to Lyon to repress the federalist revolt against the Jacobins. Thousands were brutally killed – he earned the nickname the 'Executioner of Lyon'. Robespierre was appalled by the scale of death. He planned to dismiss Fouché, but Fouché contributed to 9 Thermidor, the arrest and death of Robespierre. He changed sides several times in the Directory and with Sieyès plotted the 1799 coup. As minister of police he was powerful but had no popular support. He did not always obey Napoleon and Napoleon had other secret police to spy on him. Fouché's main role was to control plots and contain Napoleon's enemies. The gendarmerie was given an increased role and Napoleon had his own palace guard. Military tribunals took over from civil courts in areas such as the west where brigandage remained a problem. To complete the image of a police state there was no freedom of association or press; book and theatre censorship became absolute. In 1800 the number of newspapers in Paris was reduced from 73 to 13. By 1811 there were only four, all speaking for the government. Even painters like David had to toe the line. Napoleon was always painted riding a leaping white charger.

Bureaucracy and Revolution

In 1789 the revolutionaries took apart all the corporations of the absolute state and decentralised, allowing local citizens to elect their officials. Elected local institutions gave way to a centralised regime in which there were no local liberties or consultation. Napoleon was responsible for a notable increase in the state bureaucracy. The central bureaucracy grew from under one thousand before 1789 to 25,000 by 1810. At the centre was the Council of State, a new body of experts, consisting of men from the old regime as well as revolutionaries. It supervised local administration, wrote administrative law and was responsible for the large increase in bureaucrats. Elected local councils, so important at the start of the Revolution, also disappeared. A prefectoral system was created based on the new departments. Prefects were appointed by the minister of the interior in Paris. This was not totally new – commissioners had been sent out from the capital since 1793. They were heirs of old regime intendants, except intendants did not wear a uniform. Prefects began their training in the Council of State. They were never appointed to their own locality, although sub-prefects were. They were responsible for everything in their departments: tax collection, economic growth, securing support in any voting such as plebiscites and conscription. Trying to keep army numbers up used one-third of their resources. Napoleon also made the judicial system more centralised; the minister of justice dictated who would run the local courts. Napoleon played an active role in completing the codification of law. The codes were short. They kept most of the revolutionary gains: equality before the law (if you could afford a lawyer), abolition of privilege, property to be equally subdivided among heirs, including girls. But women had virtually no civil rights. The right to divorce was restricted.

Why was the denial of political rights embodied in the 1799 coup accepted? Bonaparte seemed popular for his military successes, particularly as they were mostly financed by the conquered territories. Former supporters of the Directory backed Napoleon because they hoped to complete existing reform projects, because he offered them jobs and because a successful general was the best guarantee that French conquests would be retained and the civil war in western France brought to an end. Ordinary French people were less enthusiastic; typically fewer than half of the voters took part in the plebiscites. Napoleon's brother, Lucien, in charge of the voting, always doubled the figures to make them look good. The consulate made France secure. Liberty was gone, but had not really existed for several years; ending persistent civil war was more important. Brigandage, especially in the west and south-west was still a massive problem in 1799. Napoleon's Concordat with Pope Pius VII in 1801 was welcomed.

In 1802 a plebiscite confirmed Napoleon consul for life. In 1804 a plebiscite (3.5 million voting yes, 2,500 no) relabelled France an empire. Napoleon declared the revolution over. It was claimed that the empire was not a military dictatorship because France and the conquered lands were run by civilians. In 1807 two of the 'representative' bodies lost out. The Tribunate was abolished and the Senate was managed by imperial decree. In 1808 Paris University acquired control over higher education and Napoleon appointed its head. In 1809 Napoleon divorced Josephine and wed Marie-Louise, daughter of the Habsburg Emperor, to secure an heir. In the name of protecting the revolution, the original revolutionary ideal of liberty had been superseded by Napoleonic dictatorship. Expediency and the need to eliminate civil war triumphed over philosophy. The Empire was based on military success; when this fell apart in 1814, so did the Empire. In 1814, thanks to Bonapartist propaganda, the republic came to signify only violence and anarchy. The political legacy of 1789 viewed from 1814 was tormented, confused, contradictory and violent.

Social Revolution

On the face of it 1789 brought significant social change. In 1788 the abbé Sieyès, who became one of the most successful revolutionaries, declared that the third estate was the nation. The term morphed soon into the middle class, leaving scope for the very Revolution itself to be termed *bourgeois*. By 1793, *sans culottes* in Paris asserted that they, the poor, had been ignored by the new *bourgeois* elite. Feudal rights became a big issue in the summer of 1789 when tenants attacked chateaux and burned feudal records, and sometimes chateaux themselves, in the Great Fear. Reformers in the Assembly, influenced by enlightened ideas, committed themselves to the abolition of all traditional privileges, which included feudal rights. Originally these had been rights owned by a noble lord who in return promised protection for his tenants. During the eighteenth century these rights had been more and more separated from ownership of land and had become commodities to be bought and sold, especially by wealthy non-nobles who then exploited tenants for what they could get. In August 1789 tenants were freed from demeaning obligations, such as paying a sum of money when son succeeded father, the obligation to allow the noble to hunt over their land and to permit his birds to live off their land. In fact, although feudal dues ended, leases on land were later rewritten and tenants actually paid more rent, so the end of feudalism was merely symbolic. Clerical privilege, the tithe, which obliged people to give a tenth of their income to the Catholic Church, and a host of other privileges held by towns and guilds and which wealthy people had bought or been given over centuries were also abolished. The abolition had a profound impact on the modernisation both of the state and society, separating power based on a range of feudal traditions (including the Church), and the power of the state, based on control of centralised administrative and judicial institutions and tax raising. Peasants no longer paid a variety of extra levies to their landlord on the land they farmed. However until September 1792 they had to pay compensation to be free of seigneurial obligations, when after repeated violent protests from peasants, compensation was terminated. However by 1820 they were paying up to 50% more rent. With a higher percentage of their crops and hence its profit in their hands and in their stomachs, six million peasant families treasured 1789 as their revolution. Before 1789 peasants held titles to one-third of French land. As a direct result of the 1789 revolution, the figure rose to two-fifths. When peasants no longer paid tithe or seigneurial dues, they were no longer forced to grow grain, and could adapt their farming to suit the land. They often started to grow vines. It was the beginning of rural capitalism. Far more peasant families owned land or were free tenants than elsewhere in Europe.

Pre-revolution official posts were venal – individuals paid the Crown for the office, which became hereditary. The revolutionaries abolished venality and compensated its owners with a massive 800 million livres (McPhee, 2002, 41). Paper money, assignats, were printed as compensation (Spang, 2015). Many former office holders bought Church lands with their assignats. The Civil Code eventually decreed equal subdivision of property at inheritance. Female children were included, although the rich found ways to circumvent equal subdivision. Less well-off farmers responded by limiting the size of their families. In the long term, the noble landed elites did much better than might have been expected when, in 1790, the nobility was abolished. Noble landownership fell from around 25% of the land of France in 1789, but had stabilised at 20% by 1814. Although noble heads of households forfeited their land if they emigrated, their agents were able to buy Church and noble national land. However the loss of seigneurial rights, which might represent sometimes up to 60% of income, could be crippling, particularly when the new 16% land tax was added. In 1802 Napoleon created a new elite, the *légion d'honneur*, employing nobles and wealthy bourgeois in his governing system and hence investing them in the mechanics of the new French state – and presumably rescuing some from bankruptcy. In 1814, and even more at the Second Restoration a year later, the noble element reinstated itself as the dominant power in the state, with the support of the Church. Wealthy non-nobles, who had bought Church lands (expropriated during the 1789 revolution), were fearful of their security and were invested in the continuation of their new status quo. From 1814 social conflicts aggravated political arguments.

From Subject to Citizen: Individual Rights

The Declaration of the Rights of Man of August 1789 was the most important legacy of the Revolution. It set out the rights that the Assembly demarcated to the individual citizen. All Frenchmen (not women) were declared equal, free citizens, with equal access to codes of law to be written. In future no-one could be imprisoned without due process of the law. Everyone became a citizen, 'tu' – the first person plural was no longer used for an individual. However in defining voting rights, Sieyès announced a distinction between active citizens, who qualified to vote if they paid tax equivalent to three days labour, and passive citizens who did not pay the required tax and thus did not vote (Serna, 2019). Direct and indirect taxes were centrally prescribed and all citizens were obliged to pay.

In 1795 the journalist Babeuf, a feudal lawyer before 1789, convinced that political change was inadequate, plotted a social revolution. He put together a secret group, the Conspiracy of Equals, to carry through a social revolution to share national wealth equally among all. It was calculated that every family would receive 18 hectares, a guarantee of perpetual misery. Babeuf and his associates were arrested, betrayed by fifth columnists amongst the small Parisian membership. Babeuf was guillotined. His associate Buonarroti, who served a long prison sentence and was released in 1828, promoted his ideas among republicans.

Women

Women did not vote for the Estates-General unless they were single or widows when their property rights qualified them to delegate a man to exercise a vote based on those rights. The revolutionaries did not even consider voting rights for women. On 5–6 October 1789 up to 6,000 Parisian market women joined the National Guard in obliging the King and Queen to move their quarter from Versailles to the capital. A drawing depicted them marching with determined faces. It was one of the very few instances of women participating in the Revolution, unless one counts the royalist Charlotte Corday murdering Danton (in this case counter-revolutionary activity). Olympe de Gouges and a few other women claimed that women were citizens and attended club meetings. De Gouges published a declaration of the rights of women. She was guillotined, but as a royalist, not a spokeswoman for female rights. Madame Roland was an active supporter of the Girondins where her husband was a leading figure. When the Jacobins replaced the Girondins as the dominant force, Madame Roland was guillotined along with leading Girondins. The Jacobins had no time for woman power and in October 1793 women were banned from joining clubs. In March 1795 women could no longer attend the meetings of the Convention or even assemble in groups in public. Women were suspect because two women leaders, Claire Lacombe and Pauline Léon, had been *enragés*, supporters of extreme radicalism; also, on the opposite side of the political spectrum, because many women defended the Catholic clergy and hid refractory priests. Women did not gain from the revolution, except briefly in the new divorce law. Introduced in 1792, it helped women escape from unsatisfactory husbands who had deserted them. Around 70% of those who applied for a divorce were women. The right to divorce was later restricted and was abolished in 1816. The civil code of 1804 reduced the status of women to that of children. Women were the property of their father, then their husband, and could not own property or retain any income they might inherit. They had no say in the upbringing of their children and certainly had no right to custody upon separation.

The Economy

At the Revolution France was the most united and wealthy economic area in continental Europe with a thriving export trade in Bordeaux and Nantes based notably on sugar and coffee from Saint-Domingue. France was the hub – the arbiter of taste and the main producer of luxury goods exported throughout Europe. But internal trade was held back by a myriad of tariff barriers. Goods moved from Lorraine to the Mediterranean would have attracted 34 duties. The Encyclopaedists urged rationalisation and standardisation. The Revolution was in part the product of drastic harvest failures in 1788 and a serious economic recession set off by the 1786 commercial treaty with Britain from which British manufactures benefitted disproportionately. Revolutionary debate and restructuring aggravated the situation in town and country. Initially revolutionary governments were committed to standardisation and economic freedom. France acquired a single decimal system of weights, measures and currency, even though market stallholders still talked of 'pounds' and 'pence' in the 1980s. All tolls and internal tariffs were abolished. People expected radical changes in taxation, so avoided paying. A uniform system of taxation to replace independent farmers-general buying the right to collect taxes for the state was rapidly enacted. In 1790 in the name of a free economy traditional guilds were abolished and in 1791 the Le Chapelier law banned any association of workers or employers.

Colonial trade was much damaged by slave rebellion in Saint-Domingue, 1791, and by the British blockade July 1793; foreign trade, which had contributed 25% of national wealth, fell to 9%. Luxury goods dominated industrial production and this was devastated by the Revolution. Rich foreign visitors kept away and wealthy monarchists emigrated. War and the British blockade destroyed the export trade in luxury items. On the other hand war increased the demand for metal, wool and cotton to make arms and uniforms. But recovery was very slow. Even by 1798 there were only 146 master weavers in the Bas-Rhin, compared with 1,800 in 1790 (McPhee, 2002, 79). Even political extremists in the Convention were hostile to interference in the economy. But there was pressure in Paris for profiteers to be punished and maximum prices were brought in for essential food. Grain was requisitioned by government agents. A war economy was decreed. Labour was conscripted into war industries. By July 1793 the army had grown to 650,000 and by October all French land was liberated. But the economic crisis worsened. In April 1795 assignats were down to 10% of their original value, 1% by end of year. In 1797 two-thirds of state debt had to be repudiated. Indirect taxes were reintroduced. Napoleon imposed a Continental System which obliged all conquered territories to trade with the mother country and not with Britain, which helped the French economy. Cotton, iron and coal industries recovered.

Religion

In a divisive time, religion reigned supreme as the most divisive issue in the revolutionary years. Counter-revolution began when reformers attacked the social and economic privileges of the Roman Catholic Church. In the summer of 1789 the majority in the Assembly, following the ideas of Voltaire and other enlightened thinkers, was determined to curb the political and economic power of the first estate, the Church. In addition, the Assembly, facing a revenue crunch as people avoided paying taxes in times of disorder, declared Church lands to be national property and promptly sold many of them, pocketing the funds and creating a new class of wealthy landowners which owed their land rights to this act of the state. The Church, which owned 10% of the land, had been the biggest single landowner in France, with archbishops, bishops and those who ran religious orders, all drawn from noble families, managing large estates, with consequent political, social and economic, as well as religious power. Following this expropriation, the state claimed many Church buildings and marked them, as some still are today, 'property of the state'. In this new order, the clergy were now paid by the state, supplementing the old *dîme* system (payment of a tenth of parishioners' income to the Church). Clergy were asked to take an oath of allegiance to the state. Half refused, including many in western France, and were termed refractory clergy. In July 1790 a Civil Constitution of the Clergy was enacted which provided for the election of bishops and priests. The Catholic Church was proclaimed a constitutional Church. A few, including the abbé Sieyès, whose pamphlet *What Is the Third Estate?* had a major impact in asserting the dominant role of the middle classes in the Estates-General, took a lead in Church reform, but most clergy were hostile, as were most nobles. Religious orders were dissolved, members became free to marry.

In the autumn of 1793 Sunday and the Christian week were abolished and a new revolutionary calendar launched backdated to 'year one of the Revolution' with a ten day week and ten month year. The months were given names suitable to the seasons, for example Brumaire for November. Working people resented the extra work days and having only one day's holiday each week. Civil baptism, marriage and funerals at the town hall replaced Christian ceremonies in the church. These civic ceremonies were resented by many women, who lost their role in helping to organise these family rites of passage. For a time in 1793 radicals pushed for official dechristianisation. Robespierre, who was anxious to make France a 'republic of virtue', instead organised a festival in honour of the Supreme Being, which was held on 8 June 1794 (Smyth, 2016, 14). The Panthéon in central left bank Paris, formerly a church, was used for the re-burial of Voltaire, Rousseau and select revolutionaries, beginning with Mirabeau. Danton was later kicked out.

The attack on the Church provoked civil war in western and southern France and in Brittany, which persisted well beyond 1800. Ordinary people defended their local parish priests with whom they felt affiliation, because priests tended to come from a similar poor rural social background to their own. It was not until 1801 that a Concordat or settlement with Pope Pius VII was reached. It was seen as a positive Napoleonic achievement, but it reduced the role of individuals in the Church. Bishops were no longer elected by their lay members, but appointed by Napoleon. They were responsible to prefects. The Pope agreed to consecrate the bishops Napoleon named, but in reality papal authority increased. Religious orders including the Jesuits came back. Just by chance the day of Assumption, 15 August, was also Napoleon's birthday. The Church accepted that the sale of their lands was permanent and that their salaries were paid by the state. Roman Catholicism was declared the 'religion of the majority'. In 1805 the Pope was invited to crown the Emperor, although, in his presence, Napoleon actually put the crown upon his own head. The Church resumed its role running primary schools. The social influence of the Church, notably in education, and particularly primary education, was to remain a matter of passionate dispute throughout the next century. The revolutionaries extended the toleration of other religious groups. In 1791 France's 40,000 Jews and Protestants (2% of the population) were accorded the same civil rights as Catholics and became equally eligible for state employment. However, anti-Semitism remained a constant after 1814, surfacing notably in the Dreyfus Affair in the 1890s.

Empire

By 1789 France's first empire had almost disappeared as a consequence of disastrous wars. She had lost Quebec and the French private trading companies in India had been sold. French explorers sailed around the Pacific from Japan to Australia. Since Ferdinand Magellan (c. 1480–1521) set out to circumnavigate the globe, there was little European exploration of the Pacific. In the mid-eighteenth century French explorers searched for areas of the Pacific not already claimed by other European powers that could be made French. These included Antoine Raymond Joseph de Bruni, Chevalier d'Entrecasteaux (1739–1793), who visited Australia and neighbouring regions; Louis-Antoine de Bougainville (1729–1811), who explored the islands around Indonesia and New Guinea. In August 1785, Louis XVI sent La Pérouse to the Pacific, to visit all the lands that had escaped the vigilance of Cook. Jean-François de Galaup, comte de La Pérouse (1741–1788?) left with two ships, *La Boussole* and *Astrolabe*, sailing around much of the Pacific as well as around Japan. He sailed first around Cape Horn, then to Easter Island, the Sandwich Islands (now Hawaii), and up the coast of North America. His aim (like many) was to find the Northwest Passage between the Atlantic and the Pacific, but he gave up when he reached the southern shore of Alaska. Turning south he sailed to San Francisco before crossing the Pacific. In early 1787 he arrived in southern China and sailed north, arriving in Japan in early summer. He sailed north through the Sea of Japan. He discovered a new strait, named the Straits of La Pérouse, between the islands of Sakhalin and Hokkaido which connects the Sea of Okhotsk and the Sea of Japan. He stayed in Petropavlosk on the Kamchatka Peninsula, where he sent notes and journals back to France. The two ships stopped at the Navigators' Islands (now Samoa) en route, where 12 of his crew were killed by natives. He then sailed to Botany Bay in New Holland (now Australia). On the shores of Botany Bay, where Lieutenant James Cook first landed in 1770, is Frenchmans Bay, where La Pérouse landed in January 1788, days after the arrival of the First Fleet. He stayed for six weeks in an area later given the name La Pérouse. He constructed a stockade and planted a small garden. They set forth again on 10 March 1788. Neither La Pérouse nor his crew were seen again and, until 1826, nothing more was known of them. Then French and English explorers found that his ships had apparently been wrecked near New Guinea in the Solomon Islands. Some crew members were killed by natives; others escaped but seem to have died at sea. He then left for the southern seas and did not return. A monument to this visit was erected on the headland and the La Pérouse Cable Station museum tells the story of the La Pérouse expedition, that it met the First Fleet and that no-one knows why he left and did not return.

Although La Pérouse never returned to France his notes did get back, and they included scientific and geographic information about areas previously undocumented by Europeans. The evidence included animal, plant and geologic specimens, along with detailed notes and journals about weather and sea conditions, maps of the coasts visited, and information about much of the Pacific Ocean, gathered over the better part of two years. Together with evidence from other expeditions, a much more complete and detailed picture was gradually assembled. Some of these observations were of scientific interest only. Other evidence was useful for French commerce and the military, when they moved into the area later. La Pérouse's voyages were the start of the French gaining a stake in the Pacific. Thanks to La Pérouse, France acquired territory which was of strategic rather than commercial significance. France still has territories in the Pacific including the atolls where France tested the atomic bomb as recently as the 1990s which provide bases where French ships can be provisioned, shelter and make repairs. In 1791 Bruni d'Entrecasteaux left France on a search and rescue mission to locate La Pérouse. His journey took him across the Indian Ocean to Tasmania, then called Van Diemen's Land, and into the South Pacific before returning to France via the south-western coast of Australia. He failed to find La Pérouse, but he did discover a vast amount of Australian coastline, leaving behind a rich legacy of French place names including D'Entrecasteaux National Park, a wild and untouched place on the south-western tip of Western Australia that hasn't changed much since Bruni put it on the map. Further east along the coast Esperance was named after one of the two ships on the expedition. In Tasmania Bruni's name lives on, in Bruny Island south of Hobart and the D'Entrecasteaux Channel that separates it from mainland Tasmania. South of Hobart, the town of Huonville on the Huon River in the Huon Valley was named in honour of the Admiral's second in command, Captain Huon de Kermadec. Recherché near the far south-eastern tip of Tasmania is named after his other ship, La Recherche. The expeditioners set up a temporary village and scientific observatory on the edge of the bay and stayed for several weeks in 1792 and again in 1793, and the remains of a vegetable garden planted by the French not only as a resource for other sailors, but also for indigenous people, were unearthed by archaeologists in 2003. The next major French exploring party to spend time in Australia was the Baudin expedition, with orders to try and find out if there was a strait between the New Holland (West Australia) and NSW and to claim Southern Australia, which they called Terre Napoleon, for France. They hit the west coast first, and Cape Naturaliste and Geographe Bay near the wine-producing region of Margaret River are both named after the two ships, Le Naturaliste and Le Géographe. Several places on the north-western coast still have French names, including Faure Island and the Peron Peninsula, named after the expedition's zoologist who gathered more than 100,000 specimens, creating one of the most comprehensive Australian natural history collections of its type. Francis Peron National Park is part of the Shark Bay World Heritage Area near Monkey Mia. Baudin headed next to Tasmania. The Freycinet Peninsula on the east coast is named after one of the two Freycinet brothers on board the ship. They named many more places along the south coast of

Australia west of Wilson's Promontory, only to discover that Matthew Flinders had beaten them to the rest of the coast when they ran into him in what is now known as Encounter Bay near Victor Harbor on the Fleurieu Peninsula (named by Baudin) in South Australia; Baudin heading west, Flinders heading east. England and France were at war at the time (François Peron is believed to have prepared a secret espionage report for Napoleon on ways to invade and capture the British colony at Sydney Cove), but despite this the meeting between the two scientists was friendly – Flinders was welcomed aboard *Le Geographe*, and he shared charts and swapped travel tips, like where to find fresh water on nearby Kangaroo Island and the Eyre Peninsula. Between them, Flinders and Baudin were responsible for around 70% of the names of Australia's coastal features, and even though the French maps were published three years before Flinders', many of the French names were later supplanted by the English ones chosen by Flinders by virtue of the fact that he got there first, but only just.

Several French navigators and naturalists named and charted part of New Zealand's coastline. In 1840 a ship of French settlers aboard the Comte de Paris arrived on the Banks Peninsula (named by Cook, after his botanist, Joseph Banks), around an hour's drive south-east of modern-day Christchurch, to establish a French colony, only to find that the British had arrived first and had already claimed sovereignty. The 60 or so settlers decided it was too far to go home, so stayed on to establish the harbour-side town of Akaroa, which still has French street names, and local restaurants pay homage to French cuisine. Despite extensive French exploration and a proliferation of French place names, it was Britain who acquired both Australia and New Zealand (Cooper, 2000).

Empire, Slavery and the Rights of Man

The Declaration of Rights helped to make slavery a major issue in the Revolution. Enlightened writers considered slavery immoral and inefficient although some, including Montesquieu, while hostile to slavery, justified it on economic grounds. In 1781 Condorcet noted that slaves could become citizens by gradual emancipation. In the 1780s opposition to slavery grew among the French elite, including future revolutionary leaders Mirabeau, Lafayette and Sieyès. They noted emancipation in northern states in North America as an example. Slavery was an integral part of the triangular trade and economy of French islands in the West Indies, Martinique, Guadeloupe and Saint-Domingue. The slave trade constituted 25% of the industry of Nantes and other western seaboard ports like Bordeaux and La Rochelle. Sugar, coffee and tobacco were exported to France and then re-exported. Sugar from Saint-Domingue was a major feature of French trade.

In 1788 the *Amis des Noirs* was founded by Mirabeau, Condorcet, Brissot, Clavière and the abbé Grégoire, all future revolutionary leaders. The 1789 Declaration of Rights had no impact at first. White plantation owners continued to dominate in 1789–1792 in the Caribbean, with only whites owning at least 25 black slaves being admitted to the island assemblies. In March 1790 the colonies committee of the National Assembly promised self-government for the colonies; the franchise was to be based on property owning, as in France, and free blacks would not get to vote. Slavery was to continue. Violent confrontation spread in all French Caribbean islands. A free black rebellion rose up in Saint-Domingue, dividing the island into white and free black competing areas. There were prolonged debates in the colonial committee of the National Assembly in which Brissot and the leaders of the Society of the *Amis des Noirs*, with especially Grégoire, Pétion and Destutt de Tracy, urged by the Saint-Domingue free black leader Julien Raimond, demanding rights for free blacks. Julien Raimond (1744–1801) was a slave-owning indigo planter from Saint-Domingue, son of a white planter and a free white woman (the daughter of a planter) who had been resident in Paris since 1785 where he had been working with various bodies to raise the legal status of free blacks and free mixed race people in the French Caribbean.

In May 1791, the National Assembly ruled that free blacks should receive full voting rights when they met the requisite property qualifications, which very few did. In September the Assembly decided to leave the decision over slaves and mixed race people to planter-dominated colonial assemblies, which were very hostile. On 27 September 1791 slavery was abolished in France but not in the colonies. In April 1792 political equality was declared for those of mixed race and free blacks. An expeditionary force of 6,000 was sent to the West Indies to enforce the decree.

August 1791 Insurgency, North Saint-Domingue

This was the start of the Haitian Revolution (1791–1804), inspired by 1789, which threw the entire Caribbean into turmoil and affected relations between whites and blacks throughout the New World. Saint-Domingue (French part of Hispaniola) and the French colonies of Martinique and Guadeloupe were very important in the French economy. Caribbean trade yielded £9 million year profit compare to the British Caribbean £5 million. Saint-Domingue was especially important in the French economy, producing 40% of the world's sugar. In Saint-Domingue there were over 400,000 African slaves, with a white population of 32,000 in 1789, a tiny elite of white French plantation owners, backed by some small-scale white farmers, plus 28,000 mixed free race and creoles – black slaves born locally, often house servants. One hundred thousand slaves were owned by free Africans. Free mixed race people were already demanding full civil rights in the 1780s before the 1789 Revolution. There was a constant fear of rebellion by groups of escaped slaves. In August 1791, a combined free black *and* slave revolt of 100,000 broke out in the northern interior of Saint-Domingue. Its leader was Pierre Dominique Toussaint Louverture (1743–1803), a Roman Catholic son of an educated slave and himself a literate former slave. He learned French from the Jesuits;

he also used Haitian Creole and African tribal languages. Toussaint was a sugar plantation steward, freed in 1776. He joined the French army in Saint-Domingue and became an officer in 1794. At first unsure of the rebellion, he helped his former master escape, then joined and led the revolt. The revolt was joined by 15,000 slaves and free blacks. Hundreds of coffee and sugar plantations were devastated. Fighting over the next several months left 2,000 whites and 10,000 black slaves dead.

In April 1792, the French Assembly officially ended the white colonists' previously extensive autonomy by dissolving the colonial assemblies. It was part of the campaign in France aimed at defeating Caribbean French white conservatism, aristocratism and monarchism. The edict was partly a response to the initial Haitian revolt. All free men were declared equal, whatever their colour. In August an army of 6,000 troops (bringing 30,000 rifles) was dispatched to Saint-Domingue to assert the new French Republican Assembly's authority. With the troops arrived a civil commission chosen by the new republican regime. The commission was headed by republican anticlerical Léger-Felicité Sonthonax (1763–1813). Sonthonax made the colony's assembly democratic for free blacks, free mixed race people and poor whites. Planters were hostile and conspired with exiled monarchist leader Malouet (now in London) – his family fortune consisted of land and slaves on the island to bring Saint-Domingue under British control. Sonthonax set up a revolutionary government, including traditional-minded free blacks to the republican cause. The slave revolt in the hills persisted. Black rebels were fond of the king and religion, and indifferent to republican politics. Priests were influential in the insurgent districts. In October 1792 Sonthonax dissolved the colonial assembly, replacing it with a provisional commission of 12, comprising six whites and six blacks co-opted by the commission. The commissioners also introduced a mixed race political club at Cap Français affiliated to the Brissotins. Royalist and other protesting white officers were purged. On 2 December 1792, Sonthonax summoned a force of several hundred mixed race and free black National Guard to face down a white militia unit encamped on the Champ-de-Mars outside the town. An armed clash occurred resulting in the deaths of 30 whites and six free blacks that only narrowly avoided becoming a pitched battle.

In the summer of 1793 the Jacobins gained power in France; they were not interested in black emancipation. Sonthonax was hostile to the continuing insurgency of the blacks. The white oligarchy of the colony's other main town, Port-au-Prince, meanwhile, also defied the revolutionary regime and, in April 1793, had to be blockaded with the aid of local free blacks and bombarded into submission. As the town fell, hundreds of royalist, counter-revolutionary whites fled into the interior; others were caught and imprisoned. Jacmel was similarly reduced with black help. But with the commissioners and their troops operating in the northern interior and then the south, the situation in Cap François too deteriorated. As at Port-au-Prince and Jacmel, the chief agents of subversion were neither free blacks nor slaves but recalcitrant whites defending the colonists' supremacy and the old colonial assembly. Sonthonax's Cap Français opponents, often white refugees from the black insurgency in the interior, or monarchist seamen and merchants whose trade was now heavily disrupted by the maritime war with Britain, became increasingly aggressive.

In March 1793 war broke out between France and Spain. Spanish troops were dispatched to help Toussaint unite Hispaniola. Two small British forces also landed. A deteriorating situation exploded into a full-scale crisis in June 1793. While the Cap Français sailors mutinied and set siege to the commission's headquarters, the governor's house, units of free black militia rallied to the commission's defence. Fighting erupted and spread. At the height of the Cap Français violence, and on their own initiative, initially just as a local emergency measure, Sonthonax and Polvérel offered local slaves their freedom if they would fight for the Revolution. Sonthonax's famous printed edict of 21 June 1793 released Cap Français' slaves from bondage in exchange for help in saving the embattled Brissotin régime. Many responded with alacrity, rushing into the streets armed with knives and other implements. With Sonthonax still besieged, the shooting and killing spread. Fires started. Numerous houses were pillaged. Finally, like Port-au-Prince earlier, the entire town was burnt to ashes, mixed race and blacks often assisted fleeing or wounded whites. But others cut their throats so that besides several thousand blacks, well over a thousand whites were butchered. Whites escaped to New York.

October 1793, All Former Slaves Freed

Black insurgents in the interior were still hostile to the Republic. Toussaint L'Ouverture allied with the Spaniards to manage their eastern part of the island (today the Dominican Republic- see map) in hostility to the French, which independence he defined as liberty. Toussaint fought with Spain to defend monarchy and religion. He allowed black rebel leaders to fight independently. He opposed the French revolutionaries because they had guillotined the legitimate king, were opposed to the Roman Catholic Church and were running a bloody dictatorship. The Brissotin government, with little support from the blacks, had to fight Spain, Britain and the white planters. The British and Spanish invaded Saint-Domingue, the British seizing Port-au-Prince in the early months of 1794. The British also took French Tobago in 1793. French émigrés from Saint-Domingue and France also joined the British to fight the French in the Caribbean.

In May 1794 Toussaint Louverture dumped the Spanish and agreed to a military alliance with the French republicans in response to the Convention's abolition of slavery in French colonies. Toussaint accepted the tricolour flag and the revolutionary calendar; officers learned slogans and procedures of the new French revolutionary military code. Toussaint got powder and weapons with American help. Plantations were in ruins and numerous blacks and whites continued to be displaced by incursions of Spaniards and British, and their *émigré* allies. A few whites who had abandoned their property and had it confiscated were allowed back after swearing allegiance to the Republic, including former planters returning from the United States in the hope of evading sequestration of their lands under the Revolution's punitive laws against recalcitrant *émigrés*. Toussaint's open-door policy toward exiles returning from the United States figured among the points of disagreement that subsequently provoked his bitter quarrel with Sonthonax.

Expansion of Insurgency/War in the Caribbean

During the mid-1790s, the revolutionary contest became a pan-Caribbean conflict. The 1795 revolution in the Dutch Republic, and overthrow of the Orangist regime there, deepened the already bitter rift between Orangists and democrats convulsing all six Dutch Caribbean islands as well as in the Guyanas (most of which were then in Dutch possession). Curaçao became the focus of furious strife and while neither side, Orangists or republican Patriots, favoured emancipating the slaves, the latter, as French allies, could not prevent revolutionary papers and propaganda or Guadeloupe mixed-race privateer crews assuming a prominent profile on the island. Major slave and free black revolts erupted on Curaçao and at Coro later in 1795 which were among the biggest in the Caribbean during the revolutionary era.

The British response, one of the largest military expeditions ever sent across the Atlantic, comprised nearly 100 British ships and 30,000 troops to join the existing fleet. They regained Grenada and Saint Vincent and eventually occupied Curaçao (in 1800), but otherwise the expedition was a failure. The French dispatched far smaller expeditions, but these sufficed to hold the line in Guadeloupe and, more tentatively, in Saint-Domingue. Yellow fever and malaria exacted an appalling toll on the British forces. Up to 60,000 British troops and sailors died or disappeared.

Saint-Domingue

Assisted by the Franco-Spanish peace (1795) which transferred Spanish Santo Domingo (where slave numbers were relatively small compared to the western part of the island) to France and in theory extended black emancipation to the entire island, counter-revolutionary pressure on Haiti waned during 1796–1798, and the work of restoring order and agriculture proceeded, despite continuing disturbances, conspiracies and lapses of order often instigated by the British and Spaniards (towards whom Toussaint remained highly suspicious). In May 1796 Toussaint was appointed Lieutenant-Governor of the island. Meanwhile the French recaptured Martinique and Guadeloupe from Britain, and conquered Saint-Vincent, Saint-Lucia and most of Grenada. Control of Saint-Domingue was gradually slipping from the grip of the Directory in Paris. The turning point came in 1797 after Toussaint suddenly broke with Sonthonax (who had returned to head the administration of Saint-Domingue in the spring of 1796), sending him and other French commissionaires and officials back to France. Raimond, the last remaining commissionaire, supported Toussaint. He claimed to be firmer in his loyalty to France than Sonthonax and to be insulted that anyone should suppose Sonthonax more upright and republican than he, or 'more of a friend to the liberty of the blacks'.

Although between 1794 and 1799 the Paris French National Assembly still contained elected black and mixed race members, but in Sainte-Domingue by 1798 black leaders were in control. Toussaint was in power in the centre and north and in the south André Riguad (1761–1811). Rigaud was the son of a slave and a rich planter. Most of Toussaint's army were former slaves. Riguad was keen to work with the French. Toussaint cooperated with the USA and encouraged settlers to return from America. Like Brissot and Condorcet Toussaint was convinced that blacks and whites were fundamentally equal. By August 1800 Toussaint was in control. (Document 5).

1799 Consulate – Military Coup in France

Napoleon made himself First Consul in the coup of 1799 and was supreme. Toussaint responded by organising Haitian autonomy. Toussaint sent troops into the eastern two-thirds of the island ceded by Spain to France in 1795. He proclaimed revolutionary values and declared slavery abolished in the area. This was in defiance of Napoleon's aim of giving the land back to Spain in return for an alliance. Toussaint encouraged freed slaves to go back to work the land. He promised to protect their income. As Napoleon consolidated his own power in France in 1800, Toussaint, having overcome Rigaud's influence, developed his own power on the island. In 1801 he called a constitutional convention to unite the island in a single government. A constitution was proclaimed, 8 July 1801. He declared slavery abolished forever, proclaimed himself life governor. He had basically declared self-rule, although he insisted he still recognised French sovereignty.

In 1801 Napoleon withdrew the Lieutenant-Governorship from Toussaint and sent two powerful fleets to the Caribbean, a smaller fleet to Guadeloupe, Tobago and Saint-Lucia (all of which were recovered, though the latter two only briefly, being retaken by the British in June 1803), and a larger fleet, prepared in Brest, sent to Haiti under the command of General Charles Victor Emmanuel Leclerc (1772–1802), husband of Napoleon's favourite sister, Pauline. Leclerc had figured among Humbert's officers during the 1798 Irish expedition and had also participated in the coup of Brumaire. The First Consul furnished him with exceptionally detailed instructions as to how to proceed in Haiti.

The fleet which arrived off Cap François in February 1802 was the biggest French force ever sent to the Caribbean. There were 22,000 fighters. Napoleon increased the total to 40,000. His aim was to create a French Empire in the New World including Haiti, New Orleans and Louisiana, which France had just acquired from Spain. The French commander declared that all inhabitants of Saint-Domingue, whatever their colour or origin, were French, and equal before God and the Republic. But the French troops and former slaves soon fought, the slaves being provided with weapons by American merchants., encouraged by Jefferson. The French tried to ban American merchants using Saint-Domingue ports, and to ensure they supplied the French, but found the Americans uncooperative. After three months Toussaint was defeated and forced to surrender, but slavery was not restored immediately. In the Anglo-French Peace of Amiens, March 1802, Britain gave Martinique back to France after ten years' occupation. Two months later the French declared slavery re-established in Guadeloupe and Cayenne. Toussaint was deported to France, imprisoned in a solitary celi in an icy, lightless underground prison in the Jura. He was denied visitors and died, probably starved, in April 1803. (*Memoir of General Toussaint Louverture written by Himself*).

An 1802 decree forbade the free entry of free blacks and mixed race into France which had been permitted since 1791. The slaughter of blacks on Saint-Domingue continued, but the French were decimated by yellow fever including Leclerc, who died in November 1802. The island was in total revolt. Black troops, encouraged by USA, drove the French troops to the Spanish side of the island. In January 1804 Haitian independence was proclaimed by the new black insurgent leader, General Jean-Jacques Dessalines (1758–1806), Toussaint's former lieutenant. The massacre of the remaining 3,000 to 5,000 or so whites still residing in Haiti occurred between February and April 1804. In October Dessalines had himself crowned, Jacques I, Emperor of Haiti. He was assassinated in October 1806. Britain recognized Haiti immediately, but the USA only in 1862 (Forrest, 2019, 1–11). France thus lost Saint-Domingue and its valuable trade, and a free black government emerged in Haiti (Document 5). This was seen as a major impact of 1789, although slavery persisted in the rest of the French Caribbean.

Having lost Saint-Domingue, Napoleon sold Louisiana. The negotiations for the sale to the USA commenced in April 1803 with Monroe acting as agent; the talks, following Napoleon's sudden change of heart, went smoothly and swiftly with Volney strenuously urging the First Consul and his foreign minister, Talleyrand, to agree. These secret negotiations transpired without Napoleon so much as consulting his scorned ally, Spain, despite the circumstance that the projected transfer would greatly weaken Spain's strategic stance in both North America and the Caribbean, leaving the entire Spanish American empire vulnerable to penetration by American contraband trade and settler immigration. Signed in Paris, on 10 May 1803, this astounding agreement doubled the area of the United States at a stroke, transferring from France to the United States in perpetuity the entire Louisiana territory, encompassing an area corresponding to the present-day states of Louisiana, Arkansas, Missouri, Kansas, Oklahoma, Nebraska and the Dakotas, in exchange for 50 million francs. The purchase embraced New Orleans, and control of the Mississippi estuary and navigation, along with no less than 828,000 square miles of land stretching to New Spain and the Canadian border. The USA was massively enlarged embracing a puzzled French Catholic population. Why? With Haiti independent and control of the other French islands precarious, France lacked the naval and military power to develop a new American Empire. Napoleon was far more interested in maintaining the newly conquered European empire – which in 1804 he was keen to extend – and did so with enormous if short-lived success in the Holy Roman Empire, including Prussia. Louisiana was not regarded as particularly valuable and its retention likely to provoke conflict with the USA and Spain.

European Empire

During the revolutionary years, whilst claiming to liberate the peoples of Europe, France acquired the biggest European empire since the days of Charlemagne in the eighth century. In 1792 war with the rest of Europe threatened Paris, but quickly the tables were turned, as France's enemies quarrelled among themselves, leading to the French conquest of the Low Countries, most of the Italian lands, the dissolution of the three hundred or so Germanic states and, in 1806, the breakup of the Holy Roman Empire. The frontiers of France expanded into Dutch, German and Italian territories, while Napoleon's relatives took over much of the rest. A Grand Duchy of Warsaw was established. The attempt to extend this continental empire into Spain in 1807 and Russia in 1812 led to military defeat and the elimination of the whole European French Empire (1814–1815).

The legacy of 1789 can be summed up as the emergence of institutional structures – administrative, judicial, legal, educational and military – which survive today. In other respects there was major division, over politics and religion, which help set off upheaval in the next century. A European empire was won and lost. France's overseas empire, already devastated before 1789, was seriously weakened by Haitian independence. We will now turn to look at how the memory of revolution was expressed in monuments and symbols.

2 Memory, Monuments and Symbols of 1789

It was in 1989 that Pierre Nora, historian and publisher, launched *Lieux de Mémoire* (*Realms of Memory: Rethinking the French Past* translated 1996), which meant French history would never be the same again. Throughout the nineteenth century the memory of 1789 was political, polarised into left and right. Monarchy was opposed to democratic republicanism, the Catholic Church to secularism. How 1789 was to be remembered was defined at the centenary when in 1880 the *Marseillaise* became the national anthem and Bastille Day a national holiday. In 1885 a lectureship in revolutionary history was established at the Sorbonne, Alphonse Aulard (1849–1928) gaining the appointment. Aulard had written a detailed account of the revolutionary orators based on the archives (1882) and went on to publish four volumes on the political history of the Revolution (1901). His hero was Danton, not Robespierre. He created a society for the study of revolutionary history. Meanwhile the new lay primary schools set up after 1881 established 1789 as the birth of the nation. As socialist history emerged with Jean Jaures and Albert Mathiez this political interpretation of 1789 was still acceptable as the start of revolution. In 1935 Bastille Day was chosen to launch the Popular Front of Radicals, Socialists and Communists, and Communists joined in the singing of the *Marseillaise* alongside *The Internationale*. The Vichy regime replaced liberty, equality and fraternity with Travail, Famille, Patrie, but retained Bastille Day as a public holiday to honour the war dead. Vichy and Fascists generally acknowledged that 1789 was important in challenging the power of old elites. The Constitution of the Fourth Republic included the 1789 Declaration of the Rights of Man and Citizen. Charles de Gaulle was able to reconcile his right-wing Catholic views with his acknowledgment of France as a republic. Opinion polls taken in the mid-1980s revealed that three-quarters of the French people accepted 1789 as a positive event, but only 49% said they would have helped storm the Bastille (Gough, 1992, 811–816). The memory of 1789 is far less vague than is 1688 in Britain. Historians and intellectuals still argue with passion over issues like the Terror. The collapse of Communism may have reduced the appeal of Marxist views that 1789 heralded social change, but Furet's stress on the Revolution and divisions in political culture continues to spark debate in scholarly journals.

DOI: 10.4324/9781003460596-2

The split between the left and right which dates from 1789 is still real. That the French retain a memory of 1789 was shown at a superficial level in 2023 when Parisian crowds built and burned barricades to resist President Macron's long-running attempt to raise the pension age from 62 to 64.

The Classical World and 1789

The revolutionaries of 1789 knew they were building a new world, but did so using the language and concepts of ancient Greece and Rome, frequently citing leading personalities from those centuries. This section will first demonstrate how antiquity figured in the performance of revolution and secondly will ask why this was so. In 1937 Harold T. Parker, inspired by Carl Becker (*Cult of Antiquity and the French Revolutionaries: A Study in the Development of the Revolutionary Spirit*), recalled frequent references made to the ancient world, mentioning Madame Roland's regret that she had not been born a Spartan. But Parker did not consider that the revolutionaries believed they were imitating their ancient brethren. He put their frequent references to their classical education, in colleges or with the Jesuits, down to a substantial time reading and discussing classical Roman writers such as Cicero, Livy, Virgil, Horace and others – the syllabus seemed very similar in the different institutions. They do not seem to have read the Greeks, such as Plato or Aristotle. The Roman writers they read were discontented with Rome in their own time and looked back to what they saw as a more admirable past. The eighteenth century then read enlightened writers, Rousseau, Voltaire etc., who also sang the praises of the classical world, but with no suggestion that the ancient past should be imitated. Few late eighteenth century contemporaries wrote in detail about their views on classical writers. Only Roland, Desmoulins and Mercier thought reading about the ancient past increased their discontent with the present and helped make them republicans. In her memoirs Roland remembered that at age nine she took Plutarch to church instead of her prayerbook. Claude Mossé's *L'antiquité dans la Révolution française* (2006) examined the role of antiquity in the Revolution, but without considering the possibility that the revolutionaries really believed they were experiencing a recurrence of a previous age. A much more recent book by Francesco Benigno and Daniele Di Bartolomeo (2022), *La magie du passé: l'idée de la répétition historique dans la Révolution française* claims that the 1789 revolutionaries consciously imitated their predecessors. The parliamentary archives (first 82 volumes, 1787–1794) are full of historical references and parallels, particularly to Greece and Rome, for instance Solon (105 hits), Catiline (95 hits) and Lycurgus (79 hits). Brutus, who assassinated Julius Caesar and founded the Roman Republic, tops the lot (588 times), but we note that the name also refers to a 1789 militant Parisian *section*, to French communes renamed with classical names, and contemporaries who took on classical names. Revolutionaries also recalled, but with distaste, more recent revolutionaries in seventeenth-century England, especially Cromwell (86 hits).

The authors noted that most historians of the Revolution have taken their cue from Marx, who dismissed revolutionaries' invocations of ancient history as mere attempts at acquiring legitimacy by casting themselves as heroic Romans. 'Revisionists', notably Furet, argued that revolutionaries repudiated the past. *La magie du passé* takes a contrary view, invoking both rational and emotional explanations in a cyclical interpretation of history. Commenting on the Varennes flight of Louis XVI in June 1791, the authors compared the King to Tarquin the Proud, King of Rome deposed by Brutus, or England's Charles I. They warned of possible dictatorship, comparing Lafayette's attempt to restore Louis XVI with the Roman general Sulla who marched on Rome in the first century BCE claiming that history was repeating itself, even though Lafayette's attempt to restore the king failed. They compared Robespierre with ancient tyrants. Jacobins denounced General Dumouriez as a Cromwell or a Caesar, particularly when he went over to the Austrians having failed to turn his troops on Paris. Finally came the example of a successful general, Napoleon seizing power, proclaiming himself consul then emperor. The degree to which revolutionaries cited the ancient world was undoubtedly substantial, but perhaps their aim was to justify their strategies, rather than claim they were actually imitating their ancient predecessors.

Links with the American Revolution

Leading individuals in both countries welcomed links between them. The Marquis de Lafayette (1757–1834) was one of the most outstanding French nobles. He fought under George Washington (a fellow freemason) against the British (1777–1779 and 1780–1782). They became close friends. Lafayette's eldest son was named George Washington Lafayette. Lafayette also became close to Alexander Hamilton and Thomas Jefferson. Jefferson, the US ambassador in Paris in 1789, helped Lafayette draft the Declaration of Man and Citizen (11 July 1789). Lafayette was appointed the commander of the new Parisian National Guard (13 July 1789) which had a major role in trying to maintain revolutionary order. Subsequently he was accused of royalist sympathies and spent several years in Austrian prisons. His estates were confiscated. He opposed Napoleon and the 1814 Restoration. In 1824 he was invited as an honoured guest by the American government and toured all the 22 states. He was an iconic figure in the 1830 Revolution and was again made commander of the National Guard in August 1830. Other French politicians who saw America as a positive influence were the Marquis de Condorcet (1743–1794), a respected Enlightenment and revolutionary philosopher. His mathematical and scientific work brought him close to Benjamin Franklin in the 1760s. He worked for the Controller-General Turgot. He joined the *société des noirs* and was a keen abolitionist. He was elected by Paris to the Legislative Assembly in September 1791 and chosen as its secretary. He was an enthusiast for liberal, anti-clerical educational reform and women's rights on which he published. Science brought him close to Benjamin Franklin. He supported the American Revolution. He was close to the Girondins and was arrested in 1794. He died in prison. Jacques Pierre Brissot (1754–1793), the Girondin leader, was an enthusiast for the American Revolution. He opposed the death of the King. He died in jail, possibly by suicide/murder; he was too popular to guillotine.

Benjamin Franklin (1706–1790), a freemason, Enlightenment enthusiast and polymath scientist, spent long periods in Europe. He was in Britain from 1750 to the mid-1770s, and was American ambassador in Paris 1776–1784. He was a close associate of the revolutionary noble leader Mirabeau. When he died in April 1790 the French National Assembly declared that they should all wear black for three days of state mourning, which coincided with part of the Fête de la Fédération.

Thomas Jefferson (1743–1826) replaced Franklin for a year as effectively American ambassador in Paris. He was very close to Lafayette. When he went back to America in 1785 he expected to return to Paris, but Washington made him Secretary of State. He remained sympathetic to the French Revolution, but not the Terror.

The American Revolution itself, their Declaration of Rights and Constitution were taken as direct examples by the French, although subsequently less was made of the comparison. America was a lesson not only of a revolt against the established ruler, but also the replacement of monarchy by a republic. Because the French Republic led to the Terror the Americans quickly lost interest in French matters.

Symbols of Revolution

Tricolour: Red Flag

Throughout the nineteenth century, the choreography of revolution in France dictated the symbolism of revolution to the whole of Europe. Two flags stood sentinel; the tricolour flag being specifically French, the red flag increasingly international. The tricolour was invented at the Hôtel de Ville on 16 July 1789 by General Lafayette for the new National Guard, although the precise combination of stripes of blue and red (Paris) and white (king, or according to Lafayette, France itself) took some time to emerge. It was used at the Fête de la Fédération, 14 July 1790, and officially adopted as the French national flag in 1794. In 1814, it was replaced by the Bourbon white fleur de lys. Many revolutionary and Bonapartist sympathisers tucked their tricolour flag away, just in case. In 1830, the Orleanist monarchy re-adopted it. The red flag remained a symbol of radical, later socialist, revolution. Louis Blanc's argument that a red flag had been the standard of the Gauls during the Hundred Years' War and should be the symbol of the Second Republic was unconvincing. Partisans always asserted that it symbolised the blood of the nation and patriotic unity, but the 1790s left the red flag with the opposite aura of divisive violent class war. The tricolour came to be seen as the middle class revolutionary standard; the red flag that of workers. The latter was the symbol of the 'social' republic between 1848 and 1851, and again in the Paris Commune of 1871. The Communard experience helped to turn it into the international flag of the workers' revolution.

The red Phrygian liberty cap, reminiscent of the headgear of freed slaves in the Roman Empire, was another favourite French revolutionary symbol of the 1790s. Like the red flag its lawless and extreme connotations persisted, especially in official memory. In 1830 the rather conservative liberals who made Louis-Philippe king were keen to mothball Phrygian caps, especially when adorning newly planted liberty trees. The cap fared no better after the 1848 Revolution. Whereas the seal of the First Republic pictured a female figure carrying a pike surmounted by a Phrygian cap, the female on the seal of the Second Republic sports innocuous headgear representing the sun's rays, similar to that later affixed to the Statue of Liberty in America. The Phrygian cap continued to cause so much alarm that in 1876 a large statue wearing one, erected in Dijon to commemorate the repulsing of the Prussian invader in 1870, was destroyed. In this new world, even playing cards were re-worked to exclude kings and queens. In addition to the Revolutionary cockade and tricolour flags appeared a gallic cockerel. Why a cockerel? The word for Gauls and for a cockerel is the same in Latin, and Ancient Romans made the connection. French Revolutionaries connected their ideas on liberty with their enthusiasm for the classical world and began to use the cockerel as a symbol.

Liberty Tree

The liberty tree was another symbol of revolution, often erected in a village to replace a crucifix. Usually small saplings, the trees might be decorated with a Phrygian cap and a tricolour flag and villagers would sing suitable revolutionary songs – a substitute for church services. The trees rarely survived less radical episodes, but new ones were planted after the July Days, 1830, when the crucifixes of the religious revival of the Restoration were uprooted from the edge of a village and returned to church grounds. Liberty trees were also planted in 1848, but there is no mention of this happening in the Paris Commune.

Revolutionary Song

Revolutionary tradition was passionately sustained in song. The 'Marseillaise', written by Rouget de l'Isle as a marching song for the army of the Rhine in 1792 and adopted as the national anthem in 1795, was rejected by Napoleon. It was only one of a number of stirring patriotic and radical songs of the 1790s; the 'Ca Ira', written in 1790 with anti-aristocratic verses added in 1793, and the 'Carmagnole' were equally appreciated. All were subsequently suppressed as subversive, giving way to tedious Bonapartist marching music.

Police reports never failed to shiver at the sound of the 'Ca Ira' in the years before 1848. The Third Republic reinstated the 'Marseillaise'.

Marianne: Revolution as Female

Marianne came to be used as a symbol of liberty, equality and fraternity, not to mention revolution and the republic very gradually after 1792. The name was drawn from Marie and Anne, the two most used girls names, and was thought up as an insult, meaning a low class woman, by those hostile to the republic. This is curious, given the similarity to the name of the Queen Marie-Antoinette. Those favourable to the name Marianne very often thought of it as close to Mary, mother of God, and the religious and revolutionary contexts increasingly intertwined. Marianne was also used as a synonym for 'goddess' in a classical/revolutionary sense. She became the republican equivalent of Joan of Arc for monarchists. During the nineteenth century there were two rival versions, depending on the politics of the regime, one rather warlike, wearing a Phrygian cap, carrying a pike, breast sometimes part-unclothed; one more peaceful-looking, in classical robes, carrying symbols of the Law and with a sun's rays headdress, similar to the American Statue of Liberty.

In 1792, the new Republic needed to agree on a image to replace that of the king. The first issue was what to put on the State Seal. The Convention set up a committee. Hercules, semi-divine son of Jupiter, was first considered. Abbé Grégoire, president of the Convention and constitutional bishop of Blois, insisted that the image of the Republic should be Liberty 'so that our emblem, circulating all over the globe, should present to all peoples the beloved image of Republic liberty and pride' (J. Renouvier, *Histoire de l'art pendant la Révolution, considéré principalement dans les estampes*, 1863, p. 391). The Convention decreed 'the State Seal should be changed and should bear the image of France in the guise of a woman dressed in the style of Antiquity, standing upright, her right hand holding a pike surmounted by a Phrygian cap or cap of Liberty, her left hand resting upon a sheaf of fasces (classical symbols of judicial authority): at her feet a tiller... and as an inscription the words: In the name of the French Republic' (Decree of 21 September 1792, quoted by Agulhon, 1981, 18). A badge was devised to be worn by the members of the Convention with a seated woman, similarly adorned. In Year III the badge worn by the deputies also included a second female figure, Equality, seated next to the altar of Law and carrying a pair of scales. Female statues of Liberty proliferated. One was erected on the Place de la Révolution, formerly Place Louis XV, now Place de la Concorde. Upright she sports a Phrygian cap and holds a pike, presumably for fighting. Another plaster female figure was raised on a column in the Place Vendôme. She was later to be replaced by Napoleon. He was pulled down together with the column during the Paris Commune, 1871. Sometimes an actual woman was used to represent Liberty, the most well-known being at the Festival of Reason in 1793. This lady was described as a goddess of liberty. Statues gradually became less assertively republican and more harmlessly classical in imagery.

The most famous depiction of Liberty is by Eugène Delacroix, 'Liberty leading the people at the barricades', painted immediately after the July Revolution, 1830. Liberty is a tall young woman, bare-breasted, wearing a Phrygian cap, a tricolour flag in her right hand, a bayonet in her left. Fighting with her on her right is a citizen, complete with bayonet and top hat. At her left a *gamin*, young lad of the people, armed with a rifle in each hand. At her feet are dead young men, some in National Guard uniforms. Delacroix exhibited his painting at the Salon early in 1831. It was bought by the Minister of the Interior, Casimir Périer, and deposited in the basement of the Louvre. Conservative supporters of the new monarchy, now in power, thought the painting too radical a personification of their revolution. It was first displayed after the 1848 revolution. After the 1830 revolution the medal worn by deputies had the king's head on one side and on the other, five figures, the central being a standing woman holding the tablets of law and on her head, to symbolise Liberty, the rays of the sun. Surrounding her were four figures: Commerce (Mercury), Agriculture (a woman carrying sheaves of wheat), the Acts (Apollo with a lyre) and Science.

The July Monarchy was notable for statue construction. The most famous, and still in place, was the Colonne de Juillet. The original plan was to surmount it with a female Liberty, but in the end a male Mercury took her place – and still survives. The Arc de Triomphe made a huge contribution to female representation. Commissioned by Napoleon in 1806, the statuary was completed by François Rude in the 1830s. 'The Departure of the Volunteers 1792', usually called 'La Marseillaise' is dominated by a massive winged female warrior, crowned with Phrygian cap, one of the most impressive symbols of Liberty ever made.

In February 1848 new representations of the republic were essential to replace images of the king. The Second republicans were not as successful as the First in this objective, perhaps because they were spending so much on the unemployed in the national workshops, or more likely because the republic was short-lived. A full-size model, laid on what looked like a market stall, that accompanied those killed in the February revolution to their burial under the July Column was neither real nor plaster but made of papier-maché. Fortunately it didn't rain. A quickly built plaster model was assembled for the Concorde Festival (20 May 1848). She was a huge upright figure, in long classical robes, wearing a Phrygian cap. Her left hand was laid on an altar to the Motherland, on which was inscribed Liberty, Equality and Fraternity. In her right hand were a long sword and a wreath. A similar massive statue was constructed to celebrate the proclamation of the Constitution on 12 November 1848 and erected on the Place de la Concorde. She held a lance in her right hand and the tablets of constitutional law in her left. She was crowned with laurel and had a bare left breast. In 1793 her predecessor had stood next to the much-used scaffold. The Second Republic abolished the death penalty, so this female celebration of the republic stood next to the obelisk from Luxor, given to Charles X by the Egyptian ruler in return for a clock, which never worked. One obelisk was moved to Paris at the cost to

France of $19 million (2021 money) and erected on the Place de la Concorde in 1836. The other was never moved, perhaps because of the cost.

No female figure appeared on the medal and insignia of the Constituent Assembly elected in April 1848, but simply a fasces and a hand of justice. The legislative assembly elected in May 1849 decorated its insignia with a woman wearing what looked like a cross between a lion skin and a Phrygian cap. The new republic held competitions, first to design a painting to be copied and installed in town halls to replace that of the king; next an image for a medal to commemorate the republic and one to appear on the new postage stamp. The committee could not agree on the best painting. Daumier offered a seated mother feeding her (rather large) babies for the preliminary round but never finished the portrait. The victor in the competition for a medal/seal of the Second Republic showed a seated woman in classical robes (no bare breast), wearing a crown of sun's rays, holding a fasces. Around the edge of the seal was written 'The French Republic, democratic and indivisible' (no mention of social). Around her is a sheaf of corn and a voting urn, among other objects less easy to identify and the Gallic cockerel, which had been an important symbol of the previous regime. The new stamps appeared on 1 January 1849 with an image of the goddess Ceres, facing left, with a crown with ears of corn, grapes around her ears, and laurel, presumably indicating the abundance of food produced in France. It became known as the 'Ceres' stamp. Soitoux won the competition for the sculpted figure. She was standing, with a headdress of laurel leaves with a star in the centre (signifying the Enlightenment), with ribbons inscribed with Republic, Democracy and February. Her body was fully clothed in classical fashion. She held a sword and on a plinth the constitution, a triangle and a beehive. By the time Soitoux had completed his finished model in 1850 the republic had been seriously undermined by the election of Louis-Napoleon as president. Soitoux's Republic was displayed at the Salon in 1850 but was relegated to the Depository of Sculptures and was not shown until 1880 when it was erected on the Quai Conti. Existing republican statues began to disappear. The enormous Republic in the Place de la Concorde had been replaced in 1850 by 18 neutral allegories: Justice, Science, Shipping, Painting, Sculpture, Industry etc.

The name Marianne began to appear in Languedoc and the south in 1850 to mean the Republic. In December 1851 the republicans who resisted the coup in the south-west were sometimes grouped in secret societies known as Mariannes. A couple of years later the concept was known much more widely. After the coup the bust of the Republic in the Palais-Bourbon was replaced by one depicting Louis-Napoleon. In January 1852 the Emperor began to replace the Republic on stamps and coins. The imperial eagle replaced the liberal cockerel and the Republican fasces on military insignia. In September 1870 Napoleon III was captured at the Battle of Sedan and France was again a republic – and a republic under siege. There was no time or money to make new statues. The Place de la Concorde statue and the July Column were the focus for festivities. Then in March 1871 came the Paris Commune.

A bust of the Republic in a red scarf and red fasces took its place at the installation of the Commune at the Hôtel de Ville. At the Church of Saint-Eustache in central Paris, the statue of the Virgin with a red cap on her head had to make do. The anarchist Louise Michel was named the Red Virgin. After the defeat of the Commune, in provincial town halls small statues of Marianne began to stand for the Republic. The Ceres stamp re-appeared and symbols of the 1848 Republic, usually without Phrygian caps, re-appeared, but not in large numbers.

It was only in the twentieth century that Marianne became a ubiquitous non-contentious symbol of the Republic and of France itself, appearing not only in two impressive statues in Paris (Place de la Nation and Place de la République), but also as the official symbol of the Republic in town halls, and on all government logos (together with the tricolore and liberté, égalité and fraternité), the euro currency and postage stamps. The French began to use the image of actual women to represent Marianne, starting with Brigitte Bardot. In 1999 mayors were asked to vote and Laetitia Casta, half Norman, half Corsican, model (L'Oréal brand, among many others) and actress, was chosen. There was some controversy over the choice when she moved to London for a less expensive lifestyle, but having four children with three different fathers is apparently no disqualification for her role as Marianne.

The Bastille

In 1789 the Bastille was a royal prison in a worker district of the present day 11th *arrondissement*, detested by ordinary people as a symbol of absolute royal power. Wealthy individuals could ask the Crown to incarcerate a relative, who had no recourse to law to free him or herself. Some freed prisoners wrote about their ill treatment which added to resentment. As popular unrest grew when the Estates-General began to assemble in May, suspicions grew that weapons were being amassed there and that the Bastille would be the focus of repression. When the Estates-General began to assemble there was a build-up of royal troops, considered more dependable to the Crown, with Swiss and German regiments making up half of the 25,000 troops in Paris. On 11 July the king dismissed his popular chief minister, Necker and appointed ministers considered right wing. From the next day unrest grew with gatherings in the Palais Royal. Wax busts of Necker and the Duc d'Orléans were borrowed from the Curtius waxworks, put on pikes and used in demonstrations. Royal troops were no longer in control. The regiments of the French Guards, more sympathetic to the people, refused to break up demonstrations. On 13 July the electors of Paris agreed to form a militia of 48,000 men to keep order. General Lafayette, who had also fought in the American War of Independence, was put in command. By 14 July 1789 Paris was becoming increasingly lawless. The new militia, soon to be called the National Guard, stormed the Hôtel des Invalides to try to acquire weapons, but the commander had already moved the gunpowder to the Bastille. The

Figure 2.1 Storming of the Bastille and arrest of the Governor Bernard-René de Launay, 14 July 1789. GL Archive/Alamy Stock Photo.

word spread that the fortress of the Bastille was to be the key to crushing the popular movement and that it had been reinforced with guns and powder. It was regarded by locals in the faubourg Saint-Antoine as a monstrosity of Gothic torture, where prisoners were held on the command of the government without trial. In reality, just before the Revolution there were government plans for its demolition because it no longer fulfilled any real function.

On 14 July a crowd of about nine hundred local people, including soldiers who had defected, the traditionally radical artisans of the area, cabinet makers, joiners, hatters, tailors and owners of *cabarets*, marched to the Bastille and demanded that the big guns of the fortress be put out of action and the powder store handed over. The governor was indecisive. In reality, it was unlikely that the Bastille could have spearheaded an attack on the popular movement, for the fortress had no independent water supply and rations only for a couple of days. Its very vulnerability in the heart of a volatile artisan district made it a likely focus for popular suspicion and assault. The Bastille was attacked on 14 July not because it was a threat, but because it was a soft target. Someone in the crowd cut the chains to the Bastille drawbridge. Some of those who swarmed across thought the drawbridge was being lowered by capitulating troops. Fighting became intense. The men later honoured as the leaders of the attack, Jacob Elie and Pierre-Augustin Hulin, two officers who had defected from royal regiments, arrived mid-afternoon, together with other soldiers, *gardes françaises* and a supply of arms. At 5 pm the governor, de Launay, capitulated. His alternative was to blow up the powder store, which would have devastated a densely populated artisan neighbourhood.

Ninety-eight of the attackers were killed or died from injuries, but only one defender, which enraged the crowd who blamed the governor for the death of so many of their associates. De Launay was taken to the Hôtel de Ville where he was beaten to death without any chance to defend himself. Outside the Hôtel de Ville, de Launay's head was hoisted on a pike, surrounded by a crowd of singing and laughing citizens. Within a short time a second head was added, that of de Flesselles, the *prévot des marchands* who was accused of misleading people about stores of arms. He was shot as he emerged from the Hôtel de Ville and his dripping head was speared on a pike. Although these were impromptu killings, they did not lead to uncontrolled mass slaughter. Displaying human heads was apparently treated as almost a symbolic sacrament to confirm the victory of the people. Horrific tales were told about the condition of the prisoners released from the Bastille. The *vainqueurs* found only seven prisoners, despite an extensive search of the vast underground passages, which, rumour claimed, reached as far as Versailles itself. The Bastille was subsequently demolished, Mirabeau, the leading politician in the first stages of the revolution, taking the first ceremonial swing at the walls with a pick (Lusebrink and Reichardt, 1997). By the end of November most of it had been flattened. Within nine days of the fall of the Bastille, two more heads of government officials were speared on pikes, marched in procession and speedily rendered in wax. They were Foulon, named in the government to replace Necker, and Foulon's son-in-law, Bertier de Sauvigny, *intendant* of Paris. After an ill-judged remark that the hungry poor could eat hay, Foulon was strung up from a lamp post. The *vainqueurs* were later rewarded with a gun and a certificate of attendance. The waxworker, Curtius, carefully kept his and it can be seen in the Musée Carnavalet today.

Symbolically the destruction of the fortress can be compared with the demolition of the Berlin Wall two centuries later. It became the patriotic focus of the Revolution. Like the Berlin Wall, the ruins immediately became a tourist attraction. A thriving Bastille industry was orchestrated by Pierre-François Palloy. The single fortress mushroomed into hundreds of facsimiles. Bastille-shaped dominoes, paperweights and other mementoes were hawked throughout France. The Fête de la Fédération on 14 July 1790 celebrated the first anniversary of the Revolution, giving the attack on the Bastille permanent status as the beginning of the Revolution rather than the first meeting of the Estates-General or the Tennis Court oath. Thus from the start the experience of the Bastille meant that Revolution symbolised popular violence and murder, not philosophical ideas, conversation or debate.

Although the fortress had been broken into its component stones and scattered throughout the country, the Place de la Bastille continued to be the focus of revolutionary memory. After the July Days, 1830 a Colonne de Juillet, celebrating the July revolution, was erected on the Place de la Bastille. The names of all those who fought against the Bourbon King Charles X in 1830 were inscribed on the column. Their bodies, which had been buried where they fell in the fighting, were moved and buried under the column in 1840, before the ceremonial dedication. The re-burial was done at night, the new regime fearful that reminding Parisians of the recent revolution might cause renewed unrest because many were disappointed that the new regime had introduced so little reform. On 27 February 1848 the provisional government marched from the Hôtel de Ville, where they were sitting, to proclaim the Republic at the foot of the July Column, Place de la Bastille. On 4 March, after a religious service at the Church of the Madeleine, the patriots who died in fighting the 1848 revolution were carried in procession by the National Guard, 'the symbol of the Republic on a chariot drawn by eight horses and accompanied by one or several representatives of the workers' (Agulhon, 1981, 67) to the July Column, to be buried alongside the revolutionaries of 1830. The hastily constructed chariot resembled a market stall and the symbol of the Republic in this case was made of papier-maché. After the defeat of Napoleon III in September 1870 the July Column was the focus of festivities celebrating first the declaration of the Republic and then, in March 1871, the election of the Paris Commune.

Panthéon: Symbol of Revolutionary Great Men

The Panthéon (temple to all the gods in ancient Greek) was commissioned as a church in 1758 on the orders of Louis XV. The architect Soufflot based his design on the original ancient Roman Panthéon, still well-maintained today. The Paris site was the Montagne Sainte-Geneviève on the left bank of the Seine. The new church was to commemorate the patron saint of Paris and house her remains. When it was completed in 1790 the National Assembly instead declared it a mausoleum to house the remains of notable citizens. Mirabeau, first president of the first National Assembly, was interred, as were the enlightened philosophers Voltaire and Rousseau. Voltaire's internment was the occasion of a massive procession ordered by the National Assembly and staged by the artist Jacques-Louis David in July 1791. A lengthy cortège accompanied Voltaire's body, accompanied by a waxen image, to the Panthéon. Voltaire lay on an impressive sarcophagus placed in a bronze-wheeled funeral chariot and drawn by 12 white horses. The effigy was dressed in vermilion robes, and a beautiful girl, representing Immortality, crowned him with a halo of gold-coloured stars. Unfortunately it rained and the vermilion dye streaked the effigy (Duval, 1841, I, 288–293).

There were rumours later that Voltaire's remains had been discarded into a rubbish heap, but they were still intact. Rousseau's remains were moved in 1794, 16 years after his death, in an elaborately inlaid wooden sarcophagus with classical illustrations and suitably semi-naked ladies. There is no

Figure 2.2 Pantheon, Place du Pantheon, Sorbonne district, Paris, France. Peter Forsberg/Alamy Stock Photo.

indication how many people were needed to lift the device, but there were a not insubstantial number of handles let into the base. The revolutionary politician, Marat, considered a martyr after he was murdered by Charlotte Corday, was also placed in the mausoleum. He was later removed, judged unworthy. Napoleon added over 40, half the current clientele, largely forgotten soldiers, lawyers and administrators, but including the scientist Cabanis (1808), an evolutionist and supporter of Mirabeau. During the nineteenth century the use of the Panthéon switched from church (1827–1831, 1851–1870) to mausoleum, depending on the regime. It finally settled as a mausoleum in 1885 when Victor Hugo was installed. A mixture of politicians and artists followed; in 1889 Lazare Carnot, in 1894 his grandson and former president Sadi Carnot after his murder. Émile Zola was buried there in 1908, Léon Gambetta in 1920 and the socialist leader Jean Jaurès in 1929. Félix Eboué was the first black African put in the Panthéon in 1949. He was born the grandson of slaves in Cayenne. He became a senior administrator, a supporter of General de Gaulle's Free France Resistance, and governor-general of French Equatorial Africa, 1940–1944. Another Resistance fighter, Jean Moulin, was interred in 1964, followed in 1988 by Jean Monnet, founder of the European Economic Community. In 1989, thanks to the intervention of the Socialist president François Mitterrand, came the remains of the abbé Grégoire and Condorcet, liberal, anti-Jacobin revolutionaries of the 1790s. In 1995 it was the turn of the Nobel prize-winning physicists, Marie and

Pierre Curie. Toussaint Louverture, who, in 1791, led the black slave revolt which eventually made Haiti independent, became the second black man in the mausoleum in 1998. The novelist Alexandre Dumas followed in 2002. In 2007 President Chirac inaugurated a plaque dedicated to 2,600 'Righteous among Nations', who had saved French Jews in the Second World War. Thanks to them 75% of French Jews survived the Holocaust. In 2011 came Aimé Césaire, black poet and president of the regional council of Martinique. In 2013 François Hollande, the socialist president, suggested more women be considered (it was International Women's Day), including perhaps Olympe de Gouges, George Sand or Louise Michel… Michel, anarchist, feminist, and a Paris Commune leader, has a metro station and numerous streets named after her, but is still seen as too radical for the Panthéon. There are still only six women: Baker, Marie Curie and Sophie Berthillot – the latter qualifying as the wife of the nineteenth-century chemist, Marcellin – two resistance heroines who were added in 2015, Geneviève de Gaulle-Anthonioz and Germaine Tillon, and in 2018 came Simone Veil and her husband. Veil was a distinguished politician who as Health Minister advanced women's rights in her abortion legislation (1975). She was the first women to serve as President of the European Parliament (1979–1982) and in the Constitutional Council 1998–2007. President Macron gave the welcoming oration. In 2021 the Afro-American naturalised Frenchwoman, Josephine Baker, resister and entertainer, was the first black/foreign origin woman remembered in the Panthéon (not her remains but soil from her birthplace, Missouri, and some from where she died, Monaco). Anyone can propose additions to the government commission that runs the building and they are voted on.

What does the Panthéon symbolise today? Revolution? It is interesting that only moderate revolutionaries were considered worthy of the Panthéon. There is no sign of Robespierre or St Just and definitely not Blanqui. There are only six individuals representing revolution, mainly the ideas of the Enlightenment and moderate politicians of the early 1790s. Radical Jacobin revolution is totally absent. There are no representatives of nineteenth-century revolutions. Social revolution and socialism are totally shunned. Where is Louis Blanc? A passing tourist, and the Panthéon is a free visit on the tourist route, would assume from its architecture that the building is a church. A tricolour flag flies inconspicuously quite low down on the outside, but a crucifix is at the summit of the top dome in a far more prominent position. Religious imagery dominates the gloomy interior. From the outside the only hint of revolution are the carvings of post-revolutionary patriots on the pediment, erected by David d'Angers in 1837 and commissioned by the Orleanist regime. On the left are scientists, philosophers and statesmen, including Voltaire, General Lafayette and Xavier Bichat. Bichat, anatomist, pathologist and founder of histology, died in 1802 aged 30, having caught typhoid fever from dissecting infected skin. On the right stands Napoleon, and a group of soldiers, sailors and students from the École Polytechnique. Underneath is a huge inscription, readable from the street: 'To the great men, from a grateful nation'. This inscription was chipped away during the Restoration, to be renewed in 1830. The July regime also planned to erect a female colossus 'Immortality' on the top of the main dome, just as Liberty was to be set on the dome of the Capitol in Washington, but Immortality never made it. The purpose of the Panthéon is written over the main door: on the left, Public Education, on the right Patriotic Devotion. Its reputation is enhanced by the nearby Panthéon-Sorbonne, the most prestigious university in France. Except when a new body arrives, there do not seem to be organised occasions to gather people together to remember anything or anyone. There was an exception in 1851 when the physicist Léon Foucault demonstrated the rotation of the earth with a 67 metre pendulum beneath the central dome. To the very modest extent the Panthéon represents moderate revolution, it is cheerless revolution. A mass of tombs, the Panthéon seems to symbolise death. Although one thinks of the Panthéon in association with revolution, it celebrates a motley collection of innocuous individuals, chosen because they will not cause cultural and/or political offence and united by their support for a moderate Republic.

Statues of Liberty

The original Statue of Liberty was given to America by France in 1880 to celebrate the abolition of slavery. The design was based on the French symbol of liberty, Marianne. The iron components were made by Gustave Eiffel and shipped to America to be erected. Ten or more copies were subsequently made and displayed in France. One is on the Île aux Cygnes on the Seine River in the city centre. This was a gift from the United States in remembrance of the centenary of the first French revolution in 1889. Liberty carries a tablet inscribed with the dates of the US Declaration of Independence and the date of the storming of the Bastille. She used to look towards the Eiffel Tower in the east. In 1937 she was turned west to face the New York statue. Another scale version was made for the Exposition Universelle of 1900 which is now in the entrance hall to the Musée d'Orsay, and a bronze copy stands in the Jardin du Luxembourg. Another life-size copy given by the United States is at the entrance to the Pont de l'Alma tunnel. It was made a memorial to Princess Diana after her death in the tunnel in 1997.

The memory of 1789, recorded in numerous published accounts, encouraged later revolutions and the symbols devised were also used in subsequent revolutions.

3 Narrative of Nineteenth-Century Revolutions

France experienced more major unrest than any other European state in the nineteenth century despite the stability of her institutional and social framework which had emerged from the revolutionary years. As we saw in the first chapter, revolution is a portmanteau, chameleon term which can be used to describe violent change engineered by members of the existing elite, radical popular movements, or indeed both combined, but can equally be used for authoritarian takeovers such as Louis-Napoleon's coup of December 1851 or the support for general Boulanger in the 1880s. We will define revolution as violent regime change and in this chapter we will consider revolts in France. There were repeated revolts elsewhere in Europe which had been affected by 1789 and the Napoleonic wars. We will assess the impact of French revolutions in Europe in the following chapter on shared factors in revolution. There were five episodes in France, some of which impacted on Europe. These were March 1815, July 1830, February 1848, December 1851 and September 1870. Other events alarmed established governments, but did not bring permanent political change. These were the risings of June 1832, May 1839, June Days in 1848, the Paris Commune in March 1871 and the Boulanger episode in 1886. All took place in Paris. In addition there was substantial disruption in some major cities: Lyon (1831, 1834), Marseille and Lyon (1870). Finally, there was unrest in rural areas and small towns: 1818–1823, July 1830 – March 1831, April–June 1848, December 1851 – January 1852. None of these events unseated the central authorities in Paris. Some revolutions were encouraged by the civil militia, the National Guard, some by junior officers and men in the army. All revolts were brought to an end by military force, with imprisonment, deportations and death sentences, some of which were carried out, but with fairly speedy amnesties for those incarcerated. Ideas present in the 1789 Revolution re-emerge in these later revolutionary episodes, including liberty, equality, fraternity, sovereignty, constitution, democracy and republic, but do not always have the same meanings as in 1789 or today. As we trace the four main nineteenth century revolutionary events we will assess whether they contributed to revolts elsewhere.

DOI: 10.4324/9781003460596-3

March 1815 Hundred Days

This was a coup by the Emperor Napoleon deposed in 1814 after defeat by European Allies. It was well-received by his former soldiers but not accepted by the allies who defeated Napoleon for a second time and shipped him to the remote south Atlantic island of St Helena. Napoleon's actual escape and his return to France was a piece of pure individual opportunism. His decision was determined by the propinquity of Elba which, curiously, the Allies had given him to rule, and the intelligence he received concerning French army hostility to Bourbon military demobilisation. He landed near Cannes with just over one thousand followers on 1 March 1815. The Bourbon regime melted away, the royal brothers once more went into exile in Ghent. Many new royal officials simply renewed their loyalty to the Emperor. There was no armed resistance. By 20 March, Napoleon was in Paris.

Napoleon engaged the liberal Benjamin Constant to write a constitution, the *Additional Act to the Constitutions of the Empire* (Document 6), in an attempt to promote the pretence that the Restoration had not occurred. Napoleon was obliged at least to equal the liberal tenets of the Constitutional Charter of 1814. He went further. The belligerence of foreign powers, he claimed, had prevented him from setting up a fully representative regime earlier. A plebiscite held to confirm the new arrangements attracted the usual minority of voters; 1.5 million in favour, 4,802 against. Elections were held immediately for the new Chamber, but only 33,000 of the 69,000 enfranchised voters voted. Liberals dominated the new assembly, controlling 500 of the 629 seats. Only 80 Bonapartists were chosen. Napoleon had hoped for an obedient assembly, but found himself in partnership with an argumentative one. The 'Additional Act' would probably have been forgotten had he won at Waterloo and an authoritarian empire restored.

Napoleon's attempt at a comeback was defeated, not by the French, but by the allies. Napoleon was determined to renew the war, and the allies believed that peace was inconceivable while Napoleon remained in power. On 16 June 1815, he marched his army into the Low Countries. Two days later at Waterloo, his 72,000 men were defeated by slightly fewer allied troops in a battle Wellington himself admitted was 'a close run thing'. Almost 25,000 of the French troops were killed or wounded. Napoleon escaped to Paris, where he abdicated in favour of his son. On 3 July 1815 Paris surrendered. For a second time the allies restored the Bourbon Louis XVIII to be king of France. Napoleon's attempt to revive the empire failed, but the memory of the coup was elaborated in memoirs written by several of his companions in his final exile on St Helena (e.g. Las Casas, 1835). His great nephew, Prince Napoleon-Louis, wrote eulogistically in 1839, after an abortive effort to seize power in France, 'The Emperor Napoleon has contributed more than anyone else to hasten the reign of liberty by preserving the moral influence of the Revolution and diminishing the fear that it inspired. Without the Consulate and Empire the Revolution would have been merely a great drama, leaving grand recollections but few practical results' (Gooch, 1967, 34–35). The survival of memories of Napoleon facilitated the election of Louis-Napoleon to the presidency of the Second Republic in December 1848. With military support he was able to carry out a coup which brought the Second Republic to an end in December 1851, after which a plebiscite confirmed him Emperor in December 1852. The memory of Napoleon did not die and lives on with substantial revolutionary content in French memory today (Document 6).

July Days 1830

In July 1830 Charles X, Comte d'Artois, was deposed by the liberal majority in parliament and replaced by his cousin, Louis-Philippe, Duc d'Orléans. This successful revolution was the product of a combination of economic and political circumstances. In 1814 the Restoration regime seemed a tolerable settlement to liberals who had worked with Napoleon and royalists who returned with Louis XVIII. But after the Hundred Days in 1816, liberals were violently persecuted by ultra-royalists in the White Terror. Younger clergy ran a prolonged evangelical campaign to ask forgiveness for the Revolution. A week's campaign would end with a procession carrying a cross to be erected, not on a church, but on village property. Later, in 1825, a law was passed imposing a death sentence for sacrilege to church property.

In 1820, after the murder of the Duc de Berry, son of the Comte d'Artois and the heir to the throne – by a liberal pursuing personal, not political motives – the ultra-royalist far right began to assert itself. A double vote for the 25% richest electors was adopted by decree. A mere 40 liberals were elected in 1824. Subsequently a new seven year law allowed the Chamber of Deputies to sit for seven years. On the death of Louis XVIII in 1824, his brother, the Comte d'Artois, the leader of the ultras, succeeded as Charles X. Parliament voted to raise a loan to allow *émigrés* whose land had been declared national land and sold during the Revolution to reclaim it if it became available. Liberals, who had acquired much of this national land, were apprehensive that their titles to national land might be questioned. In 1827 the small liberal group in the Assembly, led by François Guizot, set up Help Yourself and the Heavens Will Help You (*Aide-toi, le ciel t'aidera*), to protest at prefects cheating when they compiled electoral lists and also when they ran elections. The electorate had shrunk from 110,000 to 79,000 since 1816. Prefects were excising liberals from the electorate and displaying electoral lists pinned up so high that no-one could read them and taking them down after only a short time so liberals had no time to produce documentation showing they paid enough tax to qualify as a voter. *Aide-toi* published short pamphlets telling voters how to ensure their name appeared on electoral lists. At the same time an economic crisis exploded when an investment bubble broke and led in 1827 to bankruptcies, industrial setbacks and unemployment and short-term work. Harvest failures in 1828 and 1829 doubled the price of bread while taxes on wine kept the sale price of the small amount of poor quality wine impossibly high. The government's tariff policy was blamed.

Liberals began to win by-elections and in November 1827 the Chief Minister Villèle decided to hold an election early, hoping he would keep his majority. He could have waited until 1831. The result was a hung parliament, with around 180 royalists, 180 liberals and 60–80 ultras. Charles tried to compromise and appointed the centre-right Martignac Chief Minister, naming Duvergier d'Hauranne, a leading liberal, President of the Chamber of Deputies. Martignac's attempts to keep the liberals content by initiating an investigation into the economic crisis, promising that local councils would become elective and excluding the Jesuits from France, failed and he resigned. In April 1829 Charles appointed Polignac, his friend, possibly his illegitimate son, at the head of a right-wing government. The re-call of parliament was postponed from December 1829 to March 1830. New liberal newspapers including *Le National*, edited by Adolphe Thiers, campaigned for 'no taxation without representation'. In March instead of the traditional anodyne response to the speech from the throne, the Chamber of Deputies passed a motion of no-confidence in the government, with 221 deputies supporting the motion. On 19 March Charles dissolved parliament. In elections in June 1830 liberals secured a majority with 270 seats, including 202 of the 221, with 145 royalists.

The Four Ordinances, July 1830: A Royal Coup d'Etat?

Charles claimed that the liberals were a revolutionary threat and that the election results were a challenge to his own authority. He invoked Article 14 of the Charter which allowed the king to make decree laws in an emergency. On 26 July the King issued four decrees. The first ordered all liberal papers to cease publication, or risk the seizure of their presses by the police. The second dissolved the new assembly before it had even met. The third called new elections for early September, and the fourth disenfranchised 75% of the electorate, leaving only the double vote electors to vote for a Chamber which was reduced to 258 members. The remainder of the electorate were merely allowed to propose candidates.

Until August 1829, ultras, royalists and liberals had muddled along tolerably well. Why did a political crisis turn to revolution? If the liberal deputies had been the decision makers, it is likely that the ordinances would have been absorbed, with grumbling resignation, into the political game. Liberal unity collapsed as the crisis turned to revolution. Forty-four liberal editors and journalists agreed to publish a written protest, prepared by Thiers. However only the *Le National*, *Le Globe* and *Le Temps* published it. What turned a political crisis into a revolution was the intertwining of hesitant elite mutterings with more robust popular protest. This was facilitated by the geography of central Paris. The central artisan districts, which were home to the luxury trades of the capital, with tailors, hatters, shoemakers, cabinet makers and metal workers, had been in a ferment of demonstrations and protests for three years over short-term work and unemployment. The Four Ordinances drove more men and women than was usual on the streets for the traditional Monday demonstrations (there was a tendency to extend the weekend Sunday break by another day). The usual crowd was joined by the print workers and journalists, put out of work by the new decrees. What made their turbulent marches dangerous was that the central artisan quarters also contained not only the newspaper industry but also adjoining centres of government. Close by were the town houses of nervous liberal deputies. The streets in which the workers demonstrated were narrow and easy to barricade.

The King was not in Paris, but at his palace in St Cloud. He had made no plans to protect himself by bolstering the forces of law and order. Ordinary minor infringements of law and order were in the hands of the local police commissioners who were few in number. During the 1789 Revolution a volunteer civil militia or National Guard had quickly sprung up, the nucleus of which was usually made up of former soldiers, the bulk being small businessmen and artisans. After 1815 it was a symbol of revolution and a bastion of Bonapartism. The King dissolved the Guard in 1827, following a royal inspection that was accompanied by shouts, the most polite of which was 'Long live the Charter'. This meant that if a civil disturbance threatened to get out of hand, the authorities did not have the Guard to turn to, and there was a danger, which indeed occurred during the 1830 revolution, that former guardsmen would dig out their uniforms, weapons and tricolour flags, and side with the insurgents.

For the authorities, their best hope of controlling a major disturbance was to call out the local regiment of the gendarmerie. Unfortunately for Charles X, in January 1830 a substantial force had set off for Algeria, taking Algiers on 5 July, leaving the capital without reserves. Marmont, Duc de Raguse (1774–1852), a former Napoleonic marshal, was in charge of the defence of Paris. He was considered a traitor by left-wingers because he had sided with the royalists in 1814; *ragusard* had come to mean traitor. In theory Marmont had 13,000 men at his disposal, half of them the Royal Guard. He could muster fewer than half. The line regiment was so jealous of the privileged Royal Guard that many deserted to the rebels. Initially Marmont remained sanguine because in 1827 he had controlled unrest with a much smaller body of men.

The Three Glorious Days

The revolution began on 27 July, with the erection of barricades at several points in central Paris, but Marmont was so confident that he sent his men back to their barracks in the suburbs at nightfall. On 28 and 29 more substantial barricades were raised in the right-bank artisan districts, near the Hôtel de Ville, the rue Saint-Honoré, the Palais-Royal, the Tuileries and the workers' district of St Antoine. Marmont was helpless. Men in National

Guard uniforms and his own junior officers, NCOs and men deserted to the opposite side of the barricades. On 29 July the royal troops abandoned the Tuileries and with this the fighting was effectively over. No accurate figures exist of the numbers of dead and injured. Some sources claim that 2000 people were killed. Others put the figures lower, with 800 insurgents and 200 soldiers dead. The figures for the injured also vary, with the highest total standing at 4,000 rebels and 800 soldiers. About 1,750 of the 6000 soldiers deserted to the rebels. Most of the dead and injured among the insurgents were young skilled artisans. These numbers were relatively small for an uprising which changed the regime.

The artisan combatants looked to the liberal journalists and deputies for leadership, unaware that most were mere fearful onlookers to the struggle. It was only on 29 July that the deputies, after frantic and indecisive meetings, sometimes at the banker Casimir Périer's home, sometimes at the house of Jacques Laffitte, the Duc d'Orléans' banker, finally published a timid criticism of the Ordinances, in which they insisted on their loyalty to the King. Only 41 of the 73 deputies present actually signed the document. Anxious to assert themselves after they had realised that the King was losing control and the initiative was passing to General Lafayette, who had been commander of the first National Guard in 1789 and was now the champion of the Parisian artisans, some liberal deputies and journalists, especially Thiers' cohort from the *National*, declared a 'provisional municipal committee' at the Hôtel de ville. It was composed of moderates, Orleanists, republicans and Bonapartists, and included Périer and Laffitte.

Late on 29 July, Charles, who remained at St Cloud, agreed to dismiss Polignac. That night Thiers hammered up placards praising the leadership qualities of Louis-Philippe. The next day, on the urging of some of the deputies, Thiers went to Louis-Philippe's home at Neuilly to offer him the role of Lieutenant-General of the Kingdom. On 31 July, persuaded by his sister that Charles X was a spent force, Louis-Philippe returned to the capital to accept the Lieutenant-Generalcy and to take part in a staged procession to the Hôtel de Ville with Lafayette. A dramatic representation depicts Lafayette embracing the Duke on the balcony, both enveloped in tricolour flags. Captions claim that Lafayette apparently hailed the Duke's elevation as 'the best of republics'. Charles abdicated on 1 August, leaving the throne to his grandson, the Duc de Bordeaux, aged 7, but acknowledging Louis-Philippe as Lieutenant-General during his minority.

How Revolutionary Were the July Days?

The Chamber of Deputies, surrounded by National Guardsmen, named Louis-Philippe King of the French people, to show he owed his power to the nation and not to God (Document 7). The voting qualification was reduced from 300 francs in direct tax to 200 for electors and from 1000 to 500 for candidates, doubling the electorate. Local councils became elective, the qualification often as low as 80 francs to secure a quorum. Officers in the National Guard were elected by their men democratically. From 1831 men promoted to the Chamber of Peers were given a title for their life only, inheritance was abolished. The Catholic Church was no longer the state church in France. In 1833 Guizot encouraged communes to set up state primary schools. There was talk of freedom of the press, but censorship increased and from 1835 the word 'republic' was banned. Louis-Philippe tried to look like a citizen-king (Document 7). His portraits showed him standing next to a very modest throne, dressed in National Guard uniform, with his hand on a copy of the constitution. He and his wife Marie-Amelie walked freely around the gardens of their home, the Palais Royal and in Paris until several attempts on his life confined them to a coach. Children attended state lycées. Court ceremony was cut, fancy uniforms abolished. The Saint-Simonian, Thomas Urbain, mixed race son of a black slave, the government's chief interpreter of Arabic in Algeria whose wife was indigenous Algerian, stayed at Versailles and was included in a portrait with the royal family. This was quite radical behaviour for the king. Louis-Philippe's eldest son and wife were liberal reformers. These were real, if modest, changes. However liberals split into Resistance, more conservative liberals like Guizot and Périer, who grabbed most jobs, and Movement, more radical deputies, who had often held office in the Hundred Days and hoped for a bigger electorate and fiscal change, grading into Republicans who demanded a popular vote on the modified constitution and the abolition of indirect taxes, but had no precise plans for a republic.

Anti-Clericalism

Anti-clerical demonstrations were frequent in the July Days and increased in number for at least eight more months. The prime targets were senior clergy who had organised evangelical missions after 1814, and who, sensibly, left the country during the revolution. The palace of the Archbishop of Paris was sacked, his books and vestments thrown in the Seine. The palaces of other bishops in eastern France, notably in Nancy and Besançon, met a similar fate, as did seminaries. The violence was often encouraged by new prefects and mayors who last held office during the Hundred Days and whose passions were at least as much personal as religious. The climax of anti-clerical demonstrations was the wrecking of the Church of St Germain l'Auxerrois, Place du Louvre, Paris, 14–15 February 1831.

Political Opposition

The memory of the early 1790s meant that every nineteenth-century revolution in France was followed by the mushrooming of political clubs whose leaders consciously imitated their historic mentors. Clubs caused particular apprehension to the new elite, partly because the Orleanist regime was born of revolution, partly because the clubs flaunted a self-proclaimed Jacobin inheritance both in their structure and their ideas and because some clubs attracted artisan and peasant support as the economic depression deepened.

***Aide-toi, le ciel t'aidera*:** Before 1830 its mission had been to promote constitutional government by protecting the electoral system. After the July Days many of its members secured government jobs, like Guizot, and resigned. *Aide-toi* broadened its goals to include a larger electorate, economic and fiscal reform and universal education. It also continued to act as an electoral pressure group, but now for the Movement; 30,000 of their pamphlets were issued in 1832. *Aide-toi* remained legal and was a source of information and measured criticism of the unwillingness of conservative Orleanists to consider gradual reform. It always consisted of an educated elite, even though it wanted to extend the boundaries of the electoral community. Many were lawyers or professional men. In 1832, when Garnier-Pagès launched a membership drive, the initial subscription was 5 francs with an annual fee of 12 francs. These high sums would have limited its appeal to the comfortably-off.

***Amis du Peuple*:** A new club set up on 30 July 1830 as a public society with no limit on numbers in flagrant defiance of article 291 of the Code was very different. It condemned the new regime for its failure to call a constituent assembly after the revolution, commenting drily that the assembled deputies spent less time rewriting the constitution than the previous parliament had devoted to discussing river fishing. Indeed, they claimed, the text of the revised constitution was not even read before the assembly voted on it. They held large, noisy public meetings in a Paris riding stable. Their placards challenging the legality of the Chamber of Deputies led to the arrest and imprisonment of their President Hubert, Thierry, their Treasurer, and David their printer. The society, which had only 150 members on its books, was forced to adopt a clandestine structure, meeting in a building owned by the freemasons. Their leaders were implicated in the riots which followed the judicial decision merely to imprison the ex-ministers of Charles X when they had been found guilty of causing the revolution. Nineteen members were arrested, but were acquitted. In 1831 they organised a battalion to help the Belgian revolution and were the focus of most of the Parisian popular demonstrations in the first two years of the regime. They liked to present themselves as 'jacobins'. Numerous small radical clubs were founded, particularly in eastern France. An attempt to deny the right of association and to condemn the *Amis* as illegal was dismissed by the assize court in Paris in December 1832.

***Société des Droits de l'Homme*:** This society was founded at the same time. It was less active than the *Amis* until after the June insurrection of 1832, when the *Amis* were forced to close and the *Droits de l'Homme* took over as the main republican club. It had 750 members in Paris alone. It seems to have been rather a bureaucratic society, judging by its lists of rules and members discovered by prefects. There was a central committee of 11 directors, with 12 commissioners for each *arrondissement* of Paris. The sections had radical revolutionary names including Robespierre, St Just and Babeuf.

In April 1833 the leaders of one section were arrested and the whole society declared illegal by the courts, but the decision seems to have had little immediate impact. At its height it had about 3,000 members in Paris and perhaps 30,000 in France.

In addition to these two main clubs, there were other sometimes short-lived organisations set up to publicise such issues as national defence, press freedom and universal education. In the spring of 1831 a National Association was started in eastern France to protect France should the Allies try to restore Charles X.

The *Association polytechnique* was founded after the July Days by former students of the college who were involved in the fighting and had tended the wounded. They offered classes in literacy etc. and had a distinguished membership. Its successor was the *Association pour l'instruction gratuite du peuple*. Its leaders were Movement deputies. Étienne Cabet, a Movement then republican journalist, provided publicity for this society in his paper, *Le Populaire*. In 1833, 2,500 people were enrolled in its 54 classes in Paris. The scope of the organisation had broadened; doctors and lawyers offered their services free and the society also offered a job-hunting facility. There were similar charitable associations with related aims in provincial France as well as one to oppose increasing press censorship.

What sort of people became members of these radical, increasingly republican groups? There were some notables, landowners and industrialists, who had been in the liberal opposition to Charles X. Most were young. The leaders of the *Amis* included Cavaignac, son of the republican of the 1790s, Blanqui, and the radical young doctors Buchez, Trélat and Raspail. Members of parliament included Cabet, Lafayette, Lamarque, and Dupont de l'Eure. Among journalists the outstanding figures were Marrast, editor of *Le Tribune*, and Carrel, editor of *Le National*. Nearly all arrived at republicanism via the *charbonnerie*, *Aide-toi* and a family or personal commitment to the memory of the 1789 Revolution.

Republican clubs also sought out soldiers, and did well among junior non-commissioned artillery officers.

Their followers included law and medical students, young clerks, shop assistants, artisans and some peasants. There was usually a high proportion of established lawyers, not infrequently including members of the judiciary. Journalists usually founded the provincial clubs. National Guard officers were always present; in Dijon all the committee members were officers.

Newspapers were important for republicans. Orleanists constantly prosecuted editors and although juries tended to acquit, the cost of the trial undermined finances. Pamphlets were the cheapest form of publicity, sold in the countryside by hawkers. Another traditional form of publicity in this period when large-scale societies were banned was to hold banquets to honour leading sympathetic politicians, who would be invited to give speeches. The republicans exploited this medium with great success. One held in Dijon in December 1833 in favour of electoral reform was attended by six hundred diners, including mayors from nearby communes. After the meal there would be reform speeches by politicians. Republicans organised subscriptions, including one for the Poles, defeated in 1831 in their struggle for freedom from Russia. Funerals were one of the few occasions when republicans could gather legally.

Some republicans wanted to seize power. There was always an insurrectionary strand, which could never be entirely ignored, partly because the revolutionary tradition of the 1790s legitimised the violent overthrow of regimes and more tangibly because National Guard battalions were usually sympathetic to popular unrest. Clubs were ordered to drill and hold target practice (Pilbeam, 2014, *The 1830 Revolution in France*).

Lyon 1831

After Paris, Lyon was the most industrial city in France with a corresponding radical population. The silk industry, the dominant trade in the city, was at the centre of a mass dispute in November 1831. Silk was produced in small independent workshops. Over 50,000 workers, 25% of the working population of the city, were involved. Growth during the Restoration was followed by setbacks during the depression of 1827–1832. Proto-capitalist economic change led to serious social conflict. The weavers were in repeated deadlock with silk merchants who were attempting to assert themselves as employers rather than partners. The increase of rural industry outside the control of the master-weavers' organisations allowed merchants to buy woven silk cheaper, ignoring the traditional, but often neglected, concept of a *tarif* or negotiated fixed price. The development of the Jacquard loom on which the more expensive, fashionable patterned silks were woven obliged weavers to borrow capital from merchants to buy the new larger, more complex loom and acquire more spacious properties with higher ceilings in which it could be installed. In 1827 the master weavers, who had little faith in any government after the experiences of the Loi le Chapelier, banded together in the Society of Surveillance and Mutual Duty to try to protect their independence. The journeymen formed their own organisation and both groups cooperated.

After the 1830 Revolution the silk trade suffered further setbacks, but in 1831 a new prefect, Dumolard, acceded to the demands of the weavers, the *canuts*, to try to negotiate a set price for silk. Informed of the disapproval of his Parisian bosses, Dumolard retracted. The *canuts*, disappointed at the decision of the prefect not to intervene in their long-running dispute with merchants over rates of pay, and with, as was the norm in such conflicts, the National Guard of central Lyon, which had many weaver members, on their side, drove the local garrison out of town, marching with black flags emblazoned with their motto, 'Vivre libre en travaillant, ou mourir en combattant'. Paris had to send military reinforcements and a new prefect to regain control, to remain 'neutral', as they claimed. The government asserted that it was a purely economic dispute. In a pamphlet headed 'La Guerre Civile', the republican *Amis du Peuple* showed little understanding of the dispute; they referred to the weavers as 'ouvriers', which would not have pleased them. The rising in Lyon was the most dramatic of many popular disturbances in these years. It was certainly not republican, but it showed that Orleanists would not shrink from using the army to enforce the rights of the better-off.

Paris 1832

The next popular disturbance was in Paris in the summer of 1832 at the height of the cholera outbreak: 18,000 people died of cholera in a few weeks. The virulence of cholera in the worker districts led to rumours that the water was being deliberately poisoned. On 5 June, the funeral of the radical hero, General Lamarque, a cholera victim, was accompanied by 130 opposition deputies. Louis Blanc, the socialist journalist, described the episode as the first truly republican insurrection since 1815. There was pressure from rank and file members of the *Amis* to exploit the slight political uncertainty when the Chief Minister Périer also died from cholera for an armed uprising, but leaders resisted. As the long procession proceeded through central Paris to the river, the flying of the red flag, the sight of a revolutionary Phrygian bonnet and rumours that the Hôtel de Ville had fallen to insurgents, provoked troops to open fire as the funeral speeches for Lamarque were in progress. Barricades went up in the traditional central artisan districts behind the Hôtel de ville. But republican leaders refused their support and on 6 June left the artisans to a hopeless fight with the National Guard, which on this occasion remained loyal to the government. A total of 800 were killed or wounded. Paris was put in a state of siege; seven were condemned to death (commuted to deportation), four others to deportation. When the economy began to recover in the summer of 1832, both popular unrest and support for republican papers and clubs declined. But in 1833 there was another wave of industrial unrest as workers tried to improve rates of pay reduced during the depression.

Lyon 1834 and the April 'Conspiracy'

Parisian republicans targeted Lyon, but at first totally misread the situation by presenting themselves as partisans of modernisation. They misunderstood the structure of the silk industry and antagonised weavers by favouring industrial 'freedom', when weavers were anxious precisely to restrict the 'freedom' of merchants to pay the lowest rate possible for woven silk. The Orleanist ministers seemed to be running before the wind of three myths, largely of their own imaginings. They were convinced that the Lyon silk weavers were a threat to the regime; that they had been won over to republicanism and that a nation-wide conspiracy was to be launched by both groups with Lyon as the focus in the spring of 1834. A three-pronged government attack was launched: to stop the circulation of republican pamphlets, to close the clubs and to force their newspapers out of business. In February 1834 hawkers were forced to apply to the prefect to ply their wares, which permit could be revoked at any time. Legislation was introduced in parliament to force all societies to disband, whatever their size.

At the beginning of 1834 weavers of Lyon were once again in dispute with the merchants over the price to be paid for woven silk. The weavers were also aware that the proposed new legislation on associations would force their Mutual Duty and *Ferrandinier* societies to close. A strike was called once more. On 14 February, all 25,000 looms in Lyon came to an agreed standstill, under the same provocative black banners as in 1831, but there was no quick military victory this time. The society lacked strike funds and weavers were forced back to their looms within a week. The strike leaders were committed for trial.

Silk weavers were primarily concerned with the survival and prosperity of their families and their trade. They believed that successive Orleanist governments had waged war against them. Weavers were deeply resentful both of the tariff policy of the regime and the official proclamation of *laissez-faire*, which protected the employers by using troops against strikers, and banned coalitions of workers. But memories of the First Republic in Lyon did not encourage weavers to expect much from republicans. The February strike was a trade dispute. However the imminence of the new legislation made a strict separation of economic and political motivation impossible. All societies, political and trade, expected to be forced to disband. Agitation in Lyon persisted because of the inflammatory decision to hold the trial of the strike leaders at the precise time when the bill to outlaw all associations was before parliament. Artisans feared that their mutual-aid societies would be disbanded. The new legislation secured a majority of 246 to 154 in the Chamber of Deputies on 10 April. All societies, whatever their size or nature, were obliged to seek prefectoral sanction. The penalty for belonging to an illegal organisation was increased from a modest fine to one year's imprisonment and a 1,000 francs fine. Whoever owned the property where an illegal meeting was held was equally liable.

The postponed trial of the strike leaders opened on 9 April in an atmosphere which the local administration had allowed to become overcharged. Onlookers threw stones, the troops on duty around the *palais de justice* opened fire. Barricades were erected in defence, and by the 15 April, 300 were dead. Artillery was used to blast the central weaving districts with little discrimination. The newer outlying Croix Rousse weaving district had been carefully isolated by fortifications built since the last rising and was attacked separately. Most of the casualties among the troops were due to their inexperience in inner-city guerrilla tactics. The 3,000–6,000 artisans felt that they had been left with no choice but to take arms against the professional army and the merchants in the Croix Rousse National Guard – 37% of those arrested were weavers, mainly journeymen. The rest were mostly from other trades. A mere 15% were in either a political or even a workers' association. Of the 100 arrested and sent for trial on charges of conspiracy against the government, 39 were republicans. Of these a mere eight were eventually tried. The ferocity of the government's response meant that the official line had to be maintained that unrest in Lyon was part of a long-discussed republican plot republicans had been boasting about since the beginning of the year.

In reality, anxiety about the proposed legislation and how to oppose it contributed much to reviving a divided republican movement, no longer buttressed by popular unrest because the short-term economic recession had faded. Police informers convinced the government that a major republican rising was planned to coincide with riots in Lyon throughout eastern and south-eastern France. Informers invented or created conspiracies. In Paris republican leaders were unprepared for action when the news of the Lyon rioting broke. The government ordered the arrest of 500 militants in Paris and banned the publication of the *Tribune*. A small rising did take place, although the leaders tried to prevent it, considering the time quite inauspicious. On 13 April barricades went up in the artisan districts, but the next day the attempt was repressed with unnecessary bloodshed. An ordinary family in the rue Transnonain, with no links to republicanism, was massacred and depicted in a much-reproduced Daumier cartoon.

The attempted 'risings' all had a common motive, resistance to the new legislation, but they were not synchronised to be a takeover of power. The government continued to insist that there had been a conspiracy, despite all evidence to the contrary. The official web of suspicion, lies and intrigue had to be sustained. The government ordered the arrest of 2,000 so-called leaders, 164 of whom were finally tried in May 1835, not by the independent-minded assize court but by the Chamber of Peers. During their year in prison, the press depicted the accused as victims. There was never any evidence of a great conspiracy and most of those arrested were released without accusation. But those accused failed to disport themselves as martyrs; they argued amongst themselves and some refused to go to court. The republican Fieschi's bloody attempt to kill Louis-Philippe deprived them of all popular sympathy, even though they had no connection with him.

After over six months of hearings, in January 1836, the accused were sentenced. Typical was a fine of 10,000 francs and three years' jail when Trélat denied the right of the court to try him. Leading republicans, including Cavaignac and Cabet, avoided trial by sailing to England. After all the fuss, the convicted were released in 1837 and in 1840 the exiles were allowed to return to France. The relatively light sentences and the long delay in trying the 'accusés d'avril', as they were called, may be contrasted with the death sentences instantly carried out by the Restoration regime for similar 'offences'.

Laws against the radical press, urged on by the Fieschi attempt on the King, reached the statute book in September 1835 and were to remain in force, with brief intervals until 1881. The initial caution money paid by an editor was raised, new press 'crimes' were introduced, but most importantly, press cases were no longer to be tried by juries. Those indicted of insults to the king risked a fine of 50,000 francs and a year in jail. Newspapers could no longer publish the details of a trial. The word 'republic' was banned.

May 1839

This was a brief, Parisian rising orchestrated by the republican Louis-Auguste Blanqui which failed. He was a disciple of Babeuf and Buonarroti. He was nicknamed 'l'enfermé', because over half of his adult life, about 34 years in all, were spent in jail. He never lost the conviction that a tiny, conspiratorial revolutionary group could bring down the corrupt system of the July Monarchy and its successors and create a socialist republic. He set up two secret republican societies, in 1835 the Families, which ended in arrests and imprisonments, and in 1837 the Seasons, named because of its structure – grouped in weeks, months etc. No written membership lists were to be kept; acolytes took an oath to the republic: 'In the name of the Republic, I swear eternal hatred to all kings, aristocrats and all oppressors of humanity'. The monthly subscription was a modest 50 cents and the hat was passed around at meetings to meet the cost of weapons. Funds did not come easily and towards the end no membership fees were levied. There was no attempt to secure support within the army, because it was judged too risky. A high proportion of members were artisans and some groups were composed entirely from men in one trade. Tailors were the largest single element. By the beginning of 1838 they had 900 supporters, according to the Parisian police. Among the leaders were Barbès, Martin Bernard, with Blanqui as the undisputed senior figure. Like the Families, the society met in small groups on Sunday afternoons mainly in cafés.

Plans were laid for a rising on Sunday 12 May 1839, 2.30 pm. A Sunday, being a holiday, was the best hope for popular support. The coincidence of an economic recession with a prolonged ministerial crisis may have convinced Blanqui that circumstances were similar to those of July 1830. News of Chartist activities in England contributed to a belief that change was possible. Additionally, a major horse-race meeting on that day meant that few National Guardsmen would be available for duty. Finally, Blanqui was afraid that he would lose control unless a revolt was attempted. The Prefecture of Police and the main bridges were to be seized, enabling the plotters to hold the right bank of the Seine from the Marais to Montmartre. A proclamation prepared for the occasion announced a people's republic. 'The hour of doom has struck for our oppressors. People arise! Your enemies will disappear like dust in a storm. Strike! Exterminate the base henchmen and willing accomplices of our tyrants! Forward! Long live the Republic!'

The rising was to be led by Blanqui, Barbès and Martin-Bernard. Only the main leaders knew of the project. The main body of men were called to assemble as if for a regular review, starting in various cafés in the rue St Denis, rue St Martin and surrounding streets. Assaults began on key installations. Barbès himself led a column of 600 men to the *palais de justice* where he urged the troops on duty to join him. The guard-post at the palais succumbed, but the troops at the prefecture opposite resisted and reinforcements were brought in. Meanwhile Blanqui took the nearby Hôtel de Ville, but was soon in combat with the municipal guard. Men were sent to take control of the town halls in other Paris districts. Barricades went up in the artisan quarters of St Denis and St Martin and in the Temple area. Armourers' shops were sacked by the rebels. However they met with fierce resistance from the troops, who by 11 pm had re-established control. On the following day only a few isolated barricades remained in the Marais area.

Who took part? About 66 rebels were killed, or died from their wounds, including five women, with 28 dead on the government side. All the main leaders were speedily incarcerated and charged. Within 24 hours nearly 300 arrests had been made, the final total reaching almost 700. Many were speedily released, leaving just under 300 to be called for trial. Nearly 87% were workers, mainly artisans. The rest were middle class. The social profile of the participants was very similar to the crowd in June 1848, but rather different from the membership of the republican societies of the early 1830s, when even in Paris only 66% of the Society of the Rights of Man were artisans and the majority of provincial associates were middle class. The luxury trades of central Paris predominated as usual. The largest single element were textile workers (39), closely followed by workers in the high quality metallurgical trades (37) and cabinet makers (31), all of whom, like the 28 building workers and 26 leather workers, suffered in the recurring economic recessions of these years. They were young, the average age being 27. Married men with families would be actively discouraged from risking what earning potential they had. Most were not Parisian by birth; 64.5% were outsiders, mostly from neighbouring departments.

Why did the rising fail? It was planned and timed like a bank robbery. The precedent of the July Days was misleading; 1830 was not a planned revolution. In 1839 there were recognised and accepted self-chosen leaders, but there were too many who expected to exercise supreme command. The rising did not attract a spontaneous mass following as Blanqui had predicted. Later Barbès was to criticise Blanqui for hesitation. Above all, unlike 1830, the elite rallied instantly to the regime. The 1839 political crisis was a mere ministerial hiccup compared with both 1830 and 1848. The National Guard did not don its uniform on the rebel side as it had done in 1830, even though there was considerable republican sympathy in the surviving units, especially in the provinces. In contrast to 1830 the municipal guard took an active part in combating the insurrection as did the regular troops. The trial of 22 of the conspirators by the supreme court of appeal, the Cour des Pairs, opened with unprecedented speed on 27 June. Blanqui was to spend the remaining years of the constitutional monarchy in prison, starting with Mont St Michel. He was to become an international star when Lenin recognised a debt of gratitude to Blanqui in developing his own theory of the 'vanguard' party (Document 8).

Revolutions 1848, February and June

There were two upheavals in 1848, in February a successful republican revolt, in June, a failed worker protest. As in July 1830 their origins lay in the combination of political conflict and economic crisis.

Political Issues: Scandals

There were repeated accusations that the July Monarchy was corrupt. Technical progress in lithography improved visual representation immeasurably, and it was increasingly cheap, leading to the growth of cartoons in newspapers and the sale of cheap single sheet cartoons. The best remembered images of the time are critical cartoons, epitomised by Daumier's 'pear' and his representation of the massacre in the rue Transnonain. The new popular caricature newspapers, *Le Charivari* and *Le Caricature*, ridiculed the Orleanist monarchy and its ruling elite as self-serving, self-important, corrupt money-grubbers. The wide boy, Robert Macaire, was invented by Daumier; 140 lithographs of Macaire appeared in the *Charivari* from 1836 to 1841, when they were banned. Macaire also appeared in plays (Kerr, 2000). In May 1847 came a criminal trial of a mining company. Teste, President of the Court of Appeal and a peer, was accused of accepting large payments when he was Minister of Public Works in return for industrial concessions from General Cubières, then Minister of War. Teste attempted suicide while in prison. Both ministers were found guilty, jailed for three years and condemned to loss of civil rights. In 1847, August the Duc de Choiseul-Praslin was accused of brutally murdering his wife – he committed suicide in prison.

Social and Economic Issues

In 1846 the French endured a second year of harvest failures and potato blight. Bread prices went up by 50%. In addition there was an industrial recession similar to that of 1827–1833. Railway shares crashed. There was serious unemployment and short-term work in Paris, Rouen, Lyon, Limoges and other large towns, as well as in the rapidly expanding rural industry. This was followed by unrest, both in towns and rural areas, including not only complaints about food shortages, high prices and lack of work, but also including vigorous protests about issues which were a constant source of complaint, indirect taxation and the erosion of common rights, especially over forests. There was a new dimension, reformist socialism which proposed alternative ways of re-shaping the society and the economy. Three famous socialist books appeared between 1839 and 1841: Louis Blanc's *Organisation of Work*, Etienne Cabet's *Voyage en Icarie*, both of which had gone through five editions by 1848, and Proudhon's *What is Property?* By the mid-1840s Cabet was at the head of the largest worker organisation ever formed, the Icarians. Fourierist middle-class socialists were organised in groups in most main towns in France. In the 1840s histories of the First Republic sold well. Finally, the Banquet campaign for electoral reform organised over 80 banquets in 28 traditionally radical departments between July 1847 and February 1848, attended by officials, including mayors, and supported by moderate opposition deputies, like Barrot, and more radical ones, like the editor of *La Reforme*, Ledru-Rollin. The campaign was supported by 100 members of the Chamber of Deputies.

It would appear that the February revolution can be explained by political issues and the underlying economic uncertainties. Following a decent harvest in 1847 wheat prices had started to fall by the time of the revolution. However this was not accompanied by improvements in other sectors of the economy, and the destabilising effects of the fighting undoubtedly made things worse. Many towns, such as Lyon, Nantes and Rouen, had already set up temporary workshops for the jobless. No-one knew exactly how many were out of work, even in the capital. There can be no doubt that the unrest sparked off by the complex economic crisis was an immediate catalyst to revolution and that those who fought were men and women directly affected. The Banquet campaign was extensive, but had no agreed strategy. Some wanted to enfranchise those who paid 100 francs in tax, some aspired to a full-blown democracy. Those who attended the banquets habitually kept a distance from those who were agitating about the economy. Far from being undermined by determined opposition, the conservative government, in which Guizot was the dominant influence, and which had been in office since 1840, strengthened its majority in successive elections in 1842 and 1846. Only six republicans sat in the Assembly. Louis-Philippe's speech from the throne, opening the 1848 session of parliament, was welcomed by 221 votes to 9, despite his criticism of the banqueteers. Unlike 1830, neither government nor king faced a resolute and substantial opposition. So why revolution? (Document 9).

Process of Revolution: February 1848

The occasion of the February Revolution was a march, organised as a prelude to a Latin Quarter banquet. When the government heard of the march, which was to include unemployed artisans and students, the banquet was banned. On 21 February a meeting of the banquet committee was held at the offices of *La Réforme* which decided 80 to 17 to cancel the banquet. But the worker demonstration went ahead. From 8 am groups from the main artisan districts, new and old, gathered at the place de la Madeleine. They were joined by students from the Latin Quarter nearby. Student agitation had been gathering momentum for several months. Exactly a year earlier students had commemorated the Polish revolution and tempers were frayed following bans placed on popular courses given by Mickiewicz, Michelet and Quinet. On 3 January, 3,000 students had marched to parliament to protest when Michelet's lectures were cancelled. Student newspapers also complained about the failure of the Orleanist regime to alleviate the problems of the economic crisis.

That the demonstration escalated out of control was mainly due to the government's loss of confidence. It was only when Guizot and Louis-Philippe failed to take a decisive lead after fighting had broken out that expectations began to rise. Troops were stationed around the Palais Bourbon to contain the demonstration. That it spilled over into fighting and the overthrow of the regime was accidental, unplanned, but could not have been totally unexpected, given the history of the previous half-century of unrest. Orleanists were always fearful of popular upheaval. Apparently in a haphazard, unplanned fashion, nervous troops began to fire on the crowd and fighting developed. There were demands for the resignation of the government. Workers and students threw up barricades in various streets, mainly around the Palais Bourbon, but without any specific direction or immediate result. There was no escalation or major conflict on the first day.

National Guardsmen were called out to join the regular soldiers, but few showed up for duty. The next day (23 February) most legions declared for the banquet campaign. By midday, Louis-Philippe was sufficiently worried that he replaced Guizot with Molé. The National Guard and the parliamentary opposition leaders under Barrot were satisfied and urged the crowds to disperse. But Molé, at 70, twice Chief Minister in 1836 and 1837, seemed an unlikely guarantor of parliamentary reform. Jubilation in the streets gave way to disappointment. Crowds of workers, National Guardsmen and students continued their protests and finally, towards evening, marched on the Ministry of Foreign Affairs. Their way was blocked by a company of the 14th regiment who refused to let them pass. Shots were fired, without any command apparently being given, and in the exchange of fire which ensued 52 were killed and 74 injured. During the night, as protests increased, Molé was replaced by Thiers. The number of barricades grew rapidly to around 1,500. Many armourers' shops were looted in the quest for ammunition and weapons. Marshal Bugeaud, placed in command of the troops and National Guard at the start of the crisis, was notorious for his repressive tactics in Algeria. Louis-Philippe claimed later that one of his main motives in the crisis was to avoid mass bloodshed, and this seems to have been genuine, but Bugeaud was an odd choice to bring the situation under control. The increasing numbers of National Guardsmen on the other side of the barricades demoralised the soldiers, who, as in 1830, also began to change sides. Around midday of the 24th the Tuileries palace was attacked and Louis-Philippe hastily abdicated in favour of his nine-year-old grandson, the Comte de Paris. But crowds had invaded the parliament building where a scrappy debate considered first a regency under the liberal Duchesse d'Orléans, then a group of assorted republicans, representing the two main radical papers, *La Réforme* and *Le National*, gathered at that crucible of revolution the Hôtel de Ville and declared a democratic republic.

As a consequence of panic and a series of accidents, a tiny minority of republicans were able to replace the monarchy. The king's fear that fighting would escalate was prominent in his decision to go into exile. Memories of what a repetition of the 1790s might mean undoubtedly contributed to the route followed by the small number of republicans who declared themselves in control. France became a republic through accidental revolution. Aside from Blanqui, none of the republicans favoured violence and, once in power, tried to avoid any repetition of revolution.

What Did February 1848 Change?

The leading radical journalists and politicians, led by Lamartine and Ledru-Rollin, declared themselves a provisional government. Louis Blanc and crowds of artisans forced them to promise that this would be a social republic which would find work for the unemployed. The provisional government declared a democratic republic and quickly set about organising elections with 9 million instead of the existing 0.25 million voters. They voted that the republic should set limits on daily hours of work, 10 in Paris, 11 in the provinces. They created national workshops for the unemployed, set up an innovative Commission for the Workers at the Luxembourg Palace, headed by Blanc and allowed unprecedented freedom of association and debates, hundreds of clubs and papers mushrooming. Some of the unemployed were recruited into a *garde mobile*, a volunteer military unit, provided with uniforms and equipment and trained. In these early weeks socialists and former Saint-Simonians were prominent in discussing what was to be changed.

Clubs and Newspapers

The Orleanist regime had banned associations and critical newspapers, so it is not surprising that one of the first consequences of liberation was that both appeared in large numbers. Up to 300 new newspapers were launched in Paris and other towns in the early months of the republic. Their editors often had more enthusiasm than cash or readers and many had only a transient existence. In Paris over 200 clubs were set up with about 70,000 members to prepare for the elections to the Constituent Assembly. Membership lists show that they were the work of the republican leaders of the 1830s: Barbès created the *Club de la Révolution* and Blanqui the *Société Républicaine Centrale*. The two were now enemies, each blaming the other for their failure in 1839. The idealist republican doctor Raspail resurrected the *Amis du Peuple*, more usually known as *Club Raspail* with perhaps 6,000 adherents. Cabet set up the *Société fraternelle centrale*, one of the largest and most influential, with meetings of up to 5,000 people.

In addition men from the different Parisian trades held frequent meetings, originally to elect delegates to the Luxembourg Commission. That they too could group themselves in associations was an assertion that the restrictions of the monarchy were at an end and that their associations would persuade the new regime to resolve the worsening economic crisis. Engineering, leather, building and metal trades were particularly active, as they were to be in the June insurrection.

Rights of Women

Clubs run by and for women emerged. The first women's club was the *Société pour l'Emancipation des Femmes*. It was organised by Jenny d'Héricourt to promote intellectual and moral emancipation through women's education. It attracted an educated, middle-class membership. The fourierists set up a *Société de l'Émancipation des Femmes*. A *Voix des Femmes* club and newspaper was launched by former Saint-Simonians Eugènie Niboyet, Jeanne Deroin (Document 21), Pauline Roland and Désirée Gay, devoted to the rights of women, better pay, education, nurseries, votes for women and the restoration of the divorce law. The ladies were subject to incessant ridicule by cartoonists like de Beaumont and Daumier (See document 9). A contemporary hostile chronicler of the clubs, dismissing her crusade for women's education, described Niboyet as 'Jeanne d'Arc aux bas bleus'. Désirée Gay petitioned the Luxembourg Commission to include women delegates to speak for women's issues and that they authorise women's associations to organise communal restaurants and wash-houses. Successive marches of working women pressed their case; the laundresses were followed by lady spinners, trouser-makers, teachers, dressmakers and ladies who sewed the trimmings on upholstered furniture. Désirée Gay ran a group which persuaded Marie to employ women in the National Workshops. On 10 April the first workshop opened under Gay's direction. A total of 25,000 women were found work, at a cost massively in excess of what the women were paid. Gay and Deroin set up a Fraternal Association of Women Underwear Makers (see Deroin document 10). Gay further proposed the building of communal housing reminiscent of Fourier's ideas, incorporating a crèche, nursery school, reading room, laundry, baths, communal ovens, central heating and evening classes for young girls. The female socialists petitioned the provisional government to improve women workers' pay. A divorce law was discussed by the provisional government and abandoned. Ernest Legouvé lectured on rights of women at the *Collège de France*. He drew huge crowds and his book appeared in numerous editions and was much translated. The idea of battalions of 'Amazons' was one of the rumours and mockeries of the Second Republic, just as it was of the First. *Les Vesuviennes* was founded on 26 February in Belleville by Borme, as a collective of working women committed to fighting for social reform. Borme claimed 5,000 members throughout the country and led the women on marches to the Hôtel de Ville. De Beaumont found their bizarre militaristic activities excellent material for caricature. *La Voix des Femmes* became hostile and Daniel Stern in her history of the revolution was scornful. The men of 1848 showed some sympathy with the problems of women workers, but had no more interest than those of 1792 in female suffrage and were just as scathing of female militancy.

Education Reform

Hippolyte Carnot, heir of the Carnot of the 1790s, a former Saint-Simonian, became Minister of Education. His aim was free compulsory primary education, extending the Guizot law of 1833. There were to be scholarships for boys from primary schools to lycées, and reform in higher education, including a state college for administrators. The last was finally opened after the Second World War. Convinced that education would emancipate the worker, Carnot opened evening classes in towns and tiny libraries in villages. He had the immediate support of some of the newly appointed commissioners. Carnot urged primary school teachers to canvas for republican candidates in April elections. Some of Carnot's plans came to fruition in the 1870s; none in 1848.

The revolution led to a dramatic run on the Bank of France, whose gold reserves fell from 226 million francs in February to 59 million by mid-March. A temporary 45% increase in the land tax was decreed. This was massively unpopular, especially among country people who thought they were paying for idlers in the national workshops. The salt tax was abolished, the wine tax reduced, but nothing was done to protect communal forest rights demanded by the poor in rural areas. The economic crisis intensified: the Paris National workshops cost 15 million francs rather than the initial budget of 5 million. Their name sounded vaguely socialist, but the provisional government was determined that they would be like earlier workshops, temporary solutions to unemployment. They were run on semi-military lines from a deserted chateau at Monceau on the outskirts of Paris. Recruits got up to 2 francs a day, 1 franc after 17 March if no actual work was available. Officers were paid up to 3 francs a day. Bread, meat and soup, and free medical aid were made available. A nine-and-a-half-hour day was to be worked. All this in theory, for ten times the projected number rushed to apply and at no stage could work be found for more than 10,000 men. The navvying work offered was not very appropriate for men accustomed to skilled work in Parisian luxury industries and supervision was lax. The government engineers who ran them had no sympathy with the men. However, they attracted increasing numbers of unemployed to Paris, 100,000 by May. These huge numbers of men, gathered together daily but for whom no work was found, became a serious concern. Other towns like Lyon and Rouen were also obliged to run workshops.

Elections April 1848

The provisional government planned democratic elections for 9 April to vote for an assembly to write a republican constitution. At first it was assumed that the almost 9 million new voters would instinctively vote for republican candidates, but after a demonstration led by Blanqui on 17 March demanding that voters needed to be taught how to vote, the elections were postponed, but only to 23 April. Elections were traditionally run by local prefects. Orleanist prefects were replaced by *commissaires*, a term used from the summer of 1793 before the name prefect was employed (Cobban, 1943). Twenty-two of the new officials had been organisers of the banquet campaign in their local area and were enthusiasts for the new republic. At first the new Minister of the Interior, Ledru-Rollin, instructed his commissaires to be neutral in running the new national elections, but as former royalists and clergy set up committees to promote the election of their candidates, Ledru-Rollin did likewise. One commissioner reported that priests were ordering the wives of voters to withdraw sexual favours unless their husband promised to vote for the clerical candidate. Unfortunately for the republicans 23 April was Easter Sunday and priests led their congregations from the church service to vote.

The elections proved to be a disaster for the infant republic. Former monarchists, defined as republicans of the 'day after' *républicains du lendemain*, secured a majority; 439 of the 851 elected were Orleanists or Legitimists who had been active in politics before February. A distinct minority of those who were republicans before the revolution, *républicains de la veille*, were successful; only 230 moderate and 55 radical republicans were elected. Of the 880 deputies (after by-elections), 325 were lawyers, 160 landowners, 99 army officers, 65 industrialists, 53 involved in commerce and 53 doctors, while only 18 were workmen and 6 foremen. Democracy helped the notables; 700 of the new deputies paid more than 500 francs in tax a year, and 80% were over 40 and could have been deputies (165 were) before 1848. The new republic was in the hands of men who had no confidence in it. The Assembly met on 4 May. This date, not 24 February, the day of the actual revolution, was used to commemorate the foundation of the republic in the three successive years, which tells us a lot about the Second Republic. The Assembly elected an Executive Commission from the members of the provisional government, which consisted of Arago, Garnier-Pagès, Marie, Lamartine and lastly Ledru-Rollin. On 15 May there was a demonstration in the Assembly, purported in favour of the Poles, put down by middle-class National Guardsmen. Raspail and Blanqui were arrested, Louis Blanc, who had not been involved, was threatened and the authority of the new Assembly undermined.

On 13 May the Executive Commission decreed that no more men should be admitted to the workshops. All single males between 18 and 25 were to be enlisted into the army; older workers were to be removed to the provinces. Those who refused were to be dismissed from the workshops. It was not until 20 June the Assembly finally decided to dissolve the workshops. Two days later the *Moniteur* announced that workers were to be drafted into the army or moved to the provinces; by 24 June, only 400 had been moved.

The June Days 1848

A protest demonstration to the Assembly, planned by men from the workshops, and possibly also from the Luxembourg Commission, began on 22

June at 8 am. Repeated marches that day culminated in a 100,000-strong meeting at the Place du Panthéon. Demonstrations continued the next day starting with a dawn gathering at the July Column, Place de la Bastille. It was presided over by Pujol, son of a worker and leader of a secret society. He concluded by encouraging workers to erect barricades. The government decided against trying to arrest the leaders. A state of siege was declared and a military campaign was begun led by General Louis-Eugène Cavaignac, Minister of War, who after a vote was given temporary dictatorial power. General Lamoricière, another former Saint-Simonian, was brought from Algeria to be Minister of War. Cavaignac was a man of impeccable republican pedigree whose father had served as a Jacobin deputy in the First Republic and whose brother Godfrey had been a leader of the republicans until his death in 1845. General Cavaignac's military expertise, so much the worse for the insurgents, had been gained in Algeria. The workshops were to be closed within three days. That evening the marchers began to build barricades in eastern Paris and what had begun as a workshop protest became much more complex.

Four days of bitter street fighting ensued, but by the end of 24 June it was clear the workers' revolt was in check. General Bréa was asked by the workers to negotiate a settlement, but was killed, as was the Archbishop of Paris, not by the workers but by an isolated local resident when he also tried to bring peace at the Place de la Bastille. The fighting had ended by 11 am on the 25th. The June Days were a spontaneous, virtually leaderless insurrection, a protest against the imminent disappearance of the only means of livelihood for the unemployed. Who and how many fought? Marx, in his study *Class Struggles in France 1848–50*, suggested that up to 50,000 took part. Probably the figure was nearer 20,000. Who participated? Workshops members, but many were persuaded to stay off the streets by the good faith which the government demonstrated in continuing to pay the dole throughout the insurrection. Some idea of the participants can be gauged by the composition of the workshops themselves. Thomas estimated that nearly 9,000 were unskilled labourers. The rest belonged to the traditional Parisian crafts: 6,300 were joiners, over 4,000 masons and nearly 4,000 were painters – indicative of the depressed state of house building and repair. Nearly 3,000 were locksmiths, 2,500 turners and the same number were barrel makers. Shoemakers, tailors, jewellers and hatters made up a high proportion of the rest. Over 7,600 did not state their jobs. Tocqueville claimed that the rebels had links with a criminal underworld and Taine was to take up the same story. In reality the insurgents' only crime was poverty. Of those arrested nearly 67% were skilled workmen, particularly from the building, metal-working, clothing and furniture trades, while just over 10% were shopkeepers. How many were killed? The conservative estimate of the prefecture of police was 1,460, but the actual figure must have been several times that, making the June Days the bloodiest fighting ever recorded in the capital to that date. Some 15,000 were arrested, of whom 5,000 were eventually incarcerated in Algeria. No leaders emerged. Revolutionary activists Barbès and Blanqui were in jail after

15 May. Proudhon and Blanc were hostile to the workers and continued to attend the debates of the Assembly. The violence of the June Days was as distasteful to most socialists as to more moderate republicans. To contemporary socialists the June Days were the result of the failure to implement socialist measures. The insurgents were the victims of the absence of a social programme. Their rebellion lacked ideology. It happened because the government finally decided to close the workshops before the economy had started to recover and when there were still very few real jobs.

The government, chivvied by the conservative majority in the Assembly, insisted that the rebellion was an attack on the republic itself. They believed they were justified in reconquering artisan Paris with a military campaign. Aware that in July 1830 and February 1848 revolutions succeeded when troops and National Guards changed sides, they made sure that they could command the necessary force. The government had been nervously massing troops in and around the capital since 15 May, using the recently completed rail lines. There were 20,000 men garrisoned in Paris, thanks to the new forts, 10,000 in the new republican *garde mobile*, 2,600 republican guards and 2,000 regular Parisian police. In the surrounding areas there were an additional 15,000 men at the ready. The middle-class sections of the Parisian National Guard fought against the rebels. National Guardsmen were also brought in by train from 53 departments, which was of considerable psychological significance, given the hostility in rural areas to the 45 cents tax. The June barricades confirmed the fears of conservatives that the workers were intent on civil war, not just against the republic, but were radical socialists opposed to the established social order. De Tocqueville neatly summed up their worries: 'In truth it was not a political struggle, but a class struggle, a "servile war"' (Tocqueville, 1971, 169). On 3 July the Workshops were closed.

Cavaignac believed that in June the victor was the republic. On 28 June he resigned his temporary powers and the Assembly voted him Chief of the Executive Power. Provision was made for those still unemployed – Cavaignac ordered a large-scale public works programme. Further to provide for the thousands of Parisians arrested in June and for those still without work, Lamoricière introduced a plan to provide for nearly 20,000 of them to volunteer for the first mass colonisation of Algeria, which was instituted in the autumn and was envisaged by those who volunteered as a socialist project. Whole families were encouraged to go by the offer of a free passage, free accommodation in Algeria, land, tools, animals, seeds etc., to allow them to cultivate land which after three years' cultivation would be their own. The worker paper, *L'Atelier*, encouraged emigrants:

Set off without fear; Algeria
  Will become great by dint of our hard work
  Leave the sands of the Sahara
  To barbarism.

(Pilbeam, 2014, 156–167)

The majority in the Assembly were convinced that June was the consequence of allowing excessive freedom after the February revolution. In July clubs were restricted, 11 of the most left-wing newspapers were forced to close and stamp and caution money were again imposed on the press. Blanc left for London rather than risk arrest. Proudhon had been elected to the Assembly in June and continued to run his newspaper. On 31 July he asked the Assembly to back his idea of an exchange bank to provide capital for social enterprises, the finance to be taken from direct taxation. He was supported by Louis Greppo, a cloth manufacturer from the Rhône; 600 voted against. Two other socialists, Pierre Leroux and Victor Considérant, abstained. In September the Assembly reconfirmed that the government should continue to set maximum hours of work, increasing the working day to 12 hours. In July and August local elections were held for municipalities and *arrondissements*. Frequently the former Orleanist members were re-elected. Autumn saw some riots against the 45 cents tax, particularly in the south, and some strikes by workers.

Constitution of 1848

The most important task after June was to complete a constitution. The constitutional committee included members representing *Le National*, notably Marrast and Cormenin, recent republican 'converts' such as Tocqueville and Barrot, and socialists, Corbon and Considérant. They looked for examples in the constitutions of the first French republic and America. The preamble was drawn from the constitution of the first republic:

> In the presence of God and in the name of the French people, the National Assembly proclaims:
>
> I France constitutes itself a Republic. In adopting this as its definitive form of government, it aims to follow more freely in the path of progress and civilisation, to work towards an increasingly equitable distribution of the responsibilities and advantages of society, to improve the material circumstances of every individual by the gradual reduction of public expenditure and taxation and, avoiding further commotion, to raise every citizen, through the progressive and constant action of the institutions and the laws, to an ever highly level of morality, enlightenment and well-being.
>
> II The French Republic is democratic, united and indivisible...
>
> IV Its principles are Liberty, Equality and Fraternity. Its bases are the Family, Work, Property and Public Order.

There was to be a single Chamber, as in 1791–1792. The Chamber was the legislature. The legislative assembly was to have 750 members, elected by direct, male and secret suffrage for three years. Voters had to be at least 21, candidates 25. Deputies could not hold public office.

The executive was to consist of a president elected by direct universal suffrage. He would be both head of state and of the government. In this the Assembly was following the model of the United States. In March Blanc had encouraged the provisional government to acknowledge that the state recognised a right to work and its obligation to provide work for the workless. In writing the preamble for the constitution the Constituent Assembly considered this a socialist concept which had led to the workers' revolt in June. Article 8 of the constitution proposed 'by offering assistance in a fraternal spirit [the Republic] should ensure the existence of all citizens in need, either by providing them, as far as its resources allow, with work or providing succour for those unable to work, in cases where their families are unable to do so'. An attempt by the extreme left, proposed by Mathieu (Drôme), to insert a more comprehensive right to work was defeated by 596 to 187 votes.

The biggest decision reached after the June Days was how the presidency would be organised and how the president would be elected. The only universally known name was Napoleon and it was assumed that the Emperor's nephew would move to France and stand. The other likely candidates were Cavaignac, currently head of state, and the poet Lamartine, who had served as Minister of Foreign Affairs in the provisional government. Rivalry between Lamartine and Cavaignac – Lamartine believed he would win – led to the decision on 10 October (643 votes to 158) that the president would be directly elected by a democratic vote. It was known that Louis-Napoleon would stand, so as a safeguard the winning candidate would have to secure a minimum of 2 million votes. There was an assumption that this would not happen. Then the Assembly would elect the president from among the five candidates who obtained the most votes. The president was to be elected for four years and he was not allowed to stand for immediate re-election.

Bonapartism

Louis-Napoleon was little known in France, but his name was the most familiar of all the presidential candidates. His increasing popularity in 1848 was in some ways surprising; he had twice failed to seize power during the reign of Louis-Philippe. Bonapartism had a broad patriotic, nationalist appeal in early nineteenth-century France. In popular songs, plays, novels and paintings Napoleon was portrayed as the saviour of the Revolution. Republicans could honour him without embarrassment. He was also respected as the man who had brought 'order' to the Revolution. Memoirs written by Las Cases on St Helena went through six editions between 1823 and 1842. Bonapartism had become such a vague, amorphous, classless sentiment that Louis-Philippe turned part of the palace of Versailles into a museum to the Emperor. In 1833 a statue of Bonaparte was placed on the top of the Vendôme column. The return of Napoleon's ashes to France, one of the Emperor's last requests, was organised and funded by popular subscription. Louis-Philippe encouraged one of his sons to preside over the installation of the ashes in Les Invalides in 1840, which became a shrine to the Empire. On Sunday 20 December 1840, 200,000 visited the tomb. Bonapartism was the only mass sentiment in 1848, overshadowing the appeal of the republic because it was a more united historic memory. It had a particular impact on those newly enfranchised. However Napoleon's great-nephew, Louis-Napoleon, seemed no threat whatsoever to the republic in 1848. Neither as conspirator nor politician did he strike much of a figure. In 1836 he tried to secure the support of the Strasbourg garrison as a prelude to seizing power. Instead he was arrested and exiled to the USA. In 1839 he brought out a short account of the Empire in which, echoing Napoleon's own memoirs, he claimed that Napoleon had only been a dictator because of the demands of war, and had been a liberal at heart. In 1840 he landed in Boulogne with a small group of followers, but the local garrison ignored him. He was imprisoned in the fortress of Ham from which he escaped in 1846. Louis-Napoleon's first attempt to enter France at the end of February 1848 was repulsed. However the patriotic memory of the Empire was enough to secure his election in June, while he was still in London, in four constituencies, including artisan Paris. The Assembly refused to allow him into France. Then came the June Days and in the September by-elections Louis-Napoleon became a deputy. He was a poor speaker, spoke French badly and seemed no threat (Document 11).

Presidential Election

The 400 or so conservatives in the Assembly formed the Réunion of the rue de Poitiers, which included Thiers and which gained seats in the September by-elections and in local elections. They then turned to the presidency. On 26 October Louis-Napoleon said he intended to stand. A few days later Thiers addressed the Réunion, urging them to agree to back Louis-Napoleon, the obvious winner, otherwise an indecisive poll would mean that the choice would be left to the Assembly which would choose Cavaignac. Thiers convinced most of them that Louis-Napoleon's name would secure his victory and that the Réunion should back him, even though they had had no contact with him and he was hostile to them. Why? Many of the notables believed that Louis-Napoleon was simply a donkey with a famous name and would do their bidding.

There were four republican candidates. Cavaignac was the most conservative. He was little known outside Paris and there his military victory in June was hardly likely to endear him to many of the voters. Lamartine, the next most conservative candidate, had not distinguished himself as Minister of Foreign Affairs and was probably the only person confident of his success in December. Ledru-Rollin was backed by a number of clubs but had no mass appeal. The most radical candidate was Raspail, still in jail awaiting trial after the 15 May demonstration.

Presidential Election Results, 10 December 1848

The election of Louis-Napoleon to the presidency on 10 December marked the total defeat of the February republicans. It was a public display of their disunity and lack of popular appeal. He secured 5,434,226 votes out of the 7,327,345 votes cast (74%), giving him a majority of 3.5 million votes over all the other candidates. Cavaignac came second with 1,448,107. No-one else was a serious contender. Ledru-Rollin got 370,119 votes, Raspail 36,920, Lamartine 17,910 and the legitimist General Changarnier 4,790.

Louis-Napoleon – New Government 1849

Louis-Napoleon's gratitude to the Réunion was marked by the appointment of a government which suited them and included no republicans. Republican prefects and mayors were gradually purged.

Fight Back of Radical Republicans

(1) Right of Association

The official republic may have been shunted towards the right, but the comparative freedom of the early part of the Second Republic allowed a variety of socialist experiments and developments. The 'right to work' may have been excluded from the republican constitution, but the old republican concept of 'fraternity' in its new socialist clothing continued to have a profound appeal. Associations of a vaguely 'socialist' imprint prospered, attracting large numbers of artisans, with some middle class support. In total about 50,000 members joined 300 socialist associations from 120 trades during the life of the republic. Mutual-aid societies and producer and consumer cooperatives continued to grow. In August 1849 the Union of Worker Associations was formed. The Union sought to provide mutual credit and an impressive total of 104 associations joined. In May 1850 the Assembly forced it to close.

Mutual-aid schemes continued to expand; from 262 in Paris in 1846, during the Second Republic there were 348 in the capital and 114 in Lyon. Consumer cooperatives were also opened in Lyon, Nantes and Reims and other cities.

(2) Republican Solidarity: The Democ-Socs

The scale of Louis-Napoleon's unexpected success in 1848 and the realisation that he had made an enormous appeal to peasants and the less well-off awoke republicans to the need to work together in the legislative elections in May 1849. They agreed on broad issues: the urgent need to educate men for universal suffrage, social strategies, including the right to work and the creation of cooperatives, and the need to rediscover a primitive Christianity as a moral foundation for society. Their twin beliefs in a democratic and social republic earned them the rather inelegant name 'democ-soc'. Their enemies referred to them as reds, democrats, socialists or simply extremists.

On 10 January 1848 Faucher formally banned them, but the ban had only limited success. Political meetings were banned. But the democ-socs transformed themselves into electoral committees in preparation for the May elections.

Legislative Elections, May 1849

The democ-socs demanded progressive income tax, the abolition of indirect taxes on necessities, widespread nationalisation of primary industries and utilities, free and compulsory primary education and army reform to make it truly representative of the 'nation-in-arms'.

Conservative support for the new president was opportunistic and the conservative alliance very fragile. The presidential election did not make former monarchists Bonapartists. They were very divided.

The alliance of the notables won, although the unity and regional strength of the democ-socs alarmed them. Roughly 450 of the 715 deputies were conservatives, 75 were moderate republicans and about 200 were democ-socs. There were more republicans than a year earlier but the proportions of moderates and radicals were reversed. The democ-socs secured 2.36 million votes compared with 3.5 million for the conservative coalition.

Unrest after Legislative Elections: Demonstration of 13 June 1849

Paris, 13 June 1849: The next day 120 deputies signed a petition against the decision to send troops to Rome to defend the Pope against Mazzini's republic and Ledru-Rollin, with some reluctance, led a critical but unarmed demonstration of about 8,000. Seven were killed in violent repression by the troops. A state of siege was declared once more in the capital and in the surrounding 11 departments. There were many arrests, including 30 of the radical-socialist deputies.

Provincial Unrest 1849 and Government Repression

There was conflict in a number of provincial centres including Strasbourg, Valence, Grenoble, Toulouse and Perpignan. Fighting between the Lyon workers and the soldiery turned into a full-scale battle on 15 June. More than 50 were killed and 800 arrested. A state of siege was declared in the Rhône and neighbouring departments. Large numbers of people were arrested throughout the country. On 24 June 1849 all political clubs were forced to close or go underground. Cooperative associations of all kinds were forced to disband. Censorship of the press was stiffened in both 1849 and 1850. Public hawkers were prevented from selling radical literature; trees of liberty were chopped down, all reminiscent of the early 1830s. Some republican mayors and school teachers were dismissed. Prefects were encouraged to investigate all reports of democ-soc attitudes with a zeal which became a veritable witch-hunt in areas where the republicans retained support and organisation. In some cases National Guard battalions were disbanded.

There was the usual purge of officials. To underline the return to conservatism, and protect against the influence of radical school teachers, the Falloux Law of March 1850 permitted the expansion of church-run schools. But the increasing conservatism of the regime was not entirely to the taste of the Party of Order, who found that the President was far less complaisant than they had hoped. In October 1849 the Barrot ministry was replaced by the first government chosen by Louis-Napoleon, of which he was effectively the head and including his own men. Repressive action by the government after June 1849 sharpened the sense of confrontation and hostility. Most radical leaders were now in exile: Blanc, Cabet, Leroux, Ledru-Rollin etc.

Legislative Repression

However, republicans at home could not be ignored. The success of the conservative backlash was patchy. There were limits on the information against individuals which could be gathered by a prefect who was habitually a stranger in his department. To the horror of conservatives, 21 democ-socs were chosen in by-elections in March 1850, including the novelist Eugène Sue. The conservatives now resorted to the electoral tactics of the Bourbon Restoration.

Electoral Restrictions – May 1850

In May 1850 universal suffrage was undermined by a three-year instead of a six-month residence requirement for all voters. One-third (3 million) of the electorate, who were assumed to be the most radical because they were mobile through poverty, was thus disenfranchised, leaving an electoral register of 6,800,000 and the republic in tatters.

Re-Election of Louis-Napoleon

Conservatives were so determined to eliminate radical resistance that the re-election of Louis-Napoleon, specifically forbidden in the constitution, was viewed as the most desirable option. In the spring of 1850, 52 of the departmental general councils, urged on by their prefects, voted in favour of constitutional revision. In 1851 the number rose to 79. The campaign for revision concluded with a parliamentary vote in July 1851 in which the proposal to allow Louis-Napoleon to stand for a second term gained 446 votes to 278, a very clear majority, but insufficient for constitutional revision.

Between December 1848 when Louis-Napoleon was elected president and December 1851 when he seized permanent power through a coup d'état, conservative elements conspired, legislated and administered to smother the democratic republic. The behaviour of monarchist notables gave Louis-Napoleon the opportunity to present himself as the defender of democracy. During the autumn of 1851 he proposed the restoration of universal suffrage, but this was rejected by the Assembly. Conservatives were hoodwinked by tales of a 'red' rebellion planned for 30 November. The rebels were expecting British help.

Coup d'état, 2 December 1851

Louis-Napoleon's solution was a coup d'état which was executed as a military exercise and provoked virtual civil war in a substantial number of departments, particularly in the south. The Second Republic really ended on 2 December 1851, the anniversary of the battle of Austerlitz, although its formal demise was delayed for a year. Over 30,000 troops were used in the operation: 220 deputies were arrested (where were the other 38 who had voted against revision?), including Barrot, de Tocqueville and Falloux. The President proclaimed that he was acting in defence of the republic and that anyway there had been a large majority in favour of him standing for re-election (Document 10). Any argument that such a constitutional 'revision' was universally popular should have been dispelled by the unprecedented scale of resistance in many parts of France and by the number of arrests and condemnations.

The ensuing four months witnessed unprecedented political repression. On 3 December barricades went up in traditional centres of artisan radicalism in Paris, the area around the Hôtel de Ville, St Martin, rue Rambuteau and rue Transnonain, but no more than 1,200 turned out. The ferocity of the repression can be gauged by the fact that one-third of the protestors were killed on the spot. The government had laid the ground for the coup with great care, learning lessons from both 1830 and 1848. In areas where resistance might be expected mobile columns of troops were drafted in, making full use of the telegraph system and the new rail network.

Resistance to Coup: Republican Insurrection

Southern France reacted spontaneously with force. Some departments were already in a state of siege, including the Drôme, Ardèche, Cher and Nievre. Tens of thousands in two dozen departments in the centre and south rose against the coup, including seven in the south-east, two in the south-west and three in the centre. Rebellion began in the small towns, but included many rural communes. Revolutionary communes were declared in one hundred centres, which went beyond past experience. The chef-lieu of one department and 12 *arrondissements* were seized by rebel armies of over 1,000 in

13 cases. The government squashed these uncoordinated civic rebellions with mobile columns, graphically recalled by Zola in *Les Fortunes des Rougon*. A state of siege was declared immediately in the 32 rebel departments including (grouped by region) Seine, Seine-et-Oise, Oise, Seine-Inférieure, Eure, Eure-et-Loir, Loire-et-Cher and Loiret; in the centre, Aube, Yonne, Nièvre, Cher, Allier, Loire, Saône-et-Loire and Aveyron; in the east, Bas-Rhin; and further south, Jura, Ain, Rhône, Basses-Alpes, Isère, Drôme and Ardèche; in the Midi Vaucluse, Var, Gard, Hérault, Gers, Lot-et-Garonne, Lot and Gironde.

Objectives of Resistance to the Coup

What were the main issues for the rebels? Government supporters stressed immediate economic concerns. Of those arrested 44% worked in agriculture, 48% in various crafts and commerce; 80% of the rebel communes were in rural areas where peasants were producing goods for a market economy which were extremely sensitive to price fluctuations in times of crisis. Although the industrial sector had recovered from the mid-40s depression by 1851, agricultural prices had remained low and peasant producers, unable to pay their debts to urban money lenders, were sometimes threatened by expropriation. However an exclusively economic explanation of their rebellion is inadequate. Peasants in wheat-producing areas who were suffering from low prices rose in revolt; wine-producers in similar circumstances did not, although they had been volatile in the 1830s. Conversely some prosperous areas rebelled.

Political factors were far more important. Five members of parliament were sentenced to deportation, 65 were expelled as 'leaders of socialism' and 18 others were made temporary exiles because of their opposition. The rebels declared themselves defenders of the republic; Article 68 of the constitution declared the president guilty of high treason if he dissolved the National Assembly. The rebels claimed that they were acting in the name of the 'general will', which, given the coup, was the only remaining legal centre of authority. Violence was rare in their takeover of town halls. The rebel departments were ones where the democ-socs had been most active in the 1849 elections, had gone underground in the time-honoured tradition of secret societies and had suffered more than average harassment by the authorities. That is not to say that secret democratic societies only existed in rebel Provence or Languedoc. Democratic clubs were common in about 700 communes in December 1850, 500 in the south-east and 50–100 in the south-west, with 90 in the Var alone. Peasants were numerous; 'We wouldn't have any forest guard, any fishing guard, any priest. We would lower taxes, we would divide the commons', was the motivation of one peasant in southern Ardèche. Above all, the repeated declarations of communal autonomy were protests against the constant interference of Paris in local affairs. It was no coincidence that the departments which rose were some of the ones with a pronounced tradition of communal autonomy. The centralising march of the bureaucratic state, which had become increasingly interfering since December 1848, was not to their taste.

Mixed Commissions

At the beginning of February 1852 the Minister of War was empowered to create special commissions in each department to deal with opponents. The commissions consisted of the prefect, government prosecutor and military commander. They were able to impose summary punishment including transportation to Cayenne or Algeria. Those worthy of mere exile were to be sent with all speed to Belgium or England. In all 27,000 were arrested, 9,000 of whom were deported to Algeria. Republicans later suggested that government statistics deliberately underestimated those punished and Jules Simon estimated that a realistic figure might be as high as 100,000. Worker self-help associations were closed. Only 15 of 299 such organisations in existence on 2 December survived. As a consequence of the 1851 military coup and the popular response, France became an autocratic empire. Republicans could not sit in the virtually powerless Legislative Assembly. In the late 1860s the Assembly began to recover some influence but there were only 30 republicans in the Assembly in 1870 (see documents 12 and 13).

September 1870

The next change of regime was not the product of revolution but of military defeat. Napoleon III became involved in war against Prussia and the new North German Confederation in the summer of 1870 for no good reason other than Napoleon III's hurt pride when the Prussian ruler proposed a German candidate to the vacant Spanish throne, and then withdrew the offer with inadequate humility. The French high command did not anticipate defeat. Louis-Napoleon was captured at Sedan on 4 September, a republic was declared and most of northern France overrun. Paris was put to siege. A government of National Defence was declared which admitted defeat in January 1871 and ceded Alsace and most of Lorraine to the new German Empire in the Peace of Frankfurt, March 1871. France did not formally become a republic until 1875.

Paris Commune March–May 1871

The Paris Commune was a failed worker rebellion, a direct consequence of the relationship of the Government of National Defence with Paris during the siege, military defeat, the election of a conservative Assembly, and above all, the tactics employed by the new head of state, Thiers, in March 1871. The attempt by the Commune to assert the autonomy of the capital failed and was destroyed by army units brought in by Thiers. For the second time a worker rebellion in Paris had failed. Paris no longer dictated to the rest of France.

At the beginning of March 1871, in conformity with the Peace treaty, the troops stationed in Paris during the siege were given ten days' pay at the beginning of March and moved out. The army of the new German Empire remained in its siege position and prepared to occupy eastern France until the indemnity of 5 thousand million (milliard) francs had been paid. On 15 March, aware that the government meant to repossess the capital as soon as possible, 215 of the 254 battalions of the National Guard in Paris elected a central committee to try to protect their interests. On 18 March Thiers sent troops into Paris to seize cannon from the heights of Montmartre (see illustration 14 and document 15 noting comments by Louise Michel left-wing supporter of Commune). This was a disastrous error of judgement, or deliberate provocation, for the hundred odd cannon belonged to the National Guard and had been paid for by public subscription in Paris during the siege and built in the capital (Document 16). The Parisian mayors backed Thiers, but many of the troops did not and, worse, no horses were supplied to remove the cannon (Document 19). The attempt was a total and bloody failure in which generals Lecomte and Clement Thomas were shot. Thiers ordered the evacuation of Paris.

The Response of Paris

The next day the central committee of the National Guard established itself at the traditional radical heart of the capital, the Hôtel de Ville, and with the support of some of the many political clubs which had sprung up during the siege, decided to hold elections on 26 March for a municipal council for Paris. This decision recalled 1792, when France had also been threatened by invasion. The National Guard felt that they had been abandoned during the siege, the defeat and the peace settlement. They claimed that Thiers' evacuation left the capital without a government. In their proclamation of 18 March the National Guard committee declared: 'The proletarians of Paris, amidst the failures and treasons of the ruling classes, have understood that the hour has struck for them to save the situation, by taking into their own hands the direction of public affairs' (Tombs, 1999). They organised the immediate election of a municipal council for Paris. A large proportion of the middle class population had fled in the siege and afterwards and barely half the electorate voted. Workers, primarily artisans, predominated among the quarter of a million or so voters, and the 90 men elected represented them more than any previous assembly, local or national, had done: 35 were artisans; 73 had taken part in earlier revolutionary movements; 19 were moderates. They represented all strands of anti-Thiers opinion, including Blanquists, Proudhonists and Jacobins. A number had been members of the Internationale during the 1860s and of Parisian clubs (see document 16 comment by Goncourt, hostile right-wing opponent of of Commune, who remained in Paris during Commune and was an acute observer).

Policies of the Paris Commune

The new municipal council met on 28 March at the Hôtel de Ville, serenaded by enthusiastic National Guard battalions, and adopted the more revolutionary name of Commune. Asserting that Paris had been abandoned for the second time, the Commune claimed it had the right to govern Paris. On 29 March they abolished conscription and declared all fit men members of the National Guard. Restarting the economy after the siege was vital; some Communards hoped that socialist ideas could prevail, but more pragmatic considerations dominated. Thiers' decrees on rents and pawnshop goods were withdrawn. Workers' cooperatives were encouraged to continue to produce armaments as during the siege; others started to re-open small businesses shut because of the siege. Owners were to be compensated. But it was impossible to revive the traditional Parisian luxury trades while Paris was in rebellion against the central government. Most workers still depended on their National Guard pay of 30 sous a day. The Bank of France agreed to provide funds to revive the economy. Food supplies were adequate; neither Versailles nor the Germans tried to blockade trade. The separation of Church and State, an issue dear to republicans, was declared. National Guard training and parades tended to dominate life. At its most moderate, the Commune expressed the demand of Parisians for civic autonomy denied them throughout the Empire; at its most extreme it was an attempt to spark the decentralisation of France. Proudhonist socialists were enthusiastic Commune supporters, although other socialists such as Louis Blanc were not. The small number of Marxists were at first uncertain whether the Commune was a proletarian revolution. The Commune was very actively supported by women. Women had an active role in education reforms. Marguerite Tinayre, a teacher and member of the Internationale, became the first inspector of schools, Mink started a free girls' school, Michel wrote a plan for girls' education and Marie Manière started a girls' professional school. Vaillant, head of the Education Committee, equalised the salaries of male and female teachers and appointed a group of women to plan the organisation of schools for girls (Document 16 see document 17 on women and Commune; Eichner, 2022).

There were riots in support of Paris in Lyon and Marseille on 23 March, followed a day later by Le Creusot, Saint-Étienne and Narbonne, with Toulouse and Limoges on the 25th, but more active support never materialised. There was concern that the regiments of the North German Confederation, encamped in the northern suburbs of Paris, might take the opportunity to re-start the war, but they stayed aloof from the argument. The most urgent problem for the new Commune was to decide whether to try to negotiate with Thiers or fight. The Communards could not agree on a strategy. On 29 March an Executive Commission was declared, replaced on 20 April, followed by two Committees of Public Safety, two military War Delegates, and finally a civilian, Charles Delescluze. Thiers never wavered. He regarded them as rebels and called troops to Versailles to invade Paris. While the Communards issued practical decrees for recovery and idealistic ones to reform social inequalities, the government in Versailles refused all negotiations and planned a military campaign to take Paris. It almost seemed that Thiers' policy towards Paris had been so harsh as to be designed to provoke the capital to rebel. Only in late April did the Communards accept that they could not influence the shape of the new republic, merely fight for their lives. By then Thiers had been able to gather sufficient troops to launch a full attack, and to control the defiance of other towns, which were not always in sympathy either with him or the capital.

Repression of Paris Commune 22–28 May 1871

The Commune was brought to an end by the army, in what has been known ever since as 'bloody week', 22–28 May 1871, a massacre surpassing that of the June Days 1848. Versailles and Communard forces battled for the control of Paris street by street. The death toll among Communards was 25,000, for the army 900. Many Communards were summarily shot after capture. Estimates of the dead are very varied, the total offered often related to the sympathies of the writer. Some say that 2,000 soldiers died; 40,000 were arrested, of whom 270 were condemned to death and 26 actually executed; 400 were deported. During the last days of the fighting many public buildings were destroyed by fires, some accidental, some started by the Communards to halt advancing troops. Thus Thiers at the head of the elected assembly was able to reassert control of France's most rebellious city with loyal army units, in a massacre more costly than any of the Franco-Prussian war. The manner of the defeat of the Commune created its myth and an international socialist legend. Marx, after some hesitation, entitled his account of it a 'civil war'. It left a legacy of bitterness on both sides which was long lasting. Paris remained under martial law until 1878. The meaning of the Commune has been variously interpreted from the last protest of a declining artisanate to the first Marxist workers' revolution. Contemporary evidence is plentiful (documents 14, 15, 16 and 17 illustrate contemporary pro and anti Commune attitudes). Those who created the Third Republic preferred to forget the Commune. In the 1890s when Weill wrote a history of nineteenth-century republicanism he did not mention the Commune at all.

The crushing of the Paris Commune probably contributed much to the creation of a stable republic. Republicans were still very divided on their ideal republic, but left-wing aspirations, whether Blanquist or Proudhonist, were no longer a factor in realistic future plans. Paris and the militants who had backed its Commune could be discounted in any definition of the republic. None of the Parisian deputies to the National Assembly supported the Commune. The degree of uncertainty about France's political future was less than might appear from the unwillingness to rush into print with a new constitution. Thiers claimed that this was a 'republic without republicans', but he exaggerated. The by-elections of July 1871 were indicative of public opinion. Republicans secured 99 of the 114 vacancies. The old exiles of the Second Republic were among them. Ledru-Rollin returned in September 1870 a sick man. He was elected to the Assembly in February 1871, but resigned. Louis Blanc, a revered socialist veteran, became a founder of the moderate radical socialist movement. The republican leadership had passed to the generation trained in the Empire. Although still arguing, moderates were in control. Using the model of the liberal Empire in which they had served their apprenticeship, they calculated and compromised with the monarchist notables to create a conservative republic, tolerable to the elite and just about democratic enough when laced with anti-clerical policies and a secular state education system to be a convincing heir of the First Republic. There was no practical alternative to a republic. The assembly of monarchists in 1871 had been elected to make peace, not a monarchy, and in addition, they could never have settled on a claimant. The legitimist heir, Chambord, insisted on a white flag, his potential heir, his Orleans cousin, lacked monarchist ambition, and the Bonapartist, Prince Napoleon, died fighting in South Africa. A brief attempt by elements of radical republicanism and the far right to make general Boulanger a dictator fizzled out. In 1886 Boulanger was appointed Minister of War, a popular decision. A year later he was dismissed. It was a year of political and economic crisis. The President's son-in-law Daniel Wilson was accused of selling official decorations. In 1888 Boulanger was forced to retire from the army. To some on the left and the right, including Bonapartists and the right-wing *Ligue des Patriotes*, orchestrated by Déroulède, a right wing nationalist, Boulanger began to seem a solution to political arguments. The right saw him as the way of destroying Republic. A year later he was elected in several by-elections including Paris among rumours that he was about to launch a coup. Boulanger had no such ambitions; he feared arrest, fled France and later committed suicide on his mistress's grave.

Born tentatively of defeat and civil war, and positively NOT of revolution, the Third Republic was to prove the most enduring regime since 1789.

1889 Centenary

The celebration of the centenary of 1789 was used as an occasion less to philosophise about the inheritance of 1789, and more to boost the French economy and stress the modernity of France. An International Exposition was organised by the republican government to celebrate the centenary of the 1789 Revolution. A competition was held for a centenary building. Gustave Eiffel, the winner, was a noted bridge builder, who designed the framework of the Statue of Liberty, donated by the French government, which became the symbol for migrants arriving at New York harbour. The ultra-modern Eiffel Tower, challenging the Sacre-Coeur on the opposite side of the Seine, spoke for a modern, steel and glass republican inheritance. At 984 feet high it was the tallest building in the world at the time. It formed the entrance for the International Exposition which opened in May on the anniversary of the meeting of the Estates-General. It was one of the few world's fairs to make a profit. In addition to the Eiffel Tower over 80 other structures on the Champ de Mars housed exhibits, including the impressive 1,452 foot long Galerie des Machines. The fair attracted exhibits from Europe, South America, the United States and the French colonies, yet in the final analysis it was a celebration of French achievements on the centennial of the French Revolution.

In its celebration of the centenary of 1789 the republican regime tried to avoid conflict and stressed what united its heirs. The recent events of the Commune were a problem. In 1880 the Communards were amnestied and returned from exile but more extreme Communards, such as the anarchist Louise Michel, were never reconciled. She spent her later life in exile in London and even recent attempts by President François Hollande (2012–2017) to move her remains to the Panthéon failed. The 14 July was celebrated for the first time as an official holiday. In 1884 the Paris City Council erected a huge bronze of Marianne, accepted since the 1870s as the symbol of the republic on the Place de la République. Marianne wore a Phrygian bonnet, previously considered very radical. In 1889, the 14 July was again celebrated, the Marseillaise declared the national anthem, and the legacy of the declaration of the first republic in September 1792 was recognised. Sadi Carnot, grandson of Lazare, was elected President of the Republic. Third Republic presidents had no real power, but his election was a symbol of the republican tradition. In 1889 Lazare Carnot was installed in the Panthéon with two other revolutionaries. The government officially recognised Michelet's *History of the French Revolution*, which honoured Jacobins as democrats, but Robespierre was still kept at a distance because of the Terror (1793–1794). Above all, the centenary emphasised that revolution was over.

4 Shared Themes in Nineteenth-Century Revolutions

So far we have assessed the legacy and memory of 1789 and set out the narrative of nineteenth-century revolutions. This section considers what issues were common to some or all of these revolutions. We will first discuss the geography of revolution, then politics, economic and social matters and who participated. Then we'll think about other shared factors that brought change in addition to revolution.

Urban Geography and Architecture of Revolution

The centre of Paris was always the focus of revolution as were major provincial cities like Lyon. In Paris the Marais belonged to the artisans, but was close also to streets where newspapers were produced and to fine homes of elite government critics. The narrow close packed streets, near to the centre of Paris government, and especially the Hôtel de Ville, were the focus for revolution. The Hôtel de Ville had been the nucleus of radical protest for centuries. In the 1790s, but even more in 1830, 1848 and 1871, government troops struggled to control these narrow dense streets packed with tall houses.

Barricades were an essential feature of the architecture of revolts of the nineteenth century and in earlier centuries, although not of 1789 itself. Narrow streets facilitated their construction. It became the norm for protestors to build barricades across the end of their streets. Fighting at such close quarters, soldiers hesitated to fire on men, wives and children who came from the same sort of poor background as them. Traditionally troops were not stationed in central Paris, as they were in other European capitals, which made it difficult to supply them with extra ammunition, or even food and water. Barricade defenders might offer them food. It became the norm in the Three Glorious Days of July 1830 and in February 1848 for up to a fifth of regular soldiers to shift to the other side of the barricade. Cartoons show troops being pelted from houses with furniture and other objects, and defenders, men, women and children, successfully maintaining control of their barricade. Not unaware of the significance of geographical factors in protest, in 1840 the minister in charge, Thiers, ordered forts to be built in the

DOI: 10.4324/9781003460596-4

suburbs around Paris ostensibly to improve its defence from foreign troops, but equally useful to control domestic revolution.

The same streets were barricaded in 1830, 1839, February and June 1848, and 1871. From the late 1830s the construction of the rail network around Paris did two things. For the first time troops could be moved to the capital rapidly. This was significant in reinforcing Cavaignac's troops to defeat the June Days. In addition the construction meant worker houses were demolished and their occupants moved to the suburbs, removing the main insurgents from the centre.

In the 1850s, aware of the danger from narrow streets, Napoleon III set Baron Hausmann and other financiers to transform the narrow streets of the capital into wide boulevards, impossible to barricade and through which troops could be moved with ease. Central worker areas were eliminated, replaced by new department stores and apartments for the rich. Worker communities in the centre were thus eliminated for railway lines, terminals, boulevards, department stores and new luxury apartments (see document 12). Workers were forced to move to new suburbs, but many still worked, and some still lived, in the centre. Fragments of the Marais survive today, inhabited by poor Jewish and Muslim families and workshops. The suburban relocation of the poor was unplanned, their housing rough, social facilities and transport non-existent. Those who still worked in central Paris often had a round trip of about 14 miles. Worker resentment at their forced move was a factor in the Paris Commune.

The city was increasingly seen in police reports and in novels (*Les Misérables*) as a danger, a focus for crime and disease. Both were blamed on those in charge and could be factors in unrest. Migration from the countryside was depicted as socially unsettling and cities experienced higher death rates, with a new scourge: cholera. In 1832 there were 18,000 deaths in four months mainly among the poor in worker areas. Cholera was unpredictable. There was another outbreak in 1849, and another in 1892. Doctors provided no satisfactory explanation – miasmas, bad smells, were blamed, as was dirt. Healthy adults were as likely to die as the sick, young or old. No cure was found. Enthusiasm for statistics meant people saw regular placards listing the number of victims and dead in their area. This led to widespread fear. The poor accused the government of poisoning the water. Catholic priests did not discourage this view. From being the focus of revolution, the city centre became the heart of inexplicable and devastating disease (Aminzade, 1993; Traugott, 2010).

Political and Philosophical Divisions

To what extent did the political divisions that persisted after 1814 contribute to revolution? The memory of 1789 blocked compromise and negotiation. The 1789 revolutionary experience left permanent cleavages. The execution of the King and Queen made 1789 anathema to many in the conservative elite. The Terror (1793–1794) cast a long shadow. The French elite remained politically divided through the nineteenth century between those who were hostile to 1789 and those who accepted, with varying degrees of enthusiasm, the consequences of the Revolution. In 1814 the first group, which welcomed the restoration of the Bourbon monarchy, included *émigrés* including ultra-royalists and more moderate royalists. Socially they encompassed nobles and clergy, but also some bourgeois. The second group, who came to be called *doctrinaires* or liberals, included a few nobles and clergy, but were mostly bourgeois. Royalists regarded liberals as dangerous revolutionaries, which they were not. Liberals accepted the restored monarchy and wanted constitutional government, but they were convinced that royalists and especially ultras were bent on undermining the 1814 Constitutional Charter and strengthening royal power. Parliamentary government depends on compromise and a certain level of trust between opponents. Nineteenth century parliamentary disputes tended to flip into revolution; revolution seemed to become a habit. It revealed the persistent absence of trust within the fractured elite. Emotions rather than rationality tended to dominate.

The first two revolutions, 1830 and 1848, centred around the Chamber of Deputies and the size of the electorate. In the Restoration ultras and other conservative royalists argued that richer voters were more likely to vote for right-wing candidates. Hence in 1820, after the murder of the Duc de Berry, ultras pushed through a law of the double vote which gave the 25% richest voters a second vote. In reality, some of the wealthiest voters, including Voyer d'Argenson, a republican, were left wing. In the 1840s Guizot, a leading government minister, combatted a persistent campaign for a reduction in the amount of tax men had to pay to qualify to vote, on the grounds that the existing law was democratic because richer voters were more independent and able to represent poorer citizens. In May 1850 the conservative majority in the legislative assembly reduced the suffrage by restricting the vote to men who could prove a three-year residence qualification. Poorer voters tended to move home frequently. The conservatives hoped that this stratagem would allow them to change the rules for the election of the president and facilitate the re-election of Louis-Napoleon. They failed. Louis-Napoleon carried through a military coup d'état to remain president, which he confirmed by a plebiscite in which universal male suffrage was restored and never again altered. Louis-Napoleon reintroduced a democratic plebiscite and used it to confirm decisions he made a far from democratic emperor.

Turning to political philosophies, liberal, republican and Bonapartist ideas were all viewed by opponents as revolutionary. Liberals were considered revolutionary by ultras in the 1830 political crisis. Once in power in 1830 liberals quickly revealed that their enthusiasm for 1789 was very limited. France had been a republic from 1792 to 1804, but from 1799–1804 Napoleon held sovereign power. The republican legacy was extremely confused, particularly because of the Jacobin Terror of 1793–1794. In the early 1820s small cells of the *charbonnerie*, a secret organisation favouring radical political change, had some support from former leading republicans Voyer d'Argenson and Lafayette, who had participated in the American War of Independence and had been the head of the National Guard in 1789. Members were chiefly soldiers with Bonapartist sympathies. After the arrest and execution of four sergeants stationed at La Rochelle in 1822, conspiratorial enthusiasm faded. Some republicans, including Lafayette and Mauguin, joined the July Days, but quickly accepted Louis-Philippe as a 'republican' king. Republicanism began to re-emerge after the 1830 Revolution.

What did it signify to be a republican in the 1830s? Étienne Cabet was typical, with a background in the *charbonnerie* and *Aide-toi*, he took part in the July Days in Paris, was made procureur in Corsica, was fired by Périer, joined the Movement and was soon deputy for Dijon. His popular history of the 'people's' Revolution of 1830 published in 1831 was extended to two volumes in 1833 as his scorn for the Orleanists grew. He admitted that a republic would not have commanded majority support in 1830, but regretted that a Constituent Assembly had not been summoned and labelled 1830 a revolution smuggled away from the real revolutionaries, the Paris artisans. He suffered five prosecutions for this first book and quickly became the leading publicist of republican ideas. He founded and edited *Le Populaire*. The paper was partly run by workers and at 10 francs a year was relatively cheap. He reminded his readers of the Latin meaning of republic which indicated what a republic ought to be: government based on the sovereignty of the people with a written constitution and laws made by and for the nation. The republican constitution should guarantee man's natural rights to liberty, equality and security for his person and his property. The freedoms Cabet cherished included freedom of religion, of association, of the press and the abolition of monopolies and other constraints on economic freedom. All citizens should be equal in both rights and obligations in all respects, personal and political. In order to achieve such equality, Cabet demanded that the state should provide free education and medical care for the poor and ensure that there was no lack of fairly rewarded employment. To make political liberty meaningful, parliamentary deputies should receive a salary (was he influenced by the British Chartists?). An elected national assembly should be pre-eminent with an executive elected for a strictly limited period. Cabet wanted greater local autonomy and increased independence for the judiciary. Cabet's ideas were shared by many, although not all, republicans. The memory of the Convention was central to republican thinking. But their actual pronouncements were generalised and their enthusiasm for the Jacobin Republic ambiguous. Cabet was forced to flee France in 1834 because of the law against associations (Pilbeam, 1995, 95–128).

Buonarroti taught a younger generation of republicans to love the Jacobin Constitution of 1793 in his description of Babeuf's *Conspiracy of the Equals* of 1796. One of the participants who escaped the guillotine, Buonarroti, published his account he claimed to fulfil a long-cherished promise to his former associates. Buonarroti was able to settle in Paris after the 1830 Revolution.

Buonarroti presented Jacobinism as a democratic and an egalitarian revolution and laid the ground rules for a new kind of republicanism. In his book, the Jacobin Constitution of 1793, never implemented because of the demands of war and the subsequent overthrow of Robespierre on 9 Thermidor 1794, was reprinted in full as a blueprint for a future fully democratic republic. Not only the Jacobins, but also Babeuf became martyrs for the post-Imperial generation of republicans, largely as a result of Buonarroti's well-timed book (Buonarroti, 1828, 270).

The *Droits de l'Homme* reprinted the right to rebel in the Jacobin Declaration of the Rights of Man. Some republicans were also Bonapartist. The republican newspapers and clubs were shut down by legislation in the mid-1830s. Republicanism was re-shaped by Ledru-Rollin and Louis Blanc in newspapers in the early 1840s as an element in banquet campaigns to extend the suffrage and within new socialist groups. The Orleanist regime banned even the term republican, so there were never more than six deputies claiming to be republican in the Chamber of Deputies.

In February 1848 republicans were revolutionary almost by accident, taking the opportunity to claim power in the confusion when demonstrations followed a banned banquet. The members of the new provisional government were not demonstrators or fighters but politicians and journalists. Louis Blanc, Étienne Cabet, Victor Considérant and other socialists hoped that the National Workshops would be the basis for including a right to work in the new constitution, but they were appalled by the rebellion of Paris workers in June. The Paris Commune of 1871 convinced most republicans that a republic should not be revolutionary.

Socialism and Revolution

How far were socialist ideas a common factor in nineteenth-century revolution? Karl Marx looked to 1789 as the genesis for his own revolutionary creed. Everyone knows that Marx and Engels urged workers of all countries to unite in their *Manifesto of the Communist Party*, published as numerous European revolutions were underway in the spring of 1848. Neither Marx nor Engels had any substantial impact on the revolutions of 1848, but subsequently Marx wrote misleadingly that the rebellions of the Paris workers in the June Days of 1848 and in March 1871 constituted the first proletarian revolution. Contemporary conservatives were convinced that socialism was a revolutionary threat to the established order. Alexis de Tocqueville, a conservative liberal, was in accord with Marx that the June Days were a 'servile war'. The legend of June 1848 as a proletarian socialist revolution was born.

In reality the legacy of the 1789 Revolution was interpreted in contrasting ways by early socialists. The period of the constitutional monarchy was personified in the ideas of Sieyès and the abolition of feudal rights and the Declaration of the Rights of Man, over which he had a considerable influence. Sieyès gave the early socialists the language of class difference and the notion that 1789 was a bourgeois revolution. The subsequent Jacobin Republic was the lynch-pin of the Revolution for future republicans and socialists, despite its contradictory legacy. An egalitarian constitution was proposed but Robespierre's pursuit of the 'virtuous' citizen led to unprecedented persecution and Terror. In response to the Rousseauist ideal of the 'general will' and the needs of war, the machinery of the state was increasingly centralised and bureaucratised. Efforts were made to protect and provide for the needy and these were enshrined in the draft constitution, although the cost of civil and foreign war meant that little was done. Babeuf's *Conspiracy of the Equals* of 1796 embodied for some the efforts of a vanguard party to use revolution to create a communist state of equal property owners. This triple and conflicting legacy of liberty, egalitarian and repressive bureaucracy and dictatorial communism has been variously contested and applauded by socialists and communists ever since and remodelled in response to changes in communist regimes during the twentieth century, particularly that of the USSR.

However most early socialists were diametrically opposed to revolution as a philosophical construct. They claimed to be in pursuit of harmony, association, mutualism, all to be gained through cooperation, not conflict. Three of the most influential socialists, Charles Fourier, Louis Blanc and Etienne Cabet, commented on the negative practical impact of revolution in facilitating social reform. Fourier derided the achievements of 1789, Cabet and Blanc noted the limitations of the Great Revolution, while Buchez pointed out that much of the social legislation of the early 1790s, the Allarde and le Chapelier laws in particular, robbed working people of their right to associate. In 1831 Cabet described 1830 as a *révolution escamotée*, which denied benefits to the artisans who had done the actual fighting. A mere handful, clustered around Louis-Auguste Blanqui, and inspired by Buonarroti's stirring account of the Jacobin phase of the First Republic and his recollections of Babeuf's 1796 conspiracy, believed that planning and carrying out a revolution against the established order would lead to nirvana.

For all the verbal disdain of revolutionary violence, the right of rebellion, enshrined in the Jacobin Declaration of Rights of 1793, was always uppermost in the thoughts of radicals, republican and socialist. The Jacobin Declaration of Rights was constantly reprinted by radicals and socialists during the July Monarchy, from Buonarroti to Louis Blanc, who professed a hatred of revolution, but reproduced the Declaration in his critical history of the first ten years of the July Monarchy. The radical politician Ledru-Rollin quoted it to the Chamber of Deputies during an acrimonious debate on the legality of the Banquet Campaign in 1847.

Add to this evocative legitimisation of revolution, which still resonates in the streets of twenty-first century France, was the typically nineteenth-century assumption that the popular classes were always the dangerous classes. The experiences of the 1790s convinced conservatives, radicals and socialists that artisans were perpetually potential revolutionaries. That no conspiratorial activist, from Babeuf in 1796 to Blanqui, on numerous occasions between

1839 and 1871, succeeded in constructing a successful takeover of power in the name of the 'people' failed to dim either Blanqui's faith or conservative fears. The constant reinforcement of repressive legislation against associations and the press is evidence enough of the perceived danger from 'the proletariat'.

Blanqui's invented revolutions may have failed, but in these years there were two full-scale revolutions that changed regimes, numerous other episodes of unrest, ranging from bread riots to the rebellions of the Lyon silk-weavers in 1831 and 1834 and major upheavals during the Second Republic. The barricades were manned by 'the popular classes', artisans, tailors, shoemakers, weavers, hatters, cabinet makers, building workers etc. Socialists and radicals drew their support from precisely these groups, hence the fears of the established elites were perhaps not paranoia. The conservative Party of Order which took over the Second Republic in mid-1848 and the Bonapartist regime which developed were convinced that their enemies were the socialists.

There is no doubt that socialists, for all their hopes of peaceful reform, were not averse to threatening established regimes. In the early months of 1848 leading socialists such as Blanc, Considérant, Cabet and Proudhon took a not inconsiderable role in planning reform. However there was a distinction between those who believed that revolution was the prime means to achieve radical changes and the majority of socialists, who were more opportunistic profiteers from insurgency. On the other hand, popular unrest was endemic in early nineteenth-century Europe, not least in France. The artisans who formed mutual-aid groups, who became fourierists and icarians, were equally as likely to organise strikes and demonstrations, for instance, as the mutualists silk-weavers of Lyon and the cotton workers of Rouen. Small-scale wine-producers were as willing to set fire to the office of the government collectors of the detested indirect taxes as sign petitions for their abolition. When bad weather led to harvest failure, people adopted traditional strategies of grain riots and enforced the sale of grain in transit. Above all, rural inhabitants constantly protested at the withdrawal of common rights, particularly the right to use timber from communal forests. In times of major economic crisis, as in 1827–1833 and 1845–1852, a cacophony of such complaints, usually associated with anti-clerical demonstrations, the singing of the Marseillaise or Ca Ira and the waving of red flags, would alarm governments, always very aware of the revolutionary origins of their own power. Popular protest came from the very poor for whom the Forest Codes of 1827 were a disaster and who looked back to an idealised past. Equally, and more emphatically, it came from 'modernisers', more prosperous small farmers, particularly wine-producers, who were incensed by indirect taxes, the protectionist commercial policies pursued by successive governments and the high interests they were forced to pay on loans. Their motivations were both political and economic.

Historians have debated whether popular insurrection was 'archaic' or 'modernising' in inspiration. Philippe Vigier and Maurice Agulhon have shown the importance and variety of popular unrest in stimulating radical political attitudes among peasants and artisans in southern France. Agulhon emphasised that radicalism was at least as much the protest of farmers frustrated in their efforts to develop proto-capitalist agriculture as those on the margins of survival. He also stressed the importance of the traditional local sociability and communal links in maintaining independent attitudes. Alain Corbin probed conflicting 'archaic' and 'modernising' tendencies in the Limousin in his investigation of the origins of popular left-wing politics in the region and found that the focus lay in urban artisans, especially pottery workers and masons who spent the working months each year in Paris. Peter McPhee has traced the close relationship of a wide range of forms of popular unrest to the social crisis of the 1840s. John Merriman and Ted Margadant have linked popular radicalism in 1848–1849 both to resistance to the Forest Codes and the imposition of an additional 45% on the land tax in 1848. Whether those who took to the streets were modernisers or looking back to an idealised past was likely to be dictated by the development and prosperity of the economy of the region under discussion. The sort of revolution that changed regimes was urban, and essentially Parisian. Above all, revolution was an accident of geography and the absence of town planning. Cities tended to be vulnerable. In Paris the centres of government, newspapers and artisan industry were adjacent to each other. Artisan demonstrations, the demands of journalists, and the narrow streets in which both operated, made it easy to topple the highly centralised regimes of the first half of the nineteenth century. The success of the revolutions of 1830 and 1848 had far more to do with urban geography than radicalism, and even less to do with socialism.

Class Conflict and Revolution

To what extent did individuals perceive themselves as members of mutually conflicting social classes? While liberals like François Guizot, Chief Minister in the 1840s, defended the concept of class on the grounds that the new arrangement was open, equal, fair and rational, critics on the right and left presented a very different interpretation. On the right ultras like Bonald and de Maistre and liberal Catholics like Villeneuve-Bargemont lashed the bourgeois elite for their selfish, corrupt and self-seeking disregard of higher values. The first half of the century was a time of popular unrest and protest. Repeated economic crises like that of 1816–1818 in association with the more gradual impact of economic change made rural areas as well as towns the scene of repeated violent upheaval. Popular unrest became endemic, from Peterloo in 1819, the Captain Swing riots of 1830–1831, silk weavers in Lyon in 1831 and 1834, tailors and printers in Paris, Berlin and other cities in 1830, culminating in Chartism in Britain and in the revolutions of 1848. The target of protesters was 'government', which, they claimed, was responsible for iniquitous taxes, tariffs and being decreasingly willing, evidenced by recent legislation dismantling guilds and attacking freedom of association, to protect the traditional (rosily romanticised) moral economy.

Rioters were almost never committed to the overthrow of neglectful governments; they wanted government help to check damaging innovations. Grievances were specific and limited, involving attacks on property, especially new machines, forced grain sales, threats, but very little serious physical assault and almost no theft. The immediate target was often other workers, sometimes foreigners, sometimes women. Journeymen tailors complained that the growth in 'ready-made' production methods using cheap female labour reduced their income and belittled their trade. Printers were luddites and rebels because they feared that new machinery would threaten both their skills and jobs. Silk weavers resented their increasing financial dependence on merchants. Poorer peasants protested about the erosion of communal rights, the better-off that the vagaries of the market left them dependent on money lenders, or that tariffs on imported manufactures blocked their foreign wine market – and that was just in France. Factory workers were seldom involved in protests. There was no concerted 'class' consciousness, but a series of particular, often regionally limited issues which sometimes coincided in depression years. The rhetoric of 'class conflict' was aired in the cheaper, sometimes worker-run newspapers of the day, but it only had a wide audience when food prices soared and work was scarce.

Real and mythical recollections of the Terror of the 1790s in France convinced all governments of the need to repress disorder before it could escalate. Socialists had far more success in convincing ruling elites of the imminence of class war than they had in converting and uniting working people. In 1843 Flora Tristan complained of artisan indifference and hostility to her idealistic plan for a single Union of All Workers. Military repression at Peterloo, Lyon, Paris, Milan and St Petersburg did far more to create a sense of lower-class solidarity than the writings of the socialists or the inequities of the capitalist economy.

Rioting was one way of drawing attention to problems in crisis years. At ordinary times in the eighteenth century more prosperous workers had grouped themselves into small protective insurance schemes to provide death benefits etc. In some areas journeymen formed defensive, sometimes violent, groups. As the process of economic change grew in the nineteenth century, a variety of worker associations, for mutual-aid, groups of producers, employees or consumers, became more numerous and more structured. Popular associations, whether peaceful or violent, were feared by ruling elites as organised manifestations of popular opinion. In France the liberal claims of the Declaration of Rights of 1789 were gainsaid by the Civil Code which put any association larger than 20 under the scrutiny of the prefect. Craft and the mutual-aid insurance associations might be tolerated, but a vague whiff of politics or violent action brought in the army. In 1834 even associations of under 20 were banned.

Did social divisions play a part in nineteenth-century revolutions? At the time and subsequently the 1830 revolution was often referred to as bourgeois.

The socialist Louis Blanc called 1830 bourgeois, not because he considered the bourgeoisie made the revolution and profited from it, but rather because they were already in power, and failed to give way to the real revolutionaries, the artisans. A generation later Karl Marx claimed that the better-off bourgeoisie replaced the aristocracy in 1830; witness that bankers, notably Jacques Laffitte, Louis-Philippe's banker and Casimir Périer were appointed Chief Ministers in November 1830 and March 1831. Marx further claimed that less wealthy bourgeois businessmen, lawyers, doctors, state servants and journalists made the February revolution while Parisian workers made the Commune the first workers revolt. After the Bolshevik Revolution of 1917, Marxist socialists insisted that since 1789 all revolutions were the product of economic change and the resulting decline of the aristocracy, the rise and fall of the bourgeoisie and finally the success of proletarian revolution. This interpretation seemed convincing until the collapse of the USSR in 1990.

The Bourbon restoration depended on the backing of the traditional aristocracy, but was also supported by some bourgeois property owners. The Bourbon elite saw itself as predominantly noble and at odds with the Orleanist regime after 1830. However, attempts by historians in the 1960s to define those who ruled before and after 1830 in class terms were made tricky by how the nineteenth-century rich defined themselves. In the 1830s voters were asked to state their occupation on electoral lists. A man might describe himself as landowner, forge-owner, deputy, mayor etc., making simple social definitions opaque. Impoverished nobles were keen to marry their eldest son to the daughter of a rich bourgeois. Since the second half of the eighteenth century it had become the norm to talk more about *notables* than about nobles and bourgeois.

The June Days, 1848, were designated a revolt of Parisian workers as was the Paris Commune. We would be more inclined to talk about them as artisans, traditional craftsmen, not a modern industrial proletariat. In both instances the rebels considered their socio-economic status integral to their grievances with the established politicians. A democratic republic may have been declared in February 1848, but the decision of the new government to close the workshops set up to provide for the unemployed was viewed as an attack on workers' rights. The election of a democratic commune in March 1871 was a protest by Parisian workers at Thiers' unwillingness to acknowledge that the economy of the capital had been ruined during the siege. The Commune was a workers' revolt. Social cleavages were thus significant elements in nineteenth-century revolution, although class war as defined by Karl Marx did not fit the bill.

Economic Issues

Harvest failure in grains, potatoes and grapes plus industrial recession in the years 1826–1833, 1839 and 1845–1849 were always blamed on government tax and tariff policies. Governments were blamed for not taking steps to control the rise in bread prices, for instance an increase of 50% in 1828–1829 and in 1845–1849. There were constant complaints about indirect taxes, much intensified in times of harvest failure. *Droits réunis*, taxes on the producers of wine, salt and tobacco, were sharply criticised by those who had to pay them. In addition high tariffs on imported wheat led to a marked rise in the price of bread. Repeated cyclical industrial recessions in 1826–1832 and 1845–1849 led to a sharp rise in bankruptcies and resulting commercial and industrial setbacks. In 1828–1829 the Martignac government sent out questionnaires to investigate these issues. But when faced with criticism of *droits réunis* and import duties, Martignac refused to modify commercial policy. Indeed his critics were not united. Wine-producers wanted the abolition of *droits réunis* and the reduction of export duties on alcohol, while iron manufacturers demanded higher tariffs on imported iron. In 1845–1849 the main commercial issue was a boom and bust in railway development and consequent collapse of rail companies and banks. The 1789 revolutionaries had left forests, particularly in more remote areas, in the hands of the local community, their commercial value somewhat disregarded. Timber prices rose, particularly with the rapid growth of iron production, in which charcoal remained the main fuel. In 1827 Forest Laws permitted the sale of communal forests, denying the poor access to wood which they considered communal property. This became a major factor in popular unrest in more remote rural areas both in the late 1820s and the 1840s. Governments invariably favoured better-off producers over subsistence farmers, agricultural labourers and small industrial producers.

Culture Wars

Despite Napoleon's Concordat, divisions over religion persisted throughout the century. The Church gave full support to the Restoration, particularly to the ultras. In 1814 the Church aggravated divisions when young evangelical priests embarked on a campaign to get the French on their knees to apologise for the Revolution. Missionary crosses replaced trees of liberty at the entrance to villages. A feature of the 1830 revolution was an attack on the Paris archbishopric and in many communes the replacement of missionary crosses by liberty trees, adorned with tricolour flags and liberty caps. In March 1848 the clergy were encouraged to support former monarchist against republican candidates in the elections for the Constituent Assembly. In 1871 the Paris Commune followed anti-clerical policies and the archbishop of Paris was put to death in response to the execution of Communards. The Sacre-Coeur was built in Montmartre by public subscription to help people forget the Commune. Republicans remained committed to anti-clerical policies. A century of argument about primary education was resolved in 1881 by the decision to establish state-run schools. In 1905 the separation of Church and State was declared.

Participants in Revolution

Workers

Parisian workers were the most visible and numerous among those who took to the streets. Industrial change made workers aware of both their vulnerability to unemployment and government hostility to their problems. Workers were not allowed to organise or strike. The 1791 Le Chapelier law forbade workers to associate and traditional craft organisations were banned. Workers, mainly men, began to form mutual-aid societies, paying a weekly fee to provide sick, unemployment and retirement pay to members. In the 1830s some tried to strike. Lyon silk workers protested at the control merchants exercised over what they paid *canuts*, skilled silk weavers for finished silk, and the refusal of the government to protect weavers. This was the basis of weaver strikes in November 1831 which for a time allowed them to take over the city, ignoring the mayor and prefect. From 1814 people were not allowed to associate in clubs of more than 20 and all groups, whatever their purpose, required prefectoral authorisation. In April 1834 the *canuts* went on strike when new government legislation banned clubs, however small. This seemed to threaten the existence of traditional weaver craft associations.

Parisian workers were dominant in successful protests in the July Revolution of 1830 and in the February Revolution of 1848. They were also the biggest force in unsuccessful risings, in May 1839 in the June Days and in the Paris Commune. Most numerous were migrant workers, especially masons, who travelled from their homes, particularly in the Limousin, to Paris each year for the working season, March to October. They were most active in all these revolutions. They lived in specific, crowded communities in central Paris, and their work acquainted them with workers in a broader geographic area. Masons were prominent in revolts because they were particularly vulnerable to unemployment in economic depression. Martin Nadaud, Perdiguier and Turquin (Lyon) all wrote about their experiences.

Paris was the heart of French industry, particularly the luxury trades, whose workers were very susceptible to economic recession. These included weavers, hatters, shoemakers, luxury metal workers, including silver and gold, jewellers and furniture makers. By the 1860s also included were the operatives in the new iron industry in the Parisian suburb of Belleville. Highly skilled artisans were cut to short-term work or became unemployed in 1827–1832, 1845–1848 and during the siege of Paris by the Prussian army and the Commune in 1870–1871. In addition changes in the structure of some industries threatened reduction in rates of pay. Less skilled aspects of tailoring, and to some extent shoe and hat making – highly skilled male jobs, previously all done by skilled craftsmen – were 'put out' to cheap, female labour with consequent complaints from skilled men who lost work. In addition, all these skilled trades were very subject to short-term working and unemployment in economic crises.

Changes in printing techniques alarmed printers that the industry was being de-skilled. In addition the tendency of governments to try to control criticism by censoring the press and prosecuting editors forced newspapers to close. In the political crisis in 1830 the first of the four ordinances ordered liberal newspapers to cease production. The police were allowed to seize presses and force editors to cease production. Editors took the lead in organising resistance to the ordinances and their operatives joined rioters in the July Days. In 1833 when the Guizot government was alarmed by the growth of *Aide-toi* radical associations, their first target was to increase rules against newspapers, forcing radical papers to shut down. In 1848 liberal journalists were most prominent in protesting against the ban on the Paris banquet and in the provisional government which took power from Louis-Philippe.

Workers from the same trades took part in the same sort of insurrection, in the same right-bank areas near to the Hôtel de Ville in Paris in February 1848 as in July 1830. In both cases their grievances concerned reduced rates of pay and hours of work, not politics, but without their activities there would have been no revolution.

Journalists

In both 1830 and 1848, journalist critics of the regime had some impact in unseating rulers. On 27 July 1830 Rémusat and some liberal journalists defied the First Ordinance and criticised the King's policy, but others conformed to the decree. Adolphe Thiers, editor of the most radical paper, *Le National*, persuaded Louis-Philippe to meet with a revolutionary crowd at the Hôtel de Ville and accept the designation 'republican or constitutional ruler'. However, as King, Louis-Philippe showed no more enthusiasm than his predecessor for press freedom. In 1834–1835 censorship became more severe than in the previous regime.

In the February crisis of 1848 when troops had fired on crowds of the unemployed and students, and Louis-Philippe preferred to leave for England rather than risk prolonged bloodshed, it was journalists/politicians from the main left-wing opposition paper *Le National* who assembled in the Chamber of Deputies to proclaim a provisional government, making the republican journalist Ledru-Rollin Minister of the Interior. Moving on to the Hôtel de Ville, traditional focus of radical protest, they encountered journalists from more the more radical *La Réforme* and added a worker Albert to the government. The socialist reformer and journalist Louis Blanc was put in charge of a Parliament of Industry composed of workers and employers to meet in Chamber of Peers, Luxembourg Palace, to advise the new self-declared republican government on the economic crisis. Thus in 1848 journalists had a decisive role in the change to a republic. In September 1870 in the third successful change of regime journalists had no role, nor had they in the Paris Commune.

Women

The most famous depiction of revolution, painted by Delacroix in 1830, was female. Gender became a conflictual issue in the mid-century, when women replaced men in some less-skilled jobs. Former Saint-Simonian/Fourierist women, including Jeanne Deroin, promoted a women's club and worker unions and a newspaper in 1848, but found little support from men (see document 10). Hostility to women workers and revolutionaries appeared in several series of humorous cartoons in Parisian newspapers by Daumier and de Beaumont in 1848. De Beaumont's revolutionary ladies (see document 9) were all attractive, unlike those of Daumier, and particularly those drawn during the Commune. Women, including workers, joined clubs supporting the Commune, pressed for votes for women, contributed to attempts to encourage girls' education and fought to defend the Commune, but most Commune leaders were hostile to women's rights. After the Commune in 1881 girls were included in the new state primary schools, and in 1884 the right to divorce was restored. Women workers formed trade unions. At the turn of the century women's magazines edited by women appeared, but the vote eluded this 50% of the population until after the Second World War.

Army and National Guard

National Guardsmen and junior officers and soldiers took an active role in revolution in 1830 and February 1848. In 1814, and again in 1815 after the Hundred Days, when the war was over, army numbers had been drastically reduced. Bonapartists were retired on half pay. Many found it hard to find work and met in their local café with nothing to do but to regret the past. The presence of National Guardsmen and soldiers on the revolutionary side in 1830 and 1848 may have been the decisive factor in victory. It is notable that combatants were rewarded for their contribution in 1830 and the dead honourably interred. In 1848 the republican government recruited combatants into a republican guard which contributed notably to the defeat of Parisian workers in the June Days along with the guardsmen brought by train to Paris to fight the insurgents. The defeat of the Communards was entirely due to the massing of regular troops to fight against the Parisian National Guard in Bloody Week. Subsequently, aware of the contribution the National Guard had made to nineteenth-century revolution, the government completely disbanded the organisation.

Attitudes to Revolutionary Fighters

Traditionally participants in successful revolutions were rewarded by the succeeding regime. Those who contributed to the fall of the Bastille, 14 July 1789, received medals and guns. After July 1830 and February 1848 those who could prove they had fought for the revolution earned a pension. In 1848 they were referred to as *citoyens combattants*, heroes of revolution.

After the February revolution in 1848 *combattants* were encouraged to join the new *garde mobile*, or democratised National Guard, with uniform and weapon provided by the regime. However the June Days 1848 made participation in revolt dishonourable, traitorous – Tocqueville wrote about a 'guerre servile'. A similar change occurred in attitudes to those who were arrested as opponents of the regime. In the July Monarchy political prisoners were frequently released after one year; after June 1848 the insurgents were declared enemies of the republic and transported to Algeria (Hinckner, 2008). The Communards of 1871 received much harsher treatment. At least 10,000 were massacred on the spot by the 100,000 troops. The trials of those arrested in Paris lasted for four years: 93 were condemned to death, 251 to forced labour, nearly 5000 were deported, nearly 7000 imprisoned. Foreigners were most likely to be executed. Women and known criminals received the heaviest sentences, family men the lightest. But despite the harsh repression, by 1880 most prisoners had been amnestied.

Revolutionary Action as Repetition

Parisian revolution tended to start with worker marches and demonstrations complaining at government inaction over economic recession, accompanied by criticism within elite and particularly in the left-wing press. Barricades were thrown up in central areas. The National Guard plus sections of the army were reluctant to support existing regimes. At this point in July 1830 Charles X retreated. Liberal politicians backed down and it was left to liberal journalists such as Thiers to take a lead with the hero of 1789, Lafayette, meeting symbolically at the Hôtel de Ville and presenting the King's cousin, Louis-Philippe, Duc d'Orléans as a replacement 'citizen king', 'the best of republics'. Parliament reassembled and voted in a 'King of the French people'. The actual revolutionary crowd was forgotten. As the republican Cabet said, 1830 was a revolution smuggled away from the people.

In February 1848 the revolutionary process was not dissimilar to 1830. Workers marches, barricades erected in the same streets, troops failing to control unrest, the National Guard supporting the rebels, elite radicals declaring a provisional government, first at the Chamber, then at the Hôtel de Ville. It was almost as if the French were sleepwalking through an established pattern of revolt. In 1848 Louis-Philippe left for England to stop further violence. In June 1848 the second stage of the process of revolution did not happen. Worker protests at the closure of the national workshops did not attract the support of soldiers and National Guardsmen, rather the reverse. Thus, the June Days failed. In December 1851 the coup d'état engineered by the president Louis-Napoleon succeeded because he had military support, despite widespread protest in rural France. In May 1871 the attempt of Parisians to imitate the 1792 Paris Commune failed, because Thiers, the elected head of state, was able to use the army against the Parisian National Guard to suppress this second Commune with extreme violence. The military, sometimes in alliance with the National Guard, was crucial to the fate of the revolutionary process.

Why Were There No Successful Revolutions After 1848?

Despite the formation by Marx and others of the Workers International in 1862, after 1848 there were no more successful French or other European revolutions. Major technical developments may have had some impact in preserving existing regimes. The construction of rail networks and a telegraph network, together with a professional army and policing, made it easier for French governments to put down revolts. Although only a modest rail system was complete by 1848, troops and National Guard were moved for the first time by rail to help defeat the June workers' revolt. Earlier the slowness of communication allowed revolt to take hold. The telegraph made a big contribution to improving communication between central and local government by mid-century. Communication could be a factor in squashing rumour and limiting the impact of unrest. In 1849 Paul Julius Reuters initiated the first telegraphic press service (using pigeons to cover sections where lines were incomplete). Its effect was first felt, nationally and internationally, during the Franco-Prussian war and the Commune. The changing geography of Paris was significant in the decline of revolutionary action. The flattening of central Paris to build the rail terminus stations, destroying the narrow streets which could be barricaded, and replacing them with very wide boulevards, had two consequences. First the rebuilding pushed worker communities to the suburbs, making it far more difficult to gather together to protest. Second, boulevards could not be barricaded. This may have facilitated the reclamation of Paris by Thiers' army in Bloody Week, May 1871, although the conquest took a week and led to the firing of most major public buildings. By 1871 boulevard construction must have still been fairly restricted. The accidental factor in revolutions, disease, harvest failure and food shortages, had less of an impact by the 1860s. The North and South American prairie provinces and the Ukraine began to export grain, plus the canning of meat from South America ended the threat of shortage. Industrial recession did not disappear but economic growth made more work available. Increased educational opportunities for the sons and daughters of workers began to offer the chance of more varied and secure work. The growing role of national and local government as an employer provided many of these jobs. The changing structure and scope of state power, elected parliaments, eventually democratic, made revolution less easy and appealing. With the legalisation of trade unions from 1862, negotiation became an easier and less disruptive alternative to revolution.

Alternatives to Revolution: Modernity

Guided by the *philosophes* the revolutionaries of 1789 founded the modern state by rationalising institutions and modernising society through the abolition of feudal institutions. In the nineteenth century it was not that there was nothing left to stamp with modernity, but that revolution was no longer the agent. Urbanisation demanded drains, restructuring of cities, but this was the work of bureaucrats and businessmen, financed by the centralised state and private sources. The state became the biggest employer. Jobs and promotions were no longer based on traditional privilege or the four quarters of nobility. The 1789 Revolution encouraged the trend to professionalisation with the creation of higher level colleges to educate engineers, university teachers and so on, but in the nineteenth century revolution had no role in reshaping society. Instead changes were the consequence of mainly state-run education and the development of modern professional qualifications essential for posts and promotion within bureaucratic state organisations. Inheritance might still play a part, with sons following fathers as doctors and army officers, but modernising France and France modernised made revolution irrelevant. Perhaps the most important factor in the declining appeal of revolution was the alternative opportunities to violence. From 1881 all children benefitted from free primary education. The development of a parliamentary system based on universal male suffrage after 1871 permitted the growth of socialist parliamentary parties appealing to workers.

From being the example of revolution to the rest of Europe, in the nineteenth century France reassumed its eighteenth-century role as the capital of culture, providing an example to the world in everything from food and restaurants to design and fashion, literature, art and music, attracting both visitors and permanent migrants from all quarters of the Western world, particularly from America (Marrinan, 2009, 321–365). In all these arenas France probably had as much influence as the revolutionaries in the 1790s, and a more lasting influence than Napoleon.

5 France Abroad

This chapter will consider two issues. First the impact of French ideas on the rest of Europe, and second the development of a world empire after 1814 and its relationship to revolution.

Impact of French Revolutionary Ideas on Europe

Napoleon's European empire was eliminated by the Allies in 1814. However imperial conquest meant that French revolutionary institutional changes were stamped on some conquered territory and local elites came to value them. The French prefectoral system and codes of law remained in place in some Italian states and the Rhineland through the nineteenth century and had an impact on the legal systems in Egypt and elsewhere to this day. French revolutionary ideas came to dominate reforming philosophies in Europe after 1814, leading to numerous, but rarely successful, revolutions, mostly launched in part by educated young middle class enthusiasts, often members of the *carbonari* secret societies which started in the Italian states in 1820. They were joined by men who had acquired jobs during the Napoleonic conquest and had been displaced after the fall of the Empire. Revolts coincided with Europe-wide economic crises and revolts in France in 1830 and 1848. There were revolts in Spain and Greece in 1822, in Portugal and Belgium in 1830, Poland in 1830 and 1863, the Italian and German states in the 1820s, 1830 and 1848. All were influenced by the French revolutionary ideas of 1789 and by the liberal constitutional and national philosophies which emerged after 1814. For more on the French Empire see Todd (2021).

European reformers were obsessed with French liberal and national revolutionary ideas in the years after 1814 despite the efforts of the Powers who had defeated Napoleon to stamp them out. The victorious Powers were determined to avoid future French expansion. They hoped that this would best be achieved by restoring borders as near as possible to where they had been before 1792. In 1814 the peace makers had united the provinces which had previously been the Austrian Netherlands in the Holy Roman Empire with the Dutch provinces to create the United Netherlands, which meant that the Dutch, who were Protestants, ruled Catholic Belgians. William, Dutch

DOI: 10.4324/9781003460596-5

head of the House of Orange, became king. There was no elected assembly, the state was financed by high indirect taxes and strict press censorship was imposed. Neither Catholic Belgians nor French-speaking liberals were pleased. In 1827 an economic crisis gave the dissatisfied politicians popular backing. In 1828 the two groups united to force William to agree to an elected assembly and in 1830 he agreed to call an Estates-General.

Brussels was a magnet for revolutionary exiles. A leading figure was Buonarroti, revolutionary conspirator with Babeuf in 1795, who established himself in Belgium. To rally his supporters, he brought out in 1828 through a Brussels publisher his recollections of Babeuf's Conspiracy of the Equals (1796). In it he also reprinted the Jacobin democratic constitution of 1793, which had never been implemented, and urged the case for an insurrection in the name of the people. The July Days encouraged him to move to Paris, so he probably had no influence over the Belgians. It was the July Days which led directly to a nationalist, liberal revolt in Belgium. In September 1830, William, nervous, sent troops to control liberal Brussels. This set off a revolt. A provisional government was established, as in France weeks earlier, and liberals declared Belgium independent of the Dutch in October 1830. William appealed to the Great Powers who after all had caused the problem with the 1814 settlement. The Powers were quite alarmed. The French saw the chance to extend their influence in the new state. The Movement deputies wanted to march to help the Belgian revolt. Louis-Philippe feared attack by other powers if they did, but he fancied the throne of the new state for one of his many sons. Britain now became involved, as they were keen to restrain the French and visualised Louis-Philippe as another Napoleon. The Belgians were forced to accept Leopold of Saxe-Gotha (a German) the widower of George IV's dead daughter as king. Louis-Philippe contented himself with providing one of his daughters as the wife of the new king. The Belgians had successfully revolted against William, a ruler imposed on them, but the British and French imposed another ruling family on them. The Belgian affair was partly a liberal revolt, partly nationalist, partly religious. Was independent Belgium liberal? In February 1831 a National Congress was assembled by liberal and Catholic leaders. It devised a constitution modelled on that of France. Only the richest 46,000 men were enfranchised. If France was liberal after 1830, so was Belgium, but even more uneasily so because Belgian survival rested on an unlikely alliance of liberals, who were traditionally anti-clerical in nineteenth-century Europe, and Catholics who were traditionally not liberal. Civil liberties were extended. Liberal unity was fragile. We have dealt with Belgium's independence first because a new independent state emerged.

Southern Europe

Here liberals were mainly young men who had been making their way in the world in the Napoleonic regime, often in the army, sometimes in administration, and were pushed out in 1814. Some formed secret societies in the Italian states, notably the *carbonari*, which were anti-clerical and revolutionary. In 1820 there were revolts to try to restore liberal constitutions abolished in 1814 in Spain, Portugal and the kingdom of the Two Sicilies (south Italy). In 1821 there was a liberal rising in Greece and in Piedmont. None of the rulers wanted to share power with parliaments, but none had strong enough armies to hold out. The Great Powers came to their rescue. Liberal demands were squashed by Great Power agreements in a series of congresses; Laibach in 1821 agreed that Austrian troops should eliminate liberal demands in south Italy.

Italian States: Liberal and National Hopes

In the years up to 1830 nationalism was also becoming an issue in the Italian peninsula. Nationalism was not a 'popular' sentiment, but part of romantic, cultural dreams of uniting 'peoples' as counterweights to the traditional absolutist authority of rulers. Encouraged by the new conglomerate states Napoleon had created in the German, Polish and Italian lands, some thinkers and writers spun liberal and patriotic concepts together. For the moment these were rooted in history, language and culture. In the Italian peninsula the experience of French conquest gave rise to the idea of a 'Risorgimento' or rebirth of Italy. Italian literary patriots could look back to the early modern period to city states which were glorious in terms of culture and commerce. Unfortunately, they had also to look back in different languages, Italian being little used outside Tuscany. The Romantic novelist Manzoni set the tone for future attempts at mutual comprehension and harmony with the first novel in Italian, *I promessi sposi*. The author glorified Italian patriotism in a love story set in Lombardy of the 1630s. But even this much prized step to a common language had to be rewritten from the Lombardian dialect into Tuscan Italian.

Italian-exiled *carbonari*, promised support by republicans like Buonarroti in France, dreamed of the unification of the peninsula. In February 1831 a rising in Modena was followed by others in the Papal States. Harsh repression in Naples and Piedmont prevented unrest spreading. The internecine and unrealistic squabbles of the exiles and the modest and very localised expectations of the actual rebels, plus the intervention of Austrian troops in Bologna and elsewhere, ruined any chance of victory. One of the most notable revolutionaries was Giuseppe Mazzini (1805–1872). A native of Genoa, he graduated as a lawyer, representing those who could not afford to employ him. He joined the *carbonari*, a secret sect, was betrayed and arrested near Genoa and imprisoned. He was released on condition he left Piedmont. He settled in Italy. In the summer of 1831 he created Young Italy and Young Europe to work towards republican independence and democracy. He avoided linking people in secret sects because he considered them divisive. Mazzini hoped for support of 'the people', aware that earlier insurrections had lacked mass support. He did not want class war. He gained support from the poor in the main northern cities. He attracted some young idealists, but his appeal was limited. In 1837 Mazzini was forced into exile in London. His ally Garibaldi went to fight with nationalists in South America. Stimulated by economic recessions and following the example of France, the 1830s also saw revolts in other Italian states which came to nothing. There were similar divisions among radicals and moderates, which masked personal and regional rivalries.

Poland

Here the revolutionaries were nobles. In 1815 Alexander I gained control of a substantial amount of the old kingdom of Poland, split between Russia, Austria and Prussia a generation earlier. He gave them the most liberal constitution in Europe, a parliament (100,000 voters – 3% of the population) their own administrative and judicial system and army, all conducted in the Polish language.

Archduke Constantine was put in control. Poland experienced revolution in November 1830. Although Alexander's system sounded quite liberal, the Russian Tsar was not inclined to accept the decisions of the Polish parliament if it disagreed with him. After the death of Alexander in 1825 some Polish nobles were involved in the Decembrist conspiracy to promote the succession of Constantine rather than the heir Nicholas. They were put on trial. When the Poles refused to convict them, Nicholas sent them to Siberia and set about the russification of Poland, unpicking the constitution and withdrawing Polish autonomy. On 29 November 1830, close to the July Days, and involving a few Poles who had taken part in the French revolution, army officers led a rebellion in Warsaw. Their support came mainly from the 300,000 poorer nobility. They were badly affected by the series of poor grain harvests. They attracted some sympathy among the large *émigré* Polish population in Paris, and at first among liberals elsewhere in Europe, but the unwillingness of the rebels to lessen the impact of serfdom on their peasants lost this support. Their revolt failed in December 1831. The Poles lost their constitution, parliament, army, separate status and the use of Polish in government.

German States

In 1814 the Allies reduced the German states to 39 and set up a German Confederation headed by the Austrian ruler. The south German states adopted constitutions, the rest followed Austria's conservative lead. In 1832 Hambach held a festival of liberty attended by 20,000 middle class men who listened to speeches for German unity. Experiencing the economic crisis which hit the whole of Europe there were riots about manorial rights in Hesse, about high taxes in Hanover, but nothing that united Germans. In 1832, Saxony, Hanover and Brunswick adopted constitutions similar to south Germany. A meeting of the German Confederation agreed to the Austrian

Chief Minister Metternich's demands for reactionary policies, censorship and increased police surveillance after an attempted coup by Heidelberg students and academics. The ruler of Brunswick was unseated, but the Confederate Diet replaced him with his brother.

Spain

In March 1820 – junior officers 'pronounced' in favour of Spain's 1812 constitution which they looked back on as liberal compared with the post-1814 monarchy. The army officers were critical of the King and his intention to try to recapture Spain's South American colonies, although only a minority of them were liberal.

In the same month, a junta of officers in Madrid forced a constitutional government on the King – though they were scornful of civilian liberals. By summer 1820 Spain was in the hands of ad hoc liberal provincial committees when the parliament of Cortes met. Spanish liberals were not united. Urban radicals wanted democracy and to attack the power of the Church. Radicals gained a majority in the new Cortes, but could not reach a compromise with moderates, who were themselves divided. Provincial divisions were also rampant. In July 1822 the Royal Guard tried to seize power, although King Ferdinand's position was unclear. Some royalists wanted to make the King's brother Don Carlos king and dreamt of royal despotism, similar to the ultras in France. The situation was so chaotic that in a meeting at Verona the Great Powers agreed that France should intervene militarily in Spain. In April 1823 French troops moved into Spain and restored Ferdinand as absolute ruler. So France was involved in putting down, not supporting, revolution. Liberals actually did well as bureaucrats with the job of modernising Spain's economy, royalists not so well, and the army almost dissolved.

Spanish liberals in exile tried to push their case against an elderly king whose young wife had conveniently just had a child, in a strategy to disinherit his heir, Don Carlos. In September 1832 it was thought that Ferdinand was terminally ill. Don Carlos threatened civil war unless the queen renounced her infant daughter's claim to throne. To side-step her brother-in-law's bullying, the Queen (backed by Ferdinand, who recovered briefly) adopted a liberal government, amnestied up to 10,000 liberal exiles, purged the army and exiled Don Carlos himself. While it would be wrong to claim that liberalism had triumphed in Spain by 1830, it would not be unreasonable to suggest that, for the moment, the chance of thorough-going counter-revolution had been eliminated.

Portugal

Portuguese liberalism was somewhat exceptional, as was Portugal itself. In 1814 it was ruled from Brazil by the Regent John (Queen Maria was permanently insane). The country had undergone some modernisation in the previous half-century, under the dictatorial control of the King's minister, Pombal, who is traditionally included by historians among the enlightened despots. The power of the church, including the influential Inquisition, had been checked, and the Jesuits expelled. Some educational reform had been undertaken and Pombal had done battle with the dominant landed aristocratic elite. However in 1777, on the death of King Joseph and the succession of his daughter, Maria, Pombal had been forcibly retired by resurgent noble families who re-established their control. In 1792, when Maria retreated into insanity on the death of her husband, her son John took control. When Murat had led French troops into the peninsula in 1807, John moved the government of the empire to Rio de Janiero, reducing mainland Portugal almost to colonial status. He was reluctant to return in 1814.

In 1820, encouraged by unrest elsewhere, liberals in the Oporto garrison mutinied, but swore to join John if he would accept a liberal constitution. A Cortes was elected and a constitution on the Spanish model approved. The powers of the nobility and of the Church were reduced, including those of the Inquisition. John returned and promised to abide by the constitution, but two years later the entry of the French into Spain encouraged conservatives to push it aside. Liberal army officers turned to John's son, Dom Miquel, who promised to restore a constitutional regime. In Brazil John's elder son, Peter, agreed to head an independent Brazil as a constitutional king. The situation became more complicated when Peter returned to Portugal. By 1830 Portugal was in the midst of civil war between the rival royal factions.

1848 Year of Revolutions

There were revolutions in the capital cities of the German states, Austria and the Italian peninsula. They were inspired by the French tradition of revolts and the Paris February revolution. As in Paris the background was high food prices and industrial recession. Participants in cities included weavers, tailors, shoemakers, cabinet makers – highly skilled men. There was disorder also in rural areas for both long-term (the modernisation of the structure of industry) and short-term (an industrial crisis following a banking collapse) reasons; involving farmers, small-scale wine-producers and artisans who worked in rural industries such as textiles and metal trades. The biggest growth of industry in continental Europe in these years also took part in the countryside. In the short term most rulers gave in to popular unrest and agreed to constitutional changes. Frederick William IV of Prussia in response to artisan demonstrations in Berlin on 18 March 1848 agreed to a constitution and an elected *landtag*. Revolts in Austria and Hungary led to a constitution and an elected assembly. In Piedmont, Victor-Emmanuel, faced with revolt, agreed to an elected parliament with a voting qualification of 40 liras, similar to that the French had just rejected. France joined Victor-Emmanuel in a war against Austria in the name of Italian nationalism. In the Papal States Mazzini and Garibaldi helped drive out the Pope and declared a republic. In Lombardy middle-class revolutionary leaders Cattaneo, and in Venice, Manin, replaced rule from Vienna with independent republics. In the kingdom of the Two Sicilies there was also a revolt but the Bourbons, helped by Austrian troops, kept power. In the German states a Frankfurt Assembly was elected to write a German constitution, but neither of the rulers of Austria nor Prussia was prepared to head a united Germany. In Prussia the king ratified a very elitist constitution which created an elected parliament; one-third of the seats in the *landtag* were chosen by the richest 4% of voters; one-third by the next richest, around 13%, and the rest by the rest. Elsewhere in German states little changed.

In the Italian states only Piedmont kept a constitution. French troops restored the Pope to Rome. Thus in 1848 the French revolutionary example helped produced modest change, while the French army, as in Spain in 1823, shut down revolution.

Subsequently military action brought substantial change in the creation of two major nation states, Italy (1859) and Germany (1866 and 1871) under the leadership of the two most powerful states, Piedmont and Prussia. France had a role in the creation of Italy. In an alliance with Napoleon III Piedmont defeated Austria. This set off revolts elsewhere in Italy and the formation of a united Italy under Piedmont to which Rome was added in 1870. In 1866 the defeat of Austria by Prussia led to Prussia leading a North German constitution, which Prussia enlarged into an empire in 1871 after defeating Napoleon III. By no stretch of the imagination can one find any French inspiration in this empire formed in war. There was no further major political or social insurrection in the nineteenth century. It is possible to trace a French revolutionary tradition in radical leaders like Mazzini and in nineteenth-century revolutions, perhaps more in 1830 than in 1848. However that revolution occurred in a substantial number of countries was due more to the coincidence of economic crisis than the inspiration of 1789. The most tangible impact of French tradition was probably the retention of French legal and prefectoral systems in Piedmont and the Rhineland in 1814.

Empire

French governments promoted a new world empire in the nineteenth century. Nelson's victory at Trafalgar in 1805 brought France's hopes at sea to an end, devastated the economies of her Atlantic ports and their hinterland and checked her industrial growth. The Peace of Vienna put France back to her 1792 borders, and the second defeat in 1815 resulted in an indemnity and an army of occupation until it was paid (1818). France was then admitted to the Congress System (an alliance against revolution), but faced continued suspicion of her territorial ambitions. Little remained of France's first world empire. In 1814 France held the Pacific islands of the Seychelles and Réunion and in 1814 regained control of Martinique and Guadeloupe from Britain. Guiana was only returned by the Portuguese in 1817. During the revolutionary years Napoleon embarked on a disastrous (but brilliantly advertised) expedition to Egypt (1798–1799) in which polytechnic engineers mapped the area in a multi-volume *Description de l'Egypte* published from 1808 into the 1820s which stimulated nineteenth-century orientalism in Europe. In the 1950s General Nassar recalled the expedition as an inspiration in Egypt itself. The memory of Napoleon's Egyptian expedition encouraged a new emphasis on the Mediterranean in France, not surprising given the elite still learned the language and history of ancient Greece and Rome. French battleships joined British and Russian ships in the 1827 Navarino battle to help the Greeks defeat the Turks to gain their independence. Intervention in Greece involved a variety of motives, from cultural imperialism, to Great Power rivalry, to archaeology. French archaeologists had an important role. In 1821 the formation of the Geographical Society encouraged travel and exploration.

Slavery, Slave Trade and Abolition

The French, the example to the world in the Revolution and the Declaration of the Rights of Man of 1789, were much slower than the British in abolishing slavery. We left the story in Chapter 1 with Haiti independent, and slavery re-established in other French islands.

Slavery

Napoleon re-established slavery in 1802. It should be noted that there were many ex-slaves in the Caribbean. In 1796 more than half the soldiers in Guadeloupe were ex-slaves as were 11,000 who fought the British in Grenada, St Vincent and Saint Lucia and some became senior officers, e.g. Delgras. There were 35,000 French sailors who were ex-slaves. Slaves also operated as corsairs, fighting against British merchant ships. There was also work for ex-slaves in towns and some became prosperous. Those who returned to plantations did less well.

Slave Trade

In 1814 the French were pushed by the British to abolish the slave trade, but there were many loopholes and emphasis was placed on the recovery of the Caribbean economy. Abolition of the slave trade had the support only of the minority liberal opposition, including Lafayette, Grégoire, Benjamin Constant, Victor de Broglie and his mother-in-law Mme de Staël. The surviving plantocracy in the Caribbean bemoaned their lack of capital and export market.

West Indies – planters insisted on the need for slaves to recover their production of sugar etc. – 125,000 Africans were taken to the Caribbean from 1815 to 1831. Louis XVIII had assured Britain that France would end the slave trade. 1816 witnessed an attempt to colonise Senegal in which *La Méduse* with 360 colonists sank off West Africa. Passengers were abandoned on a flimsy raft and few survived. Géricault painted the tragedy *Le Radeau* *de la Méduse*. The painting secured much publicity and opposition to the colonisation of Africa, and by implication, the slave trade; 1831 saw legislation for the arrest of slavers and seizure of ships. This was the first serious law and was followed by an agreement with Britain for the mutual right of search. This ended the covert slave trade which had allowed the shipping of 77,300 black Africans to the Caribbean in the Restoration.

Abolition

In 1831 in Martinique a slave revolt resulted in the execution of 20 slaves.

In 1833 a new law offered full rights to anyone born free in the colonies, but with a ten-year wait for freedom. Voting rights in colonial assemblies was limited to those who paid 200 francs in tax – as for the Paris National Assembly. In the same year Britain freed slaves with up to six years of 'apprenticeship' and the payment of massive compensation to owners. French abolitionists made little comment. There were no slave revolts in French colonies between 1833 and 1848. It was assumed that slaves would either be freed or buy freedom, avoiding the need for compensation. Two French abolitionist associations were formed: the *Société de la morale chrétienne*, founded in 1821, and the *Société française pour l'abolition de l'esclavage*, which took over the cause in 1834. The latter was often dependent on British activists. In Britain abolition involved mass petitions, signed by thousands, including workers and women. In contrast, the French societies were never more than a few hundred strong and consisted of the male, parliamentary elite, notably liberal Catholics and Protestants. They were on the political left during the Restoration, although many became establishment figures after 1830. The French abolitionists served on parliamentary committees to debate modest changes in the laws on slavery and organised small-scale petitions. They published anti-slavery literature and tried to run a prize essay competition. In 1840 they seemed to be making progress, but faded badly. Members could never agree on whether to work for gradual or immediate abolition. They hid behind legislation limiting the formation of associations to avoid seeking mass support, which was confined to one worker petition in 1844. They scorned the most influential abolitionist of the time, Cyrille Bissette, who edited the first black-run abolitionist journal, *La Revue des Colonies*, for his radicalism and financial dependence on the British. Slave owners insisted that emancipation would ruin colonial economies, which were already under stress. The main slave-owning islands of the Antilles had narrowed their production to sugar, which was facing stiff competition from beet-sugar grown in France. The wealth of the slave-owners gave the lie to their claims; they paid out large sums for newspaper backing and to secure the voices of two of the most eloquent and influential parliamentarians. They could also rely on senior colonial civil servants. The biggest obstacle was the King, Louis-Philippe, who had been a member of the Restoration society, but, once in power, feared change and blocked any thought of reform.

Abolition – Finally

After the 1848 republican revolution the new constituent Assembly decreed the abolition of slavery. Given that the majority in the Assembly were pre-revolutionary conservative monarchist parliamentarians the emancipation decrees were surprising. Abolition applied everywhere including tiny islands: 1848 gave full voting rights, but effectively most indigenous people were excluded. Today 10 May is French National Day of Remembrance of the Abolition of the Slave Trade and Slavery (James, 1936,1963; Jennings,2000.).

Algeria

France's second overseas empire began in Algiers. In July 1830 the Turkish Regency of Algiers was invaded by 635 ships and 35,000 French soldiers. Why? Algiers' Corsairs were a pest to French ships; Britain had also bombarded the harbour for the same reason. The Dey claimed that a big debt remained unpaid on grain since Napoleonic times; in 1827 the Dey hit the French consul with a fly swat when discussing the debt. Algiers capitulated to the French invasion, but Charles X lost the throne. Resistance grew among the tribes who united under the Arab chief, Abd el-Kader in a jihad, a holy war.

Why Did a Punitive Invasion Become Colonisation?

Officers talked of a 'crusade' and were keen to advance going further than authorised in Paris. In 1831 the Foreign Legion was formed as a volunteer force. Orientalism was a passion much encouraged by Napoleon's Egyptian expedition and was another factor in the advance into Algeria. The Mediterranean was seen as a focus for France to dominate Europe economically via shipping and the development of railways and resources in Algeria. Michel Chevalier, the St Simonian leader, wrote of the Mediterranean System. He was later a main advisor to Napoleon III on economic matters, trade and organising international exhibitions. Algeria was pictured as a French Australia: it was seen as empty, with a brilliant Mediterranean climate; its economy seemed very promising for the production of European crops, wine, wheat and fruit; its mineral resources included iron and copper. Algeria was also depicted as suitable for a penal colony, particularly for political prisoners, a French Botany Bay. It was also seen as a good place to send the unemployed/politically awkward and poor. Socialists saw colonial emigration as a solution to poverty, as did Louis-Napoleon in *Extinction of Pauperism*. The government found Algeria a useful posting for military men with republican sympathies, for instance two Saint-Simonians who had become senior generals in Algeria, Cavaignac (from an old republican family, his brother a republican leader in Paris) and Lamoricière.

In 1833 because of the growing number of troops being sent to Algeria in the attempt to conquer the territory, a government enquiry was held into its potential. The decision was that prestige meant France had to persist. She would suffer international loss of face if she withdrew. In the 1830s more than 300 books and pamphlets were published on Algeria, nearly all positive. By 1840 there were 38,000 European settlers, over half not French; they were defended by 66,000 soldiers. By 1846, one-third of the French army was stationed in Algeria; 108,000 men (Document 20). In 1841 Marshal Bugeaud was made Governor-General. A century later Algerian parents said Bugeaud was a bogeyman who would eat them if they refused to go to bed. Algeria was run by the Minister of War and the army.

The numbers colonising remaining small. Bugeaud hoped retired army officers would colonise, but few agreed, despite the promise of free land. By 1845 there were 100,000 European settlers, 43% French. In the 1850s, 60,000 hectares were owned by Europeans. In 1847 Abd el-Kader surrendered. Tocqueville called him the Algerian Cromwell. He was honoured as a prisoner, especially by Napoleon III, and in the 1860s was made ruler of Syria.

Why Was Algerian Colonisation Slow?

The first answer was that the French were not enthusiastic colonisers. Population growth had been reversed by twenty odd years of perpetual war, and remained static for nearly a hundred years from the mid 1850s. The French had no need to emigrate to make a living. Quite the reverse, numbers were only maintained by European immigration into France. Over half the Europeans who moved to Algeria were not French. Attempts to persuade the French to move to Algeria turned out to be a series of myths (lies/deceptions). The biggest myth was invented by Napoleon in Egypt; that French language/culture was so superior that French occupation would civilise and modernise a barbaric people. Islam was viewed as a primitive faith to be destroyed; the main mosque in Algiers became the Roman Catholic cathedral. The French ignored Islamic culture, religion, law, education, health care and all social/economic functions. They shut mosques, Islamic schools and social welfare and appropriated property often with no compensation. The agent of colonisation was the army far more than civilian settlement.

In the 1840s the military commander, Marshall Bugeaud used the same military violence on the tribes which had been used in Spain: enfumade – smoking out an enemy hiding in a cave – and razzia – a surprise attack on an undefended native village. The French argued this was necessary to 'liberate' indigenous peoples. In 1840 Tocqueville, a liberal deputy, famous for his study of American democracy, was sent on a parliamentary mission and accepted this view, but in 1847 on a second visit he was very critical of the brutality of French policy (Tocqueville document 19). Another myth was that Algeria was another Australia, with a tiny native population (Document 21). Algeria was *not* empty. There were three million natives, mainly Arabs, some Berbers, who had been living there for centuries. In the 1830s they began to die from European diseases and war and were reduced to around 2 million by the 1850s. The French thought they might die out. Indigenous people were pushed out of the coastal plain into the desert. The French argued that the land was not owned. But the coastal plain was farmed by local families, and the rest by pastoral nomadism in which families moved and land was owned in common. The next myth was that Algeria was rich with agricultural resources, only held back by native ignorance. Algeria was not fertile in a European sense. The French condemned pastoral nomadism as simply primitive. Actually it was a sound method, given the land and climate. Europeans struggled to grow European crops. In the 1850s the French had less trade with Algeria than in Napoleonic times. In 1837 the government launched a major investigation into the mineral and economic resources of Algeria run by Colonel Berey de Saint-Vincent, similar to Napoleon's investigation into Egypt. Army officer investigators, many of them scientists, were St Simonians, including their leader Enfantin who wrote on the prospects of colonisation. Fournel wrote on minerals, Carette on ethnography. The report was published and was the main source of information on Algeria for generations.

Algeria was rich in minerals, but a big investment was needed to extract and transport them. St Simonians, including the Talabots and the bankers, Pereires, played a leading role.

The early claim that Algerian had a perfect climate for growing European crops was also soon found to be a myth. Her climate varied from extreme heat and drought to sometimes intense rain, and sometimes bitter cold.

The next French myth was racial. That the Berbers were of European stock and would work with the French. This was a myth perpetuated by the St Simonian Carette. Arabs were seen as difficult barbarians; the Berbers were Kabyles, originally from Europe. Unlike the Arabs they were settled and more educated. The French, despite the dreams described by Flaubert in *Salambô*, soon found that both Berbers and Arabs detested the French conquerors. The final myth, most offensive of all to the indigenous tribes, was that their women were sexually available. This had been perpetuated by Napoleonic soldiers in Egypt, and spread to Algeria. It was publicised in the memoirs of French soldiers and by artists, for example Delacroix, 'Women of Algiers' in 1834 (his models were actually French and the painting was done when back in Paris). The French depicted Islam as a barbaric culture, with easy divorce; multiple wives; harsh physical treatment of wives who were confined to the harem; in short, a culture where women had no role in society. Suzanne Voilquin, a St Simonian who spent time with a St Simonian expedition to Egypt, tried with only modest success to counteract this view. She worked as a midwife with Muslim women and gave a more realistic impression of the harem etc. (Voilquin, *Daughter of the People*, 1865).

An Arab Empire

A minority of Frenchmen tried to imagine an Algeria of cooperation, not conquest. A leading figure was another St Simonian, Thomas Urbain. He participated in the Egyptian expedition and in 1835 moved to Algeria. Urbain argued that Islam could live alongside French culture to their mutual benefit. Ismayl Urbain converted to Islam, married a Muslim, learned Arabic and became the leading government translator in Algeria; he grew close to Louis-Philippe whose sons were army officers in Algeria. He appeared in a painting with the royal family at Versailles. He is painted white. His mother was the daughter of a Cayenne slave, his father a French army officer. In 1848 Algeria was declared part of France, no longer a colony and divided into departments. The European areas had prefects, councils etc.; the indigenous people were ruled by the army in conjunction with *caids*, and Arab Bureaux were set up in the army. Army officers learned Arabic. In September 1848 a mass colonisation of 18,000 to Algeria was planned by Lamoricière and other St Simonians (see Chapter 3). By 1851 there were 130,000 European settlers – one-third in 130 new colonial villages. In 1856 there were 170,000 Europeans plus 21,000 native Jews. Half of the settlers worked the land, 95% under civilian rule; 90% of the 2.3 million natives were under military rule. Napoleon III was the first French ruler to visit Algeria. Urbain was his chief advisor. French settlers led by a French settler Dr Warnier were hostile to the idea of an Arab emperor. In 1865 a law was introduced to allow Muslims to become French citizens and vote. Urbain was keen, but citizenship came only if they gave up Islam. Fewer than 300 did so by 1962. Laws were passed to protect Arab property, including compensation when it was sold, but these had little impact. In the 1850s European companies developed mineral resources and railways. In 1865, 100,000 hectares was acquired by a single company for capitalist growth. Algerian cities grew up with European posh quarters, with departmental stores, boulevards. Muslim areas received no investment. Edouard Charton, a St Simonian, published illustrated magazines, including *Tour du Monde* publicising travel/colonies.

In 1869 the Suez Canal was opened, the construction of which was organised by de Lesseps (a St Simonian associate). The Empress Eugénie sailed on the canal to the sound of Ieda. In 1871 Algerian native recruits fought in the Franco-Prussian war and as prisoners were very badly treated by the Prussians. In 1871 there were rebellions in El Mokrani; Kabylia endured brutal suppression and locally held land was sequestrated. Rebel leaders were executed or sent to New Caledonia. In 1871 refugees from Alsace-Lorraine were offered 100,000 hectares for new villages. In 1874, 877 families from Alsace-Lorraine settled. The 1873 Loi Warnier (MP settler and former St Simonian) offered free land and accommodation for settlers: 2 million hectares had been distributed by 1893. All Algerian land was then declared privately owned; collective tribal land rights were abolished (Document 21). In 1870 the Cremieux decree granted French citizenship to Algerian Jews; this was resented by Muslims because there were no conditions on Jewish citizenship. In 1881 Algeria was integrated into the administrative structures of the Third Republic under the Minister of the Interior. By the 1880s there 500,000 European settlers, one-sixth of the population. Europeans owned 85% of cultivable land. In 1889 a law gave foreign settlers French nationality.

France had made Algeria part of France and had taken almost all of the land from the indigenous people with very little compensation, and no acceptance by local people that they no longer had any right to use the land. Some of the local elite tolerated French education, language and culture, but, without a vote, had no role in running what they considered their land. The prospects for their sons extended no further than the opportunity to join the French army, and for some to become officers. Poorer local people never accepted the situation, which kept them as poor labourers on foreign-owned estates. By the 1950s there were about 1 million foreign 'Algerians' and over 9 million Arabs and Berbers. Algerian colonisation provided an alternative to revolution but led to a truly revolutionary situation climaxing in bloody civil war in the mid-1950s.

The French secured colonies elsewhere in Africa, mainly in rivalry with the British. Companies keen to exploit primary resources took the lead. The army predominated, generals often pursuing strategies independent of Parisian government decisions. Few French settled anywhere other than Algeria.

West Africa

From the 1830s Senegal was absorbed into the new empire by expansion along rivers (no roads yet being built); the situation was the same in Guinea and the Ivory Coast. General Louis Faidherbe (1818–1889), governor of Senegal, hoped that the Senegal river expansion could lead to a big empire for France, linking to Algeria. He introduced ground nuts and built well defended forts, often on his own, not the government's, initiative. Equatorial Africa was also developed by expansion along rivers to exploit hard woods and primary products. Social relations were set by the traditional *Code de l'Indigénat* which formalised *de facto* discrimination by creating specific penalties for *indigènes* (local people) and organising the seizure or appropriation of their lands. The Code also applied in sub-Saharan Africa. There were summary punishments, fines and executions. A corvée, forced labour, traditional in France before 1789, included a head tax, blood tax and forced conscription. All major projects in French West Africa in this period were performed by forced labour, including work on roads, mines, and in fields of private companies. Plantations, forestry operations and salt mines in Senegal continued to be operated by forced labour, mandated by the local commandant and provided by official chiefs through the 1940s. Forced agricultural production was common in sub-Saharan Africa from the nineteenth century until the Second World War, mandated sometimes by the central French government (rubber until 1920, rice during the Second World War), sometimes for profit (the cotton plantations of Compagnie Française d'Afrique Occidentale and Unilever), and sometimes on the personal whim of the local commandant, such as one official's attempt to introduce cotton into the Guinean highlands. Unlike the Congo Free State, infamous for its nineteenth-century forced rubber cultivation by private fiat, the French government administration was bound legally to provide labour for its rubber concessionaires in French Equatorial Africa and settler-owned cotton plantations in Côte d'Ivoire. Native sub-officials also used forced labour. The French legal system (the Code Napoléon), was applied to the *évolués*, the tiny minority of indigenous people who learned French and received French education and accepted French citizenship. Otherwise sharia law prevailed for Muslims but only operated by chiefs approved by the French.

Colonies in the East

In the Pacific France acquired Tahiti. Colonial control over Indo-China began in 1858 in Saigon with exploitation via gunboats for trade – including opium. By 1862–1867 France controlled most of Cochinchina. In1863 Cambodia became a protectorate.

New Caledonia

In 1774 islands east of Australia were secured. They were named but not claimed by Cook the British explorer. Captain James Cook was the first European to sight and name New Caledonia during his second voyage saying that the northern island reminded him of Scotland. In 1853 Napoleon III claimed the 118 islands. In 1864–1897 they became a penal colony with at the largest point c. 10,500 inmates, including Communards (such as Louise Michel). Only about 40 stayed after release. Nickel was mined; labour was imported. There were very few European settlers. There were c. 60,000 local people, Kanak Melanesians (Document 20) who were cannibals. They were kept in reservations. Their population fell to one-third of the original numbers because of European diseases, but recovered gradually. In 1878 the Kanaks rebelled and the Communard prisoners fought with the French. In 1917 there was another rebellion. New Caledonia supported the Free French in the Second World War and the main Allied landing base was sited at Noumea. In 1946 New Caledonia became a Free Territory, with citizenship for all. There have been repeated attempts at independence, but always defeated in referenda, the last one being in 2020. Two MPs are elected to the Paris National Assembly and two senators. New Caledonians vote for the French president and in EU elections. New Caledonia is governed by a Territorial Assembly of 54. It is actually run by 341 tribes and tribal leaders with local customary laws for marriage etc. – except in criminal cases. The French also tried to extend their influence in Mexico during the 1860 Civil War. Napoleon III hope to make an Austrian arch-duke emperor under French control: 30,000 troops were dispatched and a scientific survey was begun. The project failed.

In 1864 Tunisia rebelled against Ottoman rule. France, Britain and Italy were rivals over who should gain control. In 1878 the Great Powers agreed that France would administer Tunisia. In 1881 Tunisia became a French protectorate with a French resident Cambon ruling with the local Bey. The

1884–1885 Berlin conference of Great European Powers decided who would own what African land, with no consultation with African chiefs. France and Belgium already had claimed chunks of North and South Congo respectively. France built Brazzaville, Belgium Leopoldville.

Madagascar became another target for French rule. In 1883 French gun boats sailed in after an incident, which had led to 20 years of fighting. Six years later Madagascar was declared a French protectorate.

There was further advance in the Far East. In 1883 the French attacked Hanoi, supposedly protecting Christians. There was considerable resistance in France to expansion in what the French called Indo-China, but in 1897 Laos was secured. No more than 150 French settled there. Despite having much ambition, including a plan for an opera house in Hanoi and other schemes for urban development, the French found it very hard to keep any control because of the distance and the number of troops needed. In 1898 the French and British made a deal in which the British accepted French influence in Morocco, while the French agreed to keep out of Sudan. In 1904, after years of colonial rivalry, a Franco-British Entente was signed. In 1911 the Moroccan Sultan asked for French help because of a rebellion. Germany responded with gunboats. A German/French deal left Germany with a chunk of Congo. Thus the European nations carved up large chunks of Africa and the world.

1914 Empire: What did it signify?

Between 1871 and 1900 France gained 3 million square miles of colonial land, mainly by deals with other West European states. Great Britain secured 4 million square miles, land equal to one-third the size of Europe. By 1912 the French Empire consisted of 10.6 million square miles and 55 million people, 15 million more than the population of France itself. The Empire was self-financing from 1900 and a big market for French goods. By 1902 trade with the colonies was more important than with Germany, Belgium and Luxembourg combined. In 1913 the colonies provided 9.4% of French imports and took 13% of her exports. Colonial companies made huge profits (companies in French Congo gained up to 38%), and French members of parliament acquired large estates in Tunisia.

What Did the Empire Signify?

In 1916 Lenin wrote in *Imperialism, the Highest Stage of Capitalism* that imperialism was an essential stage in capitalism, using surplus capital and involving class exploitation, and was a cause of the First World War in 1914. The empire provided work for local middle-class lycée-educated men. The Empire became important for them, psychologically as well as economically. Hubert Feis (a US writer), in *Europe the World's Banker* noted that most European capital was actually invested in Europe, with French banks investing in Russia, especially in government bonds, and Germany investing in her ally, the Austrian Empire. So, yes there was surplus capital, but it was not much invested in empires. Britain however had 50% of her foreign investment in her colonies.

French Foreign Investment

In 1914, French banks had 11.3 billion francs invested in Russian railways and industry, out of a total invested in Europe of 27.5 billion francs. In 1914, 4 billion francs were invested in her colonies, out of a total extra-European investment of 18.5 billion francs. International capital investment in Africa tended to be more cooperative than diplomatic national rivalries. In conclusion French colonies in 1914 produced far less profit (if any) than Saint-Domingue sugar had in the eighteenth century. But colonies had become a focus of international rivalries. The loss of Alsace-Lorraine in 1871 meant that to stay a Great Power France must expand abroad, resulting in rivalry especially with Britain in Africa. Her stagnant population, c. 40 million from the 1850s to the 1930s, meant she needed colonies to expand her imperial population; as it was commonly said, France was a nation of 40 million, an Empire of 100 million. There was much concern in France by 1914 that the German population had grown to over 60 million. France was struggling to maintain a comparable army and military service was increased from two to three years in 1912. France had a declining population only maintained by immigration from Spain, Italy, Belgium, Poland etc. The argument that an Empire was needed for surplus population was not true for France. France was a country of immigration, not emigration. The Empire was most important as an extension of mercantilist protectionist policies. Raw materials were sought abroad and owning territory secured them at the best price. Pseudo-Darwinism also had an impact; the notion that European races were superior and that the French had a 'civilising mission'. France had 40,000 Roman Catholic and Protestant missionaries in Asia and Africa. Missionary societies made conquest seem respectable. Also the French government secured education and health care on the cheap from missionaries despite the anti-clerical stance of the Republic. Exploration and discovery were longstanding motives for the elite, and engaged some middle class appeal in the mid-nineteenth century with the formation of the Geographical Society. The French society held its first international conference in 1871; illustrated journals like *Tour du Monde* and *Illustration* advertised the empire to the middle classes.

Nationalism

Imperialism aimed to make nationalism popular, capture the support of workers and offer an alternative to international socialism. Universal military service plus universal education perhaps helped to make workers supporters of empire. In reality, even at senior levels of government both France and Germany were more interested in Europe than their empires. Germany formed a Pan-German League. International rivalries did not correspond to the alliance systems that grew up. Britain and France signed an Entente Cordiale in 1904 but Britain was France's greatest imperial rival.

The acquisition of chunks of Africa and Asia offered some opportunities for employment and land acquisition, especially in Algeria, even if the French were less keen to colonise than other European peoples. In 1914 the French elite considered the acquisition of a new empire a positive achievement, both in terms of France's world status but also as promoting internal stability and avoidance of revolution. The French were told they were civilising the world. Some may have been convinced, but in the empire itself, especially in Algeria, local populations never considered French rule beneficial and were determined to use revolutionary and violent means to drive out the conqueror.

6 Historians of Revolution

The writing of the history of the 1789 Revolution began in earnest after the fall of Napoleon. In the 1820s, two of the most influential accounts were those of young liberal journalists, Adolphe Thiers (1822–1827) and François Mignet (1824), who praised the early stages of the Revolution but were very critical of Robespierre and the Terror. Thiers ended his multi-volume account with Napoleon's takeover and military successes in Europe which he explained as part of the struggle with the 'old order of things', in which (temporarily, he hoped) the revolutionaries' aspirations for liberty were put aside. Transformed into a cautious politician, Thiers served King Louis-Philippe (1830–1848) and opposed the declaration of a republic in 1848. The Revolution of 1848 and the violence and social conflict of the June Days underlined, for liberals like Alexis de Tocqueville, that revolution led to a dangerous 'servile war' which challenged the existing social order.

Also reflecting on the June Days, Karl Marx offered a structural view of revolution. For him revolution was the product of economic and social change, which contributed to class conflict; the 1830 and 1848 revolutions and the Paris Commune (1871) led to bourgeois groups taking over from the old aristocratic elites. Later, Marx's followers argued that 1789 was the beginning of this story. The Bolsheviks in Russia claimed that their revolution was part of the same continuum. Until the 1970s this analysis of revolution prevailed among most French academic historians, led by Lefebvre and then Labrousse and Soboul. In the 1780s a new bourgeois or middle class was depicted as challenging the power of the Church, the old nobles and the king; 1789 was characterised as a bourgeois revolution.

In the 1960s, the British historian Alfred Cobban argued that the third estate in the National Assembly in 1789 was not a new middle class, but a traditional bourgeoisie of doctors, state servants and other established middle elites. Influenced by Enlightenment and the eighteenth-century *philosophes* such as Voltaire and Rousseau and also by the American Revolution against British rule, he saw them as eager for a written constitution and a share in power but not more. He characterised 1789 as a political and philosophical, not a social, and certainly not an economic, revolution. In the 1970s, 1789 was depicted as the consequence of a new political culture, the

DOI: 10.4324/9781003460596-6

product of the written word and debate in the salons. At the bi-centenary in 1989 there was not a peasant or worker, or bourgeois in sight – 1789 had become a liberal revolution of ideas. The British historian, Keith Baker, and the leading French expert, François Furet, stressed changes in political culture which made reform seem possible as well as desirable. Furet revived respect for Alexis de Tocqueville's view of 1789, recorded in his *Old Régime and the French Revolution.*

Cobban's claims that, apart from the demolition of the feudal system and the acquisition of land by better-off peasants, the social consequences of 1789 were negligible, have been dissected by subsequent historians, including Chaussinand-Nogaret, André-Jean Tudesq, Maurice Agulhon, Alain Corbin, George Rudé, Richard Cobb, Olwen Hufton, Don Sutherland, Tim Le Goff, Peter McPhee and David Andress, among others. Cobban's claim that a wealthy elite of notables retained social and economic power through the nineteenth-century has been sustained, as has his assertion that, despite the abolition of feudal institutions, only the better-off inhabitants of town and country benefitted from 1789. McPhee however demonstrated that in some areas the rural poor supported the revolution.

From the mid-1960s historians were far less convinced that economic factors were dominant in shaping history. Identity became the name of the game, or rather identities. These could be region, gender, religion, ethnicity or a range of broader cultural issues such as language, education and leisure activities. Into the 1980s, micro history was often preferred to broader themes. Cheaper copying allowed historians to display the role of visual material in annoying people enough to fight in the streets. The concept of revolution itself took a bashing from Foucault and post-modernists who rejected the notion that events had precise causes or indeed results. The demand of post-modernists that historians pay more attention to language produced influential results, for example William Sewell, *Work and Revolution in France: The Language of Labor from the Old Regime to 1848* (1980 with numerous reprints). While many historians were uncomfortable with the intellectual relativism of post-modernism, contingency and chance found favour again. The outbreak of revolution tends now to be explained more by chance and personal decisions – or the lack of them – than either economic or even philosophical factors. Leading exponents are Bill Doyle and Timothy Tackett, who blame the King for his ineptitude, indecision and stubbornness in failing to reform absolutism. Peter McPhee, Malcolm Crook and others in France and elsewhere have focused on popular and regional issues. Was the Revolution dominated by Paris; did 'the people' benefit? McPhee has analysed how 'rural and small-town men and women adopt, adapt to and resist change from Paris' (McPhee, 2016; McPhee, 2002). In his day, Cobban was described as revisionist, but interpretations of 1789 moved with such speed that the term soon became out of date. McPhee, in his succinct summary of the significance of 1789 prefers 'minimalists' when describing those who, while not challenging the enormous and long-term impact of the Revolution on French institutions, continue to assert the slowness of French social change (McPhee, 2002, 178–223).

A familiar response to revolution was explored to very influential effect by Lynn Hunt (1992). The revolution, in killing King and Queen, replaced a 'family' formulation of society with a fraternal one. The Queen was vilified for her sexual experimentation. Such approaches led to a more emotional approach to 1789. William Reddy, Sophie Wahnich, Howard Brown and Sophia Rosenfeld and others stressed the emotional, rather than political content of revolution. Howard Brown (2018), an expert on 1789, is particularly apposite in taking four major violent episodes in French history to explore how their representation, particularly visual, contributed to mass trauma and the development of a sense of self. The volume focuses on the 1572 St Bartholomew Day massacre of Huguenots, a determining aspect of the Fronde in 1652, the significance of the Revolutionary Terror, 1793–1794, and Bloody Week, May 1871 which terminated the Paris Commune. His focus is not on the Terror itself but on how, subsequently, the Thermidorians helped to mould the memory of the Terror as a coordinated series of events. This helped those who brought the Terror to an end to justify the punishment they meted out to those accused as terrorists to exonerate themselves and avoid retribution. Assessing the Paris Commune, 1871, Brown asks how far the idea that the Commune was a workers' rebellion grew up afterwards in response to the scale of the retribution the army exacted on the rebels with huge numbers of arrests, on-the-spot mass shootings and the formidable destruction of the homes of the poor. Those present in Paris during Bloody Week had a restricted personal impression of events. However the unprecedented visual record liberally reproduced in this volume, in lithographs, sophisticated wood block prints, and to a lesser extent photography (taking instant shots was not yet possible) shaped contemporaries' view of events. In both words and illustrations Brown brilliantly evokes how individuals and groups responded emotionally to violent events intensifying mass trauma. Brown's book is thought provoking, not only in the way it uses multiple excellent illustrations (now possible because the cost of illustrations in books is much less than a generation ago) as well as words to interpret emotions, but also in its chronological range and use of 'mass trauma' to describe both the Terror and Bloody Week.

William Reddy (2001) asked what emotions mean for historians in the context of the French Revolution broadly (1789–1814) as well as in the subsequent age of Romanticism. He acknowledged historians can learn something from biological responses, from psychology, although historical emotions cannot be studied in a laboratory. He also recognised the contribution of anthropology and culture. His conclusion was that emotions are learned. 'History becomes a study of human efforts to conceptualize our emotional make up, and to realize social and political orders attuned to its nature' (Reddy, 2001, 34). Reddy investigated first how psychologists, then how anthropologists analyse human emotions, which is likely to be a quick flip through for a mere historian. In an apparent revolution psychologists defined emotions as culturally based 'overlearned cognitive habits' (34). Post-structuralism has apparently had a disturbing effect on anthropologists who tend now to write about 'discourses' rather than culture in defining emotions.

Historians of 1789 have focused on the Terror to demonstrate the significance of emotion. The theme was developed in David Andress, *Experiencing the French Revolution* (2013), in Jennifer Heuer and Mette Harder (eds), *Life in Revolutionary France* (2020), in Timothy Tackett, *The Glory and the Sorrow: A Parisian and His World in the Age of the French Revolution* (2021) and in Michel Biard and Marisa Linton, *Terror: The French Revolution and its Demons* (2021), especially Chapter 3, 'Terror in the Heart: The Weight of Fears and Emotions'. Those who took part in the Revolution rarely wrote about their emotions, but trying to understand how people felt as well as reasoned is vital.

In his most recent book, Tackett focused on a single person, Adrien-Joseph Colson, whom he depicted as 'an ordinary citizen in extraordinary times' (2021, 5) who gradually adopted radical revolutionary sentiments. Colson was an entirely private person. He never held an official post, no-one painted him, he was not a published author, he never married and had no descendants. We would know nothing of him or his feelings but for a huge collection of letters he wrote to a friend, Roch Lemaigre, who lived in Berry. Colson was brought up by artisan parents but because his eight brothers and sisters died in early childhood, there was enough money to educate him as a lawyer. Both of his parents died in their early fifties, so he only had himself to support. He lived most of his life in Paris near Châtelet. He describes his apartment and his friends and neighbours, although he never wrote about his personal life, and his lifetime bachelorhood. He did not employ a servant and ate his meals out. He mostly walked, so one becomes familiar with his streets. Although a convinced Roman Catholic, who had a substantial collection of pious books, he became a supporter of the Revolution and until 1793 saw no contradiction between faith and the Revolution. His emotional responses were important to him; he described himself as having a 'sensitive heart'. He became very positive about the Revolution, unlike the sword noble family, the Longaunay, with whom he associated. He was won to fraternal and patriotic sentiments and horrified at more negative and frightening events. He wrote to his friend, 'this Revolution, as stunning as it has been unexpected, both astonishes me and enormously moves me' (Tackett, 2021, 80). He noted on 22 June 1789 when he walked around the Palais Royal how the distinctions between the three estates seemed to have disappeared. He accepted the need for early violence such as the lynching of Bertier de Sauvigny, intendant of Paris, and Foulon, the conservative minister, after the storming of the Bastille, and shared fears of an 'aristocratic plot' and conspiracies. He showed no sympathy for the King after the flight to Varennes, although he did not specifically say he was a republican and never attended any political club. When General Dumouriez tried to march his troops on Paris against the

Revolution, Colson was appalled. He joined the crowd demanding the arrest of the Girondin deputies, commenting that it was a fraternal decision. But in the autumn of 1793 (he was 66), he stopped writing about politics and his relationship with both Lemaigre and Longaunay deteriorated. He destroyed Lemaigre's letters. He continued to attend his church Saint-Jacques, which was pulled down shortly before his death in 1797.

Historians of nineteenth-century revolutions have also considered the issue of the very personal, for instance Emmanuel Fureix, *La France des Larmes. Deuils politiques à l'âge romantique (1814–1840)* (2009). The cultural history of death has been resurrected from time to time since Philippe Ariès first drew our attention to it in 1975. That funeral processions were one of the few occasions when public expression of opposition was tolerated is also well known. This volume examined both the culture and the politicisation of death, contrasting the role of the Catholic Church in reconstructing a sacred image of the Bourbon Monarchy, with the emphasis after 1830 on civic and national themes. Fureix concluded with the return of Napoleon's remains in 1840, which Louis-Philippe manipulated to stress his own patriotism. Curiously this terminal date excluded the death which probably did most to weaken the regime, that of the Duc d'Orléans in 1842. Historians have also explored one of the most significant features of insurrection, the barricade, in Jill Harsin, *The War of the Streets in Revolutionary Paris, 1830–1848* (2002) and Mark Traugott, *The Insurgent Barricade* (2010) which trace its role from the sixteenth century to 1848. Revolutionary violence in Paris was explored specifically in Jean-Claude Caron's (dir.) *Paris, l'insurrection capitale* (2014). Turning to the 1848 revolution Peter McPhee explored how rural France was mobilised to support the republic and how the new empire applied a policy of state terror to repress their efforts (McPhee, 1992).

As we have noted above, scholarly accounts of regional history began to dominate in the late Marxist and post-Marxist era. One of the most impressive recent attempts began as a micro-history of Aubagne and became a major study of the Midi, earning a major 'Forum' review by four historians in 2010 (Sutherland, 2009). In June 1795 a father and his two sons were killed by a well-known local gang in this small village in Bouches-du-Rhone, near Marseille. Over the next three years they killed roughly 42 more former Jacobins and most escaped justice because they terrified local people. Aubagne was not a village with a tradition of violence. The murders were the consequence of the violent justice of local Jacobins, 1792–1793, uncontrolled by weak central government. Sutherland's analysis based on detailed archival research was reviewed by four revolutionary historians in an H-France Forum. In his response the author argued that in the Midi political extremism cannot be explained by Parisian top-down ideology, but by centuries-old local divisions, using the democratic language of the 1790s. Local people were concerned about taxes, local and national, not food shortages. Local divisions during the Revolution pre-dated the Terror, identifiable in friendship groups, sharing god-parenting (which Sutherland actually researched) and pre-Revolution penitent groups. Local divisions were partly based on wealth and occupation, but also locality and associational issues. Thus the Terror operated through local political arguments, pre-existing relationships and factions. Federalism was not a matter of class divisions but a response to the reckless behaviour of Jacobins. Opponents of Jacobins were not essentially royalist nor counter-revolutionary (Sutherland, 2009).

An H-France Salon in 2019, acknowledging the huge contribution of Tackett to 1789, illustrated the current preoccupations of historians. David Garrioch explored how ordinary Parisians experienced revolution in district committees and the National Guard, noting that even unemployed men might be admitted to the guard, to replace a wealthier individual short on time (Garrioch, 2019). Marisa Linton wrote on emotions and the Terror. Fear was the most prominent of these. Almost a third (220) of the Convention were arrested. Madame Roland wrote: 'It is very difficult to make a revolution without becoming passionate about it; no one has ever made a revolution without that emotion; there are great obstacles to overcome: you can only achieve it by means of a sort of frenzy, a devotion which comes from exaltation or which produces it. But then you avidly seize on anything which can help your cause, and you lose the ability to foresee whether these things could be harmful' (Linton, 2019, 6). Alan Forrest summarised the issue of slavery, which at first in 1789 seemed a non-issue, since slaves were property and some of the richest members of the Estates-General were Antilles' slave owners. In March 1790 the National Assembly agreed that liberty and equality did not apply in French overseas lands. The creation in 1788 of the *Société des Amis des Noirs* whose leaders included prominent figures in the early years of the Revolution, such as Mirabeau, the Girondin leader, Brissot, influential in Bordeaux and other western ports trading with the Antilles and the abbé Gregoire, gradually made slavery a significant political issue. In May 1791 free men of colour were given full voting rights in colonial assemblies. A growing number of slave insurrections, particularly in Saint-Domingue, the most valuable colony for French trade, led in 1794 to the abolition of slavery. The rebellion led by the former slave Toussaint Louverture provoked Napoleon to attempt the re-conquest of the island and the re-imposition of slavery, which itself led to the declaration of independence by Haiti. In 1807 Britain, and in 1808 America, declared the slave trade illegal. The rebellion of Saint-Domingue and the consequent independence of Haiti has attracted substantial attention in recent decades.

1789 remains a matter of significance in the detailed research and analytical scholarship of recent historians in Britain, Australia and America. Is 1789 still important to historians in France itself? In their most recent French series on the history of France, which, apparently, President Sarkozy urged the publishers Seuil to produce to ensure French national history was not forgotten, they no longer begin the contemporary age with 1789, as they did in their 1970 series. The 1789 Revolution is now the last stage of 'modern times', an end, not a beginning. '*Histoire contemporaine*' starts with 1799 and the aim, according to *Le Monde*, is to situate France in the modern world. The first volume is entitled, *L'Empire des Français 1799–1815*. There is little reference to 1789 and even the personal role of Napoleon is downplayed (Lignereux, 2012). Subsequent volumes mute the significance of revolution in the nineteenth century, for instance Bertrand Goujon, *Monarchies post-révolutionnaires 1814–1848, Histoire de la France contemporaine*, Vol. 2. Chronologically embracing the revolutions of both 1830 and 1848, the title of Volume 2, *Monarchies postrévolutionnaires 1814–1848*, blots them out. But revolutions are not like white rabbits; they do not disappear. Both of the 'post-revolutionary monarchies' fell prey to revolution. The period covered by Volume 2 includes two revolutions, 1830 and 1848, and several other episodes of popular unrest, in particular in Lyon in 1831 and 1834 and Paris in 1839. The 1830 revolution is no longer 'Three Glorious Days', but little more than a passing incident in the middle of a chapter. Volume 3, edited by Quentin Deluermoz in 2012, which covers the period of the second republic through to the end of the Commune, rejoices in the title *Le crépuscule des révolutions 1848–1871*. The title instantly invokes a different, less assured mentality than that of the volume in the earlier Seuil series, Agulhon's, *The Apprenticeship of the Republic*, or as in the Cambridge translation, *The Republican Experiment*. In the new volume, Deluermoz offers his reader a tentative and conflictual republic, an Empire which was transformed almost into a republic by 1870 and a Paris Commune, 'l'année terrible', stripped of the emotional empathy of the earlier Plessis volume. For sure revolutions are obscured in the dusk. Having abandoned a Marxist justification for revolution, the French seem puzzled to explain their tendency for repeated revolutions. They seem almost to want to smuggle revolution away just as Etienne Cabet accused the Orléanists of disposing of the 1830 revolution. The term civil war, used by Marx to describe the Paris Commune of 1871, has become a favoured description of what used to be called revolution. Insurgents are depicted as blood brothers rather than revolutionaries in *Frères de Sang. La guerre civile en France au XIXe siècle* (2009). In 2008, Hinckner analysed how the concept of 'citizen/fighter', often a member of the National Guard, changed during the nineteenth century, the individual being rewarded for participation in revolution up to February 1848, but after the 1871 Commune the National Guard being permanently disbanded (Hinckner, 2008).

Revolutions now seem sometimes to be almost embarrassing accidents, devoid of analytical substance. The decline of the French Communist and Socialist parties, for whom 1789 was central to their philosophy, offers some explanation. More recently revolution was discredited when the Arab Spring brought disastrous conflict, not liberating change, to the Middle East.

Historians have begun to stress less the exceptionalism of 1789 than the global impact of revolution from 1789 through the nineteenth century, for instance in a volume edited by Sylvie Aprile, Jean-Claude Caron and Emmanuel Fureix in 2013, *La Liberté guidant les peoples. Les revolutions de 1830 en Europe*. More recently Quentin Deluermoz has tracked the global significance of the Commune in *Commune(s) 1870–1871: Une traversée des mondes au XIXe siècle* (2020). Revolution seems to have found a new role in globalism. We have also been reminded of the importance of the empire for revolutionaries, a theme that revolutionary historians would have barely touched on in the mid-twentieth century. The fall of the USSR meant that accounts of the Commune could no longer be prophetic; it had become part of conventional history. Jacques Rougerie said it represented socialism and internationalist Marxism. American historians spoke of the crisis of capitalism and modernity, although Gould rather emphasised the variety of urban conflict. Tombs noted the impact of military defeat, Rougerie the contributions of the democratic-socialist ideas of 1848–1851 and of the Internationale. In the 1990s, writers like Kristen Ross (*Fast Cars, Clean Bodies: Decolonization and the Reordering of French Culture*, 1995) and more recently Carolyn J. Eichner (*The Paris Commune: A Brief History*, 2022) focused on the role of women. Space became an issue, with a focus on communes elsewhere, for instance Lyon and Thiers. Then came comparisons with colonial revolution in Algeria, insurrection in Martinique and transnational links. Unlike 1848, the 1871 Commune did not directly inspire revolution elsewhere, but there were connections. Garibaldi led over 30,000 volunteers (1% of the total), some from Algeria, to fight the Prussians, a strategy of more symbolic than practical importance. There were transnationals like General Cluseret, who had fought the June 1848 rebels, and some Arab Bureau officers like Dombrowski. But most foreign-born Communards were long-term Paris residents, such as the Hungarian, Leo Frankel. Members of the Internationale played a part. Originating in London in 1864 among Chartists and trade unionists, this small workers' movement was one of a number of contemporary movements focusing on international law, including the Red Cross (1863). International finance was emerging, with France and Great Britain controlling 90% of investments. The Franco-Prussian war and the Commune briefly interrupted international finance and trade, to the concern of Roman Catholic merchants beginning to trade with the Chinese in Tientsin, a port recently opened to Western trade. Napoleon III used Algerian troops in the war of 1870–1871. The Kabyles seized on this temporary weakness to revolt, but not in sympathy with the Commune.

A notable aspect of global issues which had an impact on how the Commune was remembered was the expansion in these years of the press and press agencies, such as Havas (France) and Reuters (Great Britain), steam navigation and the telegraph. The completion of the Atlantic underground cable (1851) carried news in hours rather than weeks. The Commune was the first event that newspapers in distant Mexico, or the USA, were able to comment on almost instantly. The foreign press was concerned that the Commune represented the dissolution of the nation state. The Communards were aware that they had a world audience but were far too busy with their own affairs to try to connect globally. Deluermoz makes no big claims for the universalism of the Commune. But he analyses revolts that broke out elsewhere: Martinique, Algiers, Thiers and Lyon. In September 1870, crowds in Martinique attacked a number of large estates and demanded that the republic be declared. In 1848, slavery had been abolished and the power of the governor increased. Mulattoes gained the vote, but the dominance of the white settlers remained. From 1855 to 1862, 10,000 labourers were brought in from India (Deleurmoz, 2020, 127) although some former slaves were obliged to continue to work on the estates. In December 1870, these former slaves rebelled. Rebel leaders were shot. The Martinique rebels had no links to the Paris Commune although they had similar aspirations. This is the first account of the Commune to touch on events in Martinique. In Algeria, *colons* declared a commune after news of the defeat of the French army in January 1871. In March came a revolt by Kabyles. In France in March a festive revolt of the cutlery workers in Thiers, encouraged by colleagues from Clermont, offered to help the Paris Commune (Deleurmoz, 2020, 136). A commune was declared in Lyon in September 1870 with support from the Internationale and, in March 1871, the municipal council offered help to their Parisian brethren.

What was the global perspective of the Commune? Most journalists reported on events from a Versailles angle. In June 1871 the Commune and the Internationale were seen as a barbaric menace to the civilised world. Reuters and the *Times* condemned the lack of respect for the law in the barbarism of the fires and the brutality of the massacres committed by the *Versaillais*. Journalists noted the fragility of civilisation, the attack on the Church and the plots of the Internationale. Among the plotters they included foreigners, criminals and Communists in the Internationale. Marx's *Civil War in France* was widely read; three editions appeared in two months (Deleurmoz, 2020, 274). It was translated into Spanish and Italian. The French police blocked publication; a French version was published in Belgium. The Commune may not have been Marxist, but it made Marx's name. The debate on the Commune was conducted in English, in Great Britain and in the USA. The Russian anarchist Bakunin described the Commune as 'la négation audacieuse bien prononcée de l'État' (Deleurmoz, 2020, 301). Speaking in the Reichstag the German social democratic August Bebel spoke of 'le cri de guerre du prolétariat parisien' (p. 303). Exiles carried the news of the Commune to Bolivia, Argentina, Panama, Haiti, Chile and Mexico. Exiles also had some impact in the 1873 Spanish revolution which briefly made Spain republican. In 1869, a major insurrection in Cuba against Spanish rule led to a republic and the end of slavery. To sum up, the Commune had transnational and global perspectives, less for the impact of the actual events than the new fast methods of spreading news.

The research seminars on the 1789 Revolution run by Professor Pierre Serna and the scholarly web-based journal, *La Révolution Française*, which he edits through the *Institut historique de la Révolution Française*, are the best indication of how the French now view their revolutionary history. Glancing through the themes of *La Révolution Française*, launched in 2012, the reader is struck with the breadth of coverage. Articles cover France from 1789 to the recent past, and geographically range worldwide including former French colonies, Haiti, India, and Japan, as well as other topics such as Black history, English republicanism, citizenship, images, science, the Enlightenment, pedagogy and utopianism, the press, the revolutionary assemblies in the 1790s and most recently the French Revolution in English history. In the last year Serna's seminars have focused on revolution and French colonies, South America, and Mary Wollstonecraft as well as images of revolution. It seems that one can debate almost anything under the heading 'French Revolution'.

Conclusion

In 1789 revolution was a positive concept, promising both reform and rationalisation of the state, and rights to individuals. The Declaration of the Rights of Man, encompassing liberty, equality and fraternity was inspirational and the Festival of the Federation, 14 July 1790 was widely and genuinely supported. However from the outset popular violence and the emergence of counter-revolution within the elite after legislation decreeing a state-run Catholic Church shook that first optimism. Revolution soon came to include the abandonment of negotiation and discussion, the severance of trust and compromise. Revolution came to mean fear, particularly of conspiracy, street violence and the risk of death. Revolution dominated the years from 1789 to 1814, from the sacking of the Bastille to Napoleon's defeat. It owed something to social and economic grievances, but more to contingency, the clash of personalities and the unwillingness of Louis XVI to compromise. The 'spontaneous' September massacres (1792), the legal mass killings of the Terror of 1793–1794, of the prolonged civil war in western France, seemed to make Napoleon's dictatorial regime preferable to the quest for liberty and equality, let alone fraternity. Fear of 'blood in the streets' did not prevent repeated revolutionary episodes in the nineteenth century. To summarise the insurrectionary aspects of the nineteenth-century first, the elite did not necessarily take a negative view of revolt. Until June 1848 successful insurrections led to the victorious middle-class politicians offering rewards to the combatants who facilitated their securing or retention of power. In July 1830 and February 1848 challenged rulers departed rapidly into foreign exile, meaning the bloodshed of revolution was relatively restrained. Bloody week, May 1871 gave the opportunity of revenge to soldiers from rural backgrounds who envisaged the Communards as dangerous social revolutionaries. Captured Communards were summarily massacred and public buildings were set on fire which appalled observers both in France and abroad. This was the first revolution when the news spread overseas with speed. Mass violence was quickly contained in the major nineteenth-century revolutionary episodes, July 1830, February and June 1848 and March 1871.

Were nineteenth-century revolts avoidable? In July 1830 it seems likely that liberal politicians and journalists would have tried to work within the

DOI: 10.4324/9781003460596-7

Four Ordinances, but in issuing them perhaps Charles signified that his willingness to try to work within the revolutionary changes of 1789 had come to an end. We do not know, and it seems that the Bourbon regime came to an end mainly for two non-political reasons. Protest about economic setbacks among workers willing to demonstrate in the streets and the lack of adequate military support to combat the demonstrators, partly because a large section of the army was fighting in Algiers, partly because a substantial proportion of the National Guardsmen disbanded in 1827 were willing to join disaffected workers. Was February 1848 a product of contingency? Guizot increased his majority in the 1846 election. In the 1840s attempts to push through legislation to increase the electorate constantly failed. The Banquet Campaign of 1847–1848 seemed more substantial, but banqueters disagreed on their objectives and in February when Guizot asked them to cancel a banquet they concurred. As in 1830, it seemed that in the coincidence of economic and political crises, contingency carried the day. Finally, to summarise what nineteenth-century revolutions changed. After the July Days, 1830, the dominant liberal politicians speedily made the King's cousin, Louis-Philippe, the new king, spending less time reforming the constitution than discussing fishing rights. February 1848 led to the declaration of a republic but there were only six republicans in the Chamber. This may have been the consequence of electoral laws but it was soon apparent that those who declared themselves republican did not agree about what sort of republic was desirable, a political democracy or one that involved socialist style obligations to provide work for the unemployed. The June Days added to the divisions among republicans. The republic was short-lived. In 1870–1871 political change after Napoleon's defeat by Prussia also led to prolonged disagreements on what sort of political system was desirable. The Paris Commune was the consequence of Thiers' attempt to bring Paris into line with the new Assembly. The Communal Assembly struggled to rebuild the economy of the capital and attempt modest social reforms, but was helpless faced with Thiers' determination to ignore their demands and simply turn the army against them.

There were no further revolutionary episodes in the nineteenth century; the democratically elected assembly was able to set up a stable republic. However, profound divisions remained. In 1894 Alfred Dreyfus, a Jewish artillery officer in the French army was wrongly accused of treason. It took until 1906 to secure his release from jail. Despite liberal decrees making Jews full citizens in 1791 anti-Semitism had remained a major influence among right-wing monarchists, particularly in the army. Right-wing associations such as *Action Française* offered a legitimate means of expressing such views. However the prolonged and profound clash over Dreyfus did not lead to political breakdown. The French elite remained divided but from the mid-1870s republican sentiments dominated. The dominant mood was parliamentary, no longer revolutionary. A number of competing socialist groups emerged in the assembly, the one led by Jules Guesde asserting a Marxist inheritance. However they showed no inclination to attempt a revolutionary solution.

A tiny anarchist element succeeded in assassinating President Carnot, but otherwise had little influence. In the metropole, revolution no longer seemed relevant. On the other hand colonial conquest involved the large-scale massacre of indigenous communities in the name of 'civilising the barbarian'. The ruling elite no longer saw the French lower classes as a dangerous enemy; colonial peoples had taken their place. Race, not class, became the main revolutionary issue in the twentieth century, although economic and social conflicts still bring the French onto the streets.

Documents

1 E.J. Sieyès, Qu'est ce que c'est le tiers état

In a pamphlet published in January 1789 which was to have a huge impact on the Revolution, the abbé Sieyès, elected for the Third Estate to the Estates-General, asked:

1. What is the Third Estate? – *Everything.*
2. What, until now, has it been in the existing political order? – *Nothing.*
3. What does it want to be? – *Something.*

He went on to show that the Third Estate did all the work to keep the Nation afloat:

> Who then would dare to say that the Third Estate does not, within itself, contain everything needed to form a complete nation? It resembles a strong, robust man with one arm in chains. Subtract the privileged order and the Nation would not be something less, but something more. What then is the Third Estate? Everything; but an everything that is fettered and oppressed. What would it be without the privileged order? Everything, but an everything that would be free and flourishing. Nothing can go well without the Third Estate, but everything would go a great deal better without the two others.
>
> But it is not enough to have shown that the privileged, far from being useful to the Nation, can only weaken and harm it; it is also necessary to prove that the noble *order* simply has no place at all in the organization of society – it may be a *burden* upon the Nation, but it cannot be part of it.
>
> The noble order is no less a stranger in our midst by virtue of its *civil and political* prerogatives.
>
> What is a nation? It is a body of associates living under a *common* law, represented by the same *legislature*, etc.
>
> But is it not obvious that the noble order has privileges and exemptions – which it dares to call rights – that are separate from those of the great body of citizens? As a result, it stands apart from the common

> order and the common law. Its own civil rights make it a people apart within the greater nation. It is truly an *imperium in imperio*.
>
> As for its *political* rights, it also exercises these apart from the Nation.
>
> The Third Estate thus encompasses everything pertaining to the Nation, and everyone outside the Third Estate cannot be considered to be a member of the Nation. What is the Third Estate? EVERYTHING.
>
> It is absolutely impossible for the whole body of the Nation, or even one of its particular orders, to be free unless the Third Estate is free.

Sieyès demanded that only genuine members of the Third should vote for Third candidates, excluding Robe nobles who were being excluded from the Noble estate. He also claimed that only if the numbers elected to the Third were doubled would this estate be something in the state. All the rest of the 26 million in the nation were Third Estate when the small number of first and second had been calculated. Finally he insisted that the Estates-General must vote by head and not by order. The Third should form a National Assembly. 'The representatives of the Third Estate are the true custodians of the national will. They alone can speak in the name of the whole Nation without error' (Sieyès, 2003, 150) 'A privileged class is therefore harmful not only because of its corporate spirit but simply because it exists. The more it has been able to obtain of those favors that are necessarily opposed to common liberty, the more it is essential to exclude it from the National Assembly. Anyone privileged is entitled to be *represented* only on the basis of his quality as a citizen. But for him that quality has been destroyed. He is outside the civil order and an enemy of common legality' (p. 157).

On 17 June 1789 Sieyès proposed that the Third Estate declare themselves a National Assembly. Although a clear concise theorist, Sieyès was a poor speaker. Sieyès' next contribution was that citizens should be divided into 'active' citizens who paid enough tax to vote and 'passive', less well-off men, which meant that the richer bourgeoisie held political power. Later Sieyès voted for the execution of the King but kept out of politics during the Jacobin episode. After Robespierre's fall in 1795 he was a member of the Committee of Public Safety and the Council of Five Hundred. In May 1799 he manoeuvred himself onto the five-man Executive Director. He was part of the coup of November 1799, and provisional consul with Bonaparte and Ducos. Sieyès composed the new constitution but his power then declined. Napoleon made him Grand Officier of the Legion of Honour in 1804 and Count of the Empire in 1808.

(Source: Sieyès, 2003)

2 American Declaration of Independence

The American declaration proclaimed:

> We hold these truths to be self-evident, that all men are created equal, that they are endowed by their Creator with certain unalienable Rights, that among these are Life, Liberty and the pursuit of Happiness. – That

to secure these rights, Governments are instituted among Men, deriving their just powers from the consent of the governed, – That whenever any Form of Government becomes destructive of these ends, it is the Right of the People to alter or to abolish it, and to institute new Government, laying its foundation on such principles and organizing its powers in such form, as to them shall seem most likely to effect their Safety and Happiness.

3 Declaration of Rights of Man and Citizen

Approved by the National Assembly of France, August 26, 1789

The representatives of the French people, organized as a National Assembly, believing that the ignorance, neglect, or contempt of the rights of man are the sole cause of public calamities and of the corruption of governments, have determined to set forth in a solemn declaration the natural, unalienable, and sacred rights of man, in order that this declaration, being constantly before all the members of the Social body, shall remind them continually of their rights and duties; in order that the acts of the legislative power, as well as those of the executive power, may be compared at any moment with the objects and purposes of all political institutions and may thus be more respected, and, lastly, in order that the grievances of the citizens, based hereafter upon simple and incontestable principles, shall tend to the maintenance of the constitution and redound to the happiness of all. Therefore the National Assembly recognizes and proclaims, in the presence and under the auspices of the Supreme Being, the following rights of man and of the citizen:

Articles:

1. Men are born and remain free and equal in rights. Social distinctions may be founded only upon the general good.
2. The aim of all political association is the preservation of the natural and imprescriptible rights of man. These rights are liberty, property, security, and resistance to oppression.
3. The principle of all sovereignty resides essentially in the nation. No body nor individual may exercise any authority which does not proceed directly from the nation.
4. Liberty consists in the freedom to do everything which injures no one else; hence the exercise of the natural rights of each man has no limits except those which assure to the other members of the society the enjoyment of the same rights. These limits can only be determined by law.
5. Law can only prohibit such actions as are hurtful to society. Nothing may be prevented which is not forbidden by law, and no one may be forced to do anything not provided for by law.
6. Law is the expression of the general will. Every citizen has a right to participate personally, or through his representative, in its foundation. It must

be the same for all, whether it protects or punishes. All citizens, being equal in the eyes of the law, are equally eligible to all dignities and to all public positions and occupations, according to their abilities, and without distinction except that of their virtues and talents.

7. No person shall be accused, arrested, or imprisoned except in the cases and according to the forms prescribed by law. Any one soliciting, transmitting, executing, or causing to be executed, any arbitrary order, shall be punished. But any citizen summoned or arrested in virtue of the law shall submit without delay, as resistance constitutes an offense.

4 Law of Suspects, 17 September 1793

This law encouraged the emergence of the Terror.

Art. 1 Immediately after the publication of the present decree, all suspects in the republic who are still at liberty will be placed under arrest.

Art 2 Suspects are deemed to be:

1. Those who whether by their conduct, their liasons, speech or writings have shown themselves to be adherents of tyranny, federalism or enemies of the people.
2. Those who cannot justify, in accordance with the law of the previous 21 March, their means of livelihood and the fulfilment of their civic duties.
3. Those who have been refused *certificats de civisme*.
4. Public functionaries suspended or dismissed from their jobs by the National Convention or by its commissioners and not reinstated, notably all those who have been or should have been dismissed in virtue of the law of the previous 14 August.
5. Those former nobles, including the husbands, wives, fathers, mothers, sons and daughters of *émigrés*, who have not constantly displayed their devotion to the Revolution.
6. Those who have emigrated in the period between 1 July 1789 and the publication of the law of 8 April 1792, even though they have returned to France within the time-limit stipulated by this law or previously.

(Source: Walloon, 1880, Vol. 1, 288)

5 Slavery and Colonisation

Toussaint Louverture (1743–1803)

Toussaint Louverture was the son of an African prince born in San Domingue as a slave who by the 1770s had been freed by his planter owner. His Catholic godfather made him a life-long Catholic. In 1791 he took the lead in the slave rebellion against the French, with Spanish help. In 1794 when the Convention freed slaves, he fought as a general with the French and was accepted as the leader of government until in 1802 when Napoleon reimposed slavery he declared the French part of the island the free state of Haiti. In 1804

Figure D.1 Toussaint L'Ouverture (1743–1803). Pierre Dominique Toussaint L'Ouverture. Haitian general and liberator. French lithograph, 19th century. The Granger Collection/Alamy Stock Photo.

he was captured and sent to France where he died in prison. He was recognised as a noble hero. Books were published about him, including a biography by the English radical Harriet Martineau (1856). His own autobiography was included in an 1863 biography. In 1936 the Caribbean writer H.L.R. James wrote a play, *Black Jacobin*, which was shown in the West End, with Paul Robeson, the famous black singer and actor, who also starred as Othello at Stratford, playing Toussaint. The play became a book two years later.

[Page 138–139]

> 'Resolved to persevere in a course which his judgment approved, and his position required, Toussaint L'Ouverture, as possessing the highest authority in the island, called together a council to take into consideration the propriety of drawing up a constitution, and to determine what its provisions should be. The council consisted of nine members. The composition of this deliberative assembly displays the integrity of the General-in-Chief. He might have formed it out of his officers. He might have given predominance in it to negro blood. These things, doubtless, he would have done, had he sought his own aggrandizement. But he chose its members among the men of property and intelligence. Of the nine members, eight were white proprietors, and one a mulatto; not a single black had a seat at the council-board. Even the purest patriotism might have required him to place himself at the head of the council. Its president was the white colonist Borgella, who had held the office of

Mayor of Port-au-Prince. The constitution, carefully prepared by this council, was presented to Toussaint L'Ouverture, who, having approved it (May 19th, 1800), sent a copy by the hands of General Vincent to Europe. The draft was accompanied by the following letter, addressed to 'Citizen Bonaparte, First Consul of the French Republic (16th July).

'CITIZEN CONSUL: – The Minister of Marine, in the account which he has rendered to you of the political situation of this colony, which I have taken care to acquaint him with in the dispatches which I addressed to him, sent by the corvette L'Enfant Prodigue, will have submitted to you my proclamation, convening a central assembly, which, at the moment when the junction of the Spanish part to the French part had made of Saint Domingo one single country, subject to the same government, should fix its destinies by wise laws, framed with special reference to the localities and the characters of the inhabitants. I have now the satisfaction to announce to you, that the last hand has been put to that work, and that the silt is a constitution which promises happiness to the inhabitants of this colony, which has so long been unfortunate. I hasten to lay it before you for your approbation, and for the sanction of the Government I serve. With this view, I send to you Citizen Vincent, general director of fortifications at Saint Domingo, to whom I have confided this precious deposit. The Central Assembly, in the absence of laws, and considering the necessity which exists of substituting the rule of law for anarchy, having demanded that I should provisionally put it into execution, as promising to conduct the colony more rapidly toward prosperity, I have yielded to its desires; and this constitution has been welcomed by all classes of citizens with transports of joy.

After his arrest and imprisonment in the fortress of Jouy, near Besançon, where he died, whether of hunger or cold was never identified, he wrote his version of events:

They have sent me to France destitute of everything; they have seized my property and my papers, and have spread atrocious calumnies concerning me. Is it not like cutting off a man's legs and telling him to walk? Is it not like cutting out a man's tongue and telling him to talk? Is it not burying a man alive?

In regard to the Constitution, the subject of one charge against me: Having driven from the colony the enemies of the Republic, calmed the factions and united all parties; perceiving, after I had taken possession of St. Domingo, that the Government made no laws for the colony, and feeling the necessity of police regulations for the security and tranquillity of the people, I called an assembly of wise and learned men, composed of deputies from all the communities, to conduct this business. When this assembly met, I represented to its members that they had an arduous and responsible task before them; that they were to make laws adapted to the country, advantageous to the Government, and beneficial to all, – laws suited to the localities, to the character and customs of the inhabitants. The Constitution must be submitted for the sanction of the Government, which alone had the right to adopt or reject it. Therefore, as soon as the Constitution was decided upon and its laws fixed, I sent the whole, by a member of the assembly, to the Government, to obtain its sanction. The errors or faults which this Constitution may contain cannot therefore be imputed to me. At the time of Leclerc's arrival, I had heard nothing from the Government upon this subject. Why to-day do they seek to make a crime of that which is no crime? Why put truth for falsehood, and falsehood for truth? Why put darkness for light and light for darkness?

[Page 322]

I will sum up, in a few words, my conduct and the results of my administration. At the time of the evacuation of the English, there was not a penny in the public treasury; money had to be borrowed to pay the troops and the officers of the Republic. When Gen. Leclerc arrived, he found three millions, five hundred thousand francs in the public funds. When I returned to Cayes, after the departure of Gen. Rigaud, the treasury was empty; Gen. Leclerc found three millions there; he found proportionate sums in all the private depositories on the island. Thus it is seen that I did not serve my country from interested motives; but, on the contrary, I served it with honor, fidelity, and integrity, sustained by the hope of receiving, at some future day, flattering acknowledgments from the Government; all who know me will do me this justice.

I have been a slave; I am willing to own it; but I have never received reproaches from my masters.

I have neglected nothing at Saint Domingo for the welfare of the island; I have robbed myself of rest to contribute to it; I have sacrificed everything for it. I have made it my duty and pleasure to develop the resources of this beautiful colony. Zeal, activity, courage, – I have employed them all.

The island was invaded by the enemies of the Republic; I had then but a thousand men, armed with pikes. I sent them back to labor in the field, and organized several regiments, by the authority of Gen. Laveaux.

The Spanish portion had joined the English to make war upon the French. Gen. Desfourneaux was sent to attack Saint Michel with well-disciplined troops of the line; he could not take it. General Laveaux ordered me to the attack; I carried it. It is to be remarked that, at the time of the attack by Gen. Desfourneaux, the place was not fortified, and that when I took it, it was fortified by bastions in every corner.

[Page 324]

I also took Saint-Raphaël and Hinche, and rendered an account to Gen. Laveaux. The English were intrenched at Pont-de-l'Ester; I drove them from the place. They were in possession of Petite Rivière. My ammunition consisted of one case of cartridges which had fallen into the water on my way to the attack; this did not discourage me. I carried the place by assault before day, with my dragoons, and made all the garrison prisoners. I sent them to Gen. Laveaux. I had but one piece of cannon; I took nine at Petite Rivière. Among the posts gained at Petite Rivière, was a fortification defended by seven pieces of cannon, which I attacked, and carried by assault. I also conquered the Spaniards intrenched in the camps of Miraut and Dubourg at Verrettes. I gained a famous victory over the English in a battle which lasted from six in the morning until nearly night. This battle was so fierce that the roads were filled with the dead, and rivers of blood were seen on every side. I took all the baggage and ammunition of the enemy, and a large number of prisoners. I sent the whole to Gen. Laveaux, giving him an account of the engagement. All the posts of the English upon the heights of Saint Marc were taken by me; the walled fortifications in the mountains of Fond-Baptiste and Délices, the camp of Drouët in the Matheux mountains, which the English regarded as impregnable, the citadels of Mirebalais, called the Gibraltar of the island, occupied by eleven hundred men, the celebrated camp of l'Acul-du-Saut, the stone fortifications of Trou-d'Eau, three stories high, those of the camp of Décayette and of Beau-Bien, – in short, all the fortifications of the English in this quarter were unable to withstand me, as were those of Neybe, of Saint Jean de la Maguâna, of Las Mathas, of Banique and other places occupied by the Spaniards; all were brought by me under the power of the Republic. I was also exposed to the greatest dangers; several times I narrowly escaped being made prisoner; I shed my blood for my country; I received a ball in the right hip which remains there still; I received a violent blow on the head from a cannon-ball, which knocked out

---

[Page 325]

the greater part of my teeth, and loosened the rest. In short, I received upon different occasions seventeen wounds, whose honorable scars still remain. Gen. Laveaux witnessed many of my engagements; he is too honorable not to do me justice: ask him if I ever hesitated to endanger my life, when the good of my country and the triumph of the Republic required it.

If I were to record the various services which I have rendered the Government, I should need many volumes, and even then should not finish them; and, as a reward for all these services, I have been arbitrarily arrested at St. Domingo, bound, and put on board ship like a criminal, without regard for my rank, without the least consideration. Is this the recompense due my labors? Should my conduct lead me to expect such treatment?

I was once rich. At the time of the revolution, I was worth six hundred and forty-eight thousand francs. I spent it in the service of my country. I purchased but one small estate upon which to establish my wife and family. To-day, notwithstanding my disinterestedness, they seek to cover me with opprobrium and infamy; I am made the most unhappy of men; my liberty is taken from me; I am separated from all that I hold dearest in the world, – from a venerable father, a hundred and five years old, who needs my assistance, from a dearly-loved wife, who, I fear, separated from me, cannot endure the afflictions which overwhelm her, and from a cherished family, who made the happiness of my life.

On my arrival in France I wrote to the First Consul and to the Minister of Marine, giving them an account of my situation, and asking their assistance for my family and myself. Undoubtedly, they felt the justice of my request, and gave orders that what I asked should be furnished me. But, instead of this, I have received the old half-worn dress of a soldier, and shoes in the same condition. Did I need this humiliation added to my misfortune?

When I left the ship, I was put into a carriage. I hoped then that I was to be taken before a tribunal to give an account of

---

[Page 326]

my conduct, and to be judged. Far from it; without a moment's rest I was taken to a fort on the frontiers of the Republic, and confined in a frightful dungeon.

It is from the depths of this dreary prison that I appeal to the justice and magnanimity of the First Consul. He is too noble and too good a general to turn away from an old soldier, covered with wounds in the service of his country, without giving him the opportunity to justify himself, and to have judgment pronounced upon him.

I ask, then, to be brought before a tribunal or council of war, before which, also, Gen. Leclerc may appear, and that we may both be judged after we have both been heard; equity, reason, law, all assure me that this justice cannot be refused me.

> In passing through France, I have seen in the newspapers an article concerning myself. I am accused in this article of being a rebel and a traitor, and, to justify the accusation, a letter is said to have been intercepted in which I encouraged the laborers of St. Domingo to revolt. I never wrote such a letter, and I defy any one to produce it, to tell me to whom it was addressed, and to bring forward the person. As to the rest of the calumny, it falls of itself; if I had intended to make war, would I have laid down my arms and submitted? No reasonable man, much less a soldier, can believe such an absurditywhich will not fail to be manifested afresh, when it shall be sent back invested with the sanction of the Government. With salutations and profound respect.
>
> (Source: Beard, 1863)

6 Additional Act to the Constitutions of the Empire 1815

The preamble claimed:

> In all the fifteen years since we were called upon by the will of the French people to govern the State, we have tried, always profiting from experience, to develop a constitutional system according to the needs and wishes of the nation... Our ultimate aim was the creation of a great European federation, which we believed to be in tune with the spirit of the age and with the progress of civilization. In the hope of achieving this on as large a scale with the greatest possible hope of stability, we postponed the publication of a certain amount of internal legislation, particularly that designed to protect the liberty of the individual... With all of this in mind, we now propose to develop representative institutions...

7 Louis-Philippe

Louis-Philippe was an exceptional man. ...He was endowed with all the private and many of the public virtues... He kept no Court. He walked out with an umbrella under his arm, and this umbrella was for a long time a part of his image... In the charges levelled by history against Louis-Philippe there is a distinction to be drawn. There were three types of charge, against royalty as such, against his reign, and against the king as an individual... The suppression of democratic rights, the sidetracking of progress, the violent repression of public demonstrations, the use of armed force to put down insurrection, the smothering of the real country by legal machinery and legality only half-enforced, with a privileged class of three hundred thousand.

(Source: Hugo, 1982, 713)

8 Alexis de Tocqueville

When parliament resumed in December 1847, Alexis de Tocqueville, liberal critic of the Guizot government, commented:

> It is said that there is no danger because there is no riot, and that because there is no visible disorder on the surface of society, we are far from revolution. Gentlemen, allow me to say that I think you are mistaken. True, there is no actual disorder, but disorder has penetrated far into men's minds... Do you not see that opinions and ideas are gradually spread among them and tend not simply to overthrow such and such laws, such and such a minister, or even such and such a government, but rather to the overthrow of society, breaking down the bases on which it now rests. (de Tocqueville, 1971)

9 Should I Grow a Beard? Lady Revolutionaries 1848

Figure D.2 'Should I grow a beard?' Drawn by de E. de Beaumont and appeared in the series *Les Vésuviennes* in *Le Charivari* cartoon newspaper on 7 June 1848.

10 Jeanne Deroin

Jeanne Deroin (1805–1894) was a virtually self-educated needleworker and feminist socialist who, in 1848, was the first to demand votes for women. In 1831 she joined the Saint-Simonians, writing a 44 page *profession du foi*. 'L'éducation de la femme est dirigée de manière à comprimer toutes ses facultés morales, intellectuelles. On veut la persuader qu'elle est inférieure à l'homme, et l'on s'efforce de réaliser autant que possible cette odieuse supposition'. Contemporary marriage consecrated the inferior status of women. Marriage was, she said, a continual conflict between one partner who tried to dominate by his physical strength, the other by her craftiness. 'Most marriages are based on the chance whim of love. Genuine sympathy, respect and equality are absent. It is vain for the law to assert that marriage is indissoluble, a marriage has failed almost as soon as it is made... Indissoluble unions bind the couple in an oppressive chain, humiliating for the wife. A slave can at least hope for freedom. A wife finds deliverance only in death'.

She joined a small group of former Saint-Simonian working women to run a women's newspaper, *Femme Libre* (1832–1834). One of her contributions, 'The Woman of the Future', hoped 'The time is arrived when woman shall find *her* place, her acknowledged, her useful and *dignified* place upon it [earth]... This... we can effect, both on condition of forming ourselves into *one solid union*. Let us no longer form two camps – that of the women of the people, and that of the women of the privileged class'.

In 1848 Deroin joined other former Saint-Simonian women to run *La Voix des Femmes*. She tried to stand for parliament in 1849 and ran her own newspaper, *L'Opinion des Femmes*. She ran a workers' association, and was prosecuted and imprisoned for trying to overthrow the government. When released she left for London where she spent the rest of her life, joining William Morris's *Socialist League*.

(Source: Pilbeam, 2003, 275–294)

11 Louis-Napoleon's Coup 1851 As Seen By *Punch*

Figure D.3 'All But Hatched! It was evident that the restoration of the Empire in France was only the work of time. *Vive l'Empereur* was heard at every ceremonial in which the president took part'. Louis-Napoleon is about to be accepted as Emperor in a plebiscite. Cartoon from *Punch*, October 16, 1852.

12 Demolition work in Paris in the late 1860s

Demolition work in Paris in the late 1860s

Figure D.4 Demolition work in Paris in the late 1860s.

13 Demands for change 1867

We would like to be able to organize our work in a fashion that did not reduce us to human machines... in addition we should be considered not as minors but as men, and to achieve this it is necessary to break the bonds which encircle us and [recognize] our Rights... Our duty... is without cease to reclaim the lost Liberties and to show that we are always ready to affirm the principles of 89, which every Frenchman has the right to demand. It is in virtue of these principles that we demand:

1. The right... to hold Meetings, a natural and incontestable right, which no power can rob us of.
2. Free and obligatory instruction, the foundation of a people's greatness.

3. Abolition of the *livret* (internal passport), a survival of slavery, a stigmata for the worker [which] simply serves to place him under police surveillance. The most insignificant employer does not have a *livret*, it is then in contradiction of equality between men.
4. The Right of Association.

Exposition Universel de 1867. Report of delegates of brushmakers.
(Source: Price, 2015, 138)

14 Artillery Park on the Butte Montmartre, March 1871

Figure D.5 Artillery Park on the Butte Montmartre March 1871.

15 Louise Michel

Learning that the Versailles soldiers were trying to seize the cannon, men and women of Montmartre swarmed up the Butte in a surprise maneuver. Those people who were climbing believed they would die, but they were prepared to pay the price.

The Butte of Montmartre was bathed in the first light of day, through which things were glimpsed as if they were hidden behind a thin veil of water. Gradually the crowd increased. The other districts of Paris, hearing of the events taking place on the Butte of Montmartre, came to our assistance.

The women of Paris covered the cannon with their bodies. When their officers ordered the soldiers to fire, the men refused. The same army that would be used to crush Paris two months later decided now that it did not want to be an accomplice of the reaction. They gave up their attempt to seize the cannon from the National Guard. They understood that the people were defending the Republic by defending the arms that the royalists and imperialists would have turned on Paris in agreement with the Prussians. When we had won our victory, I looked around and noticed my poor mother, who had followed me to the Butte of Montmartre, believing that I was going to die.

On this day, the eighteenth of March, the people wakened. If they had not, it would have been the triumph of some king; instead it was a triumph of the people. The eighteenth of March could have belonged to the allies of kings, or to foreigners, or to the people. It was the people's.

(Source: Michel, 1891, 64)

16 Goncourt Journal

Sunday, March 19

...A red flag on the Hôtel de Ville tower; below, the rumble of an armed populace behind three cannons

As I return, on people's faces I see flustered indifference, sometimes sad irony, most often consternation, which causes old gentlemen to raise despairing arms to the sky, though they speak in low voices and look prudently around them.

Monday, March 20

Three in the morning. I am awakened by the alarm bell, the lugubrious tolling that I heard in the nights of June 1848. The deep plaintive lamentation of the great bell at Notre Dame rises over the sounds of all the bells in the city, giving the dominant note to the general alarm, then is submerged by human shouts, which seem to me to be a call to arms.

What a reversal of all human expectation! And how God seems to laugh in his great white beard of an aged sceptic and to make sport of our feats of logic here below! How does it happen that the battalions from Belleville, so craven before the enemy, so craven before the battalions of order on October 31, have been able to take control of Paris today? How is it that the middle-class National Guard, which was so determined to fight a few days ago, has melted away without firing a shot? These days everything seems to happen pat to show the nothingness of human wisdom and experience. The consequences of events and things are a lie! in short, for the moment France and Paris are under the control of workmen'...

(Source: Goncourt, 1969, 231)

17 Commune

Paris, the central seat of the old governmental power, and, at the same time, the social stronghold of the French working class, had risen in arms against the attempt of Thiers and the Rurals to restore and perpetuate that old governmental power bequeathed to them by the empire. Paris could resist only because, in consequence of the siege, it had got rid of the army, and replaced it by a National Guard, the bulk of which consisted of working men. This fact was now to be transformed into an institution. The first decree of the Commune, therefore, was the suppression of the standing army, and the substitution for it of the armed people.

The Commune was formed of the municipal councillors, chosen by universal suffrage in the various wards of the town, responsible and revocable at short terms. The majority of its members were naturally working men, or acknowledged representatives of the working class. The Commune was to be a working, not a parliamentary body, executive and legislative at the same time.

(Source: Marx, n.d.)

18 Commune Appeal to Women

Appeal to the Women Citizens of Paris

Paris is blockaded, Paris is bombarded... *Citoyennes*, where are our children, our brothers and our husbands? ... Do you hear the cannon rumbling and the tocsin ringing the sacred alarm?

To arms! The Fatherland is in danger! ... Is it the foreigner returning to invade France? Is it the combined legions of the tyrants of Europe who are massacring our brothers, hoping to destroy with the great City the very memory of the immortal conquests that for a century we have been buying with our blood, and which the world calls Liberty, Equality, Fraternity? ...

No, these enemies, these assassins of the people and of Liberty are Frenchmen! ...

This fratricidal vertigo that has seized hold of France, this fight to the death is the final act of the eternal antagonism of Right against Might, of Work against Exploitation, of the People against its Executioners! ... Our enemies are the privileged of the present social order, all those who have always lived off our sweat, those who have always fattened off our wretchedness...

They have seen the people rise up crying: 'No duties without rights, no rights without duties! ... We want work, but in order to keep its product... No more exploiters, no more masters! ... Work is the welfare of all, the government of the people by itself, the Commune means to live free by working or to die fighting!' ...

The fear of seeing themselves called before the tribunal of the people has pushed our enemies into committing the greatest of crimes, civil war!

Citoyennes of Paris, descendants of the women of the great Revolution who, in the name of the people and of justice, marched on Versailles and brought Louis XVI back captive, we, mothers, wives, sisters of the French people, shall we endure any longer that misery and ignorance turn our children into enemies, so that father against son, brother against brother, they come to kill each other under our very eyes according to the whim of our oppressors, who want the destruction of Paris after having sold it to the foreigner!

Citoyennes, the decisive hour has come. The old world must be ended! We want to be free! And it is not only France that has risen, all civilized people have their eyes on Paris, awaiting our triumph so that they can in their turn liberate themselves. Even Germany, whose princely armies were devastating our Fatherland, swearing death to democratic and socialist tendencies, she herself is shaken and moved by the breath of Revolution! Thus, for six months she has been under martial law, and her workers' representatives are in jail! Even Russia is only watching the defenders of liberty perish so that she can salute a new generation, in its turn ready to fight and die for the Republic and for social change!

Ireland, Poland, who are dying only to be reborn with a new energy; Spain and Italy, who are regaining their lost vigour so as to be able to join the international struggle of peoples; England, whose entire proletarian and wage-earning mass is becoming revolutionary due to its very social position; Austria, whose government has to repress simultaneous revolts inside the country itself and against the Slav regimes; is not this perpetual shock between the governing classes and the people a sign that the Tree of Liberty, watered by torrents of blood shed over the centuries, has at least borne fruit?

Citoyennes, the gauntlet has been thrown down, we must conquer or perish! The mothers and wives who say 'What do I care about the triumph of our cause, if I have to lose those I love!', let them realize finally that the only way of saving those who are dear to them – the husband who supports her, the child in whom she puts her hope – is to take an active part in the struggle, so as to end once and for all this fratricidal struggle, which can only be ended if the people triumph, for otherwise it will soon have to start again!

Woe to mothers if once again the people succumb! It will be their children who will pay for the price of defeat, because the heads of our brothers and husbands are at stake, and Reaction will have free rein! … As for clemency, neither we nor our enemies want it!

Citoyennes, all resolved, all united, let us look to the security of our cause! Let us prepare to defend and to avenge our brothers! At the gates of Paris, on the barricades, in the *faubourgs*, no matter! Let us be ready when the time comes to join our efforts to theirs; if the infamous men who shoot prisoners, who murder our leaders, mow down a crowd of unarmed women, so much the better! The cry of horror and indignation from France and the world would destroy those who had attempted it! ... And if the guns and bayonets are all being used by our brothers, we shall still have the paving stones to crush the traitors...

A group of *citoyennes*.

[From *Journal Officiel* of the Commune, 11 April]

(Source: Tombs, 1999, 224–226)

19 Alexis de Tocqueville on Algeria

I came back from Africa with the pathetic notion that at present in our way of waging war we are far more barbaric than the Arabs themselves. These days, they represent civilization, we do not. This way of waging war seems to me as stupid as it is cruel. It can only be found in the head of a coarse and brutal soldier. Indeed, it was pointless to replace the Turks only to reproduce what the world rightly found so hateful in them. This, even for the sake of interest is more noxious than useful; for, as another officer was telling me, if our sole aim is to equal the Turks, in fact we shall be in a far lower position than theirs: barbarians for barbarians, the Turks will always outdo us because they are Muslim barbarians. In France, I have often heard men I respect but do not approve of, deplore that crops should be burnt and granaries emptied and finally that unarmed men, women and children should be seized. In my view these are unfortunate circumstances that any people wishing to wage war against the Arabs must accept. I think that all the means available to wreck tribes must be used, barring those that the human kind and the right of nations condemn. I personally believe that the laws of war enable us to ravage the country and that we must do so either by destroying the crops at harvest time or any time by making fast forays also known as raids the aim of which is to get hold of men or flocks'.

(Tocqueville, 1991, 704–705)

20 Colonisation – Kanak Warriors, New Caledonia

Figure D.6 Two Kanak (Canaque) warriors posing with penis gourds and spears, New Caledonia. The History Collection/Alamy Stock Photo.

21 Colonisation – Impact on Indigenous People, Algeria

The expropriation of land forced huge numbers of Algerians to endure abject living conditions as the country became the tale of two economies siting side by side. On the one side were the rich settlers whose huge enterprises comprising some 2,350,000 hectares of the best land and using the latest agricultural techniques, producing wine and food for export; on the other hand the Algerian peasantry who were forced to maintain a subsistence agriculture based on archaic methods.

(Source: Evans and Phillips, 2007, 38)

22 What Did Imperialism Signify?

Paul Leroy-Beaulieu, in the late nineteenth century considered the main French expert on the colonisation of modern peoples, wrote:

> a great part of the world is inhabited by barbarian tribes or savages, some given over to wars without end and to brutal customs, and others knowing so little of the arts and being so little accustomed to work and to invention that they do not know how to exploit their land and its natural riches... This state of the world implies for the civilized people a right of intervention... In the affairs of the peoples of the last two categories... It is neither natural nor just for the civilized people of the West to be cooped up indefinitely and jammed into the restricted spaces which were their first home. Nor is it natural and just that they there accumulate the marvels of science, the arts and civilization, that they see the rate of interest fall more each day for lack of good investment. European capitalists – and by this word we mean not only a banker, but every person putting aside a little money, a modest employee, a peasant, a worker, a spinster or a widow – can work effectively at colonization, the exploitation of the globe, without leaving their firesides.
>
> (Source: Leroy-Beaulieu, 1891)

Jules Ferry (1832–1893) PM and legislation on compulsory lay primary education.

Speech on French Colonial Expansion, Chamber of Deputies, 1884.

The policy of colonial expansion is a political and economic system... that can be connected to three sets of ideas: economic ideas; the most far-reaching ideas of civilization; and ideas of a political and patriotic sort... In the area of economics, I am placing before you, with the support of some statistics, the considerations that justify the policy of colonial expansion, as seen from the perspective of a need, felt more and more urgently by the industrialized population of Europe and especially the people of our rich and hardworking country of France: the need for outlets [for exports]... the superior races have a right because they have a duty. They have the duty to civilize the inferior races... I say that French colonial policy, the policy of colonial expansion, the policy that has taken us... to Saigon, to Indochina [Vietnam], that has led us to Tunisia, to Madagascar – I say that this policy of colonial expansion was inspired by... the fact that a navy such as ours cannot do without safe harbors, defenses, supply centers on the high seas.

(Source: Tocqueville, 1991, 704–705)

Glossary

Acte Additionnel Supposedly an amendment to Imperial constitutional decrees issued by Napoleon, 1815, advised by Benjamin Constant.

Aide-toi, le ciel t'aidera A liberal electoral association founded by François Guizot, 1827.

ancien regime The period before 1789.

Assembly of Notables Senior nobles and clergy assembled on the order of the King, 1787.

assignats Bonds issued by the government for the sale of nationalised Church lands.

Banquet campaign Launched July 1847 to run meetings urging electoral reform.

biens nationaux Church and *émigré* property sold by the state.

Chambre des deputes From 1814, elected lower house of parliament.

Chambre des pairs From 1814, upper house of parliament appointed by the king. Inherited right up to 1831; after 1831 nominated for life only.

chouans Royalist supporters, usually in western France, in the 1790s.

Dechristianisation Shutting churches, supporting the idea of replacing God with the Supreme Being, especially 1793–1794.

Estates-General Representatives of the Three Orders, elected and met May 1789.

First Estate The clergy.

gabelle Salt tax.

Hôtel de Ville Where the municipal council met.

National Guard Civic militia – started July 1789. Shut down 1827–1830. Revived after July Revolution 1830. Abolished 1872. Revived 2016. Always considered radical.

Parlements Before 1789, 13 appeal courts, also had administrative powers.

Parlementaires Magistrate members of *parlements*. They bought and inherited their office.

Philosophes Before 1789, enlightened writers and publicists.

Procureur-général Attorney general in new legal system after 1789. Appointed by Minister of Justice.

Sans culottes Militants in Paris Sections in the 1790s. Usually artisans.
Taille Direct tax up to 1789. Not usually paid by First and Second Estates.
Thermidor Coup against Robespierre 1794.
Third Estate Up to 1789, everyone who wasn't noble or cleric.
Vendée Heart of royalist rebellion, western France.
Provincial Estates Before 1789, local representative bodies which had the right to consent to taxation.
Pays d'état Before 1789, provinces run by provincial estates.

Guide to Further Reading

Agulhon, M. *1848 ou l'apprentissage de la république* (1973) (trs, *The Republican Experiment*, 1983).

Agulhon, M. *La république au village: Les populations du Var de la Révolution à la II èmeRépublique* (1979) (trs, *The Republic in the Village: The People of the Var from the French Revolution to the Second Republic*, 1982).

Agulhon, M. *Marianne into Battle: Republican Imagery and Symbolism in France, 1789–1880* (1981).

Andress, D. *The Terror: The Merciless War for Freedom in Revolutionary France* (2006).

Aprile, S., Caron, J-C. and Emmanuel, Fureix E. *La Liberté guidant les peoples. Les revolutions de 1830 en Europe* (2013).

Beard, J.R. *Toussaint Louverture: Biography and Autobiography* (1863).

Biard, Michel and Linton, Marisa. *Terror: The French Revolution and Its Demons* (2021).

Blackburn, R. *The Overthrow of Colonial Slavery, 1776–1848* (1988).

Blanc, J.J.L. *Révolution Française. Histoire de Dix Ans*, 5 vols (1841–1844).

Blanqui, L.A. *Oeuvres I. Des origines à la Révolution de 1848* (ed. D. Le Nuz, 1993).

Brown, Howard. *Mass Violence and the Self from the French Wars of Religion to the Paris Commune* (2018).

Buonarroti, P. *Conspiration pour l'Egalité dite de Babeuf, suivie du process auquel elle donna lieu*, 2 vols (1828).

Campbell, Peter R., Kaiser, Thomas E., and Linton, Marisa (eds). *Conspiracy in the French Revolution* (2007).

Caron, Jean-Claude. *Frères de Sang. La Guerre Civile en France au XIXe siècle* (2009).

Caron, Jean-Claude (dir.). *Paris, l'insurrection capitale* (2014).

Censer, J.R. and Hunt, L. *Liberty, Equality and Fraternity: Exploring the French Revolution* (2001).

Chaudonneret, M-C. *La Figure de la République. Le concours de 1848* (1987).

Clarke, J. *Commemorating the Dead in Revolutionary France: Revolution and Remembrance, 1789–1799* (2007).

Cobban, A. *In Search of Humanity: The Role of the Enlightenment in Modern History* (1960).

Cobban, A. *The Social Interpretation of the French Revolution* (1964).

Cobban, A. *Le Sens de la Révolution* (trs. 1984, French introduction by Le Roy Ladurie).

Cobban, A. 'Local government during the French Revolution', *English Historical Review*, 58(229), 1943, 13–31).
Cooper, H.M. 'French exploration in South Australia: With special reference to Encounter Bay, Kangaroo Island, the two gulfs and Murat Bay 1802–1803', *South Australian Geographical Journal*, 99, (2000), 10–15.
Corbin, A. *Archaisme et modernité en Limousin au XIXe siècle, 1845–1880*, 2 vols (1975).
Crook, M. (ed.). *Revolutionary France 1780–1880* (2001).
Crook, M. *Toulon in War and Revolution: From the Ancien Régime to the Restoration, 1750–1820* (1991).
Darnton, Robert. *What Was Revolutionary about the French Revolution?* (1999).
Deluermoz, Quentin (ed.). *D'ici d'ailleurs: Histoires globales de la France contemporaine* (2021).
Deluermoz, Quentin (ed.). *Commune(s) 1870–1871: Une traversée des mondes au XIXe siècle* (2020).
Deluermoz, Quentin (ed.). *Le crépuscule des révolutions 1848–1871* (2012).
Duval, G-L. (ed.). *Souvenirs de la Terreur de 1788 à 1793* (1841).
Eichner, Carolyn Jeanne (ed.). *Surmounting the Barricades: Women in the Paris Commune* (2004).
Eichner, Carolyn Jeanne (ed.). *The Paris Commune: A Brief History* (2022).
Evans, M. and Phillips, J. (ed.). *Algeria: Anger of the Dispossessed* (2007).
Fick, C. 'The French Revolution in Saint-Domingue: A triumph or a failure?', in D.B. Gaspar, D.P. Geggus and C.A. Clegg (eds), *A Turbulent Time: The French Revolution and the Greater Caribbean* (1997).
Flaubert, G. *Sentimental Education* (1869).
Forrest, A. 'Issues of slavery and the slave trade in the politics of the early French revolution', *H-France Salon*, 11, 2019, 1.
Forsdick, Charles and Høgsbjerg, Christian (eds). *The Black Jacobins Reader* (2017).
Forsdick, Charles and Høgsbjerg, Christian (eds). *Toussaint Louverture: A Black Jacobin in the Age of Revolutions* (2017).
Forster, R. 'The French Revolution, people of color and slavery', in J. Klaits and M. Haltzel (eds), *The Global Ramifications of the French Revolution* (1994).
Fureix, Emmanuel. *La France des Larmes. Deuils politiques à l'âge romantique (1814–1840)* (2009).
Furet, F. *Revolutionary France 1770–1870* (1995).
Furet, F. and Ozouf, M. *The French Revolution and the Creation of Modern Political Culture*, Vol 3: *1789–1848* (1990).
Garrioch, D. 'Becoming revolutionary on the streets of Paris', *H-France Salon*, 11, 2019, 1–13.
Geggus, D. 'The Haitian Revolution', in F.W. Knight and C.A. Palmer (eds), *The Modern Caribbean* (1989).
Gildea, R. *Children of the Revolution: The French 1799–1914* (2008).
Goncourt, E. de. 'Paris under Siege, 1870–1', in the *Goncourt Journal*, ed. G.J. Becker (1969).
Gooch, B.D. (ed.). *Napoleonic Ideas: Napoleon III – Des Idées Napoléoniennes par le Prince Napoléon-Louis Bonaparte 1839* (1967).
Gough, H. 'France and the memory of revolution: 1789–1989', *History of European Ideas*, 15(4–6), 1992, 811–816.
Goujon, Bertrand. *Monarchies postrévolutionnaires 1814–1848* (2012).

Greer, D.M. *Incidence of the Terror during the French Revolution* (1935).
Harsin, J. *The War of the Streets in Revolutionary Paris, 1830–1848* (2002).
Hazareesingh, S. *The Legend of Napoleon* (2004).
Hazareesingh, S. *The Saint-Napoleon: Celebrations of Sovereignty in Nineteenth-Century France* (2004).
Hazareesingh, S. *Black Spartacus: The Epic Life of Toussaint Louverture* (2020).
Hinckner, Peter Louis. *Citoyens-combattants à Paris, 1848–1851* (2008).
Hugo, V. *Les Misérables* (trs. Penguin, 1982).
Hunt, Lynn. *The Family Romance of the French Revolution* (1992).
James, C.L.R. *The Black Jacobins: Toussaint L'Ouverture and the San Domingo Revolution* (1938, 1963).
Jennings, L.C. *French Anti-Slavery: The Movement for the Abolition of Slavery in France 1802–1848* (2000).
Jones, C. *The Fall of Robespierre: 24 Hours in Revolutionary Paris* (2021).
Jones, P.M. *The French Revolution 1787–1804* (2003).
Kerr, D. *Caricature and French Political Culture 1830–1848* (2000).
Laponneraye, A. *Cours public d'histoire de France de 1789 à 1830, reprinted in Les Révolutions du XIX siècle*, Vol. 1 (1974).
Las Casas, Comte Emmanuel de, *Memorial de Sainte Hélène: Journal of the Private Life and Conversations of the Emperor Napoleon at Saint-Helena* (1823, trs. 4 vols. 1835).
Leroy-Beaulieu, Paul. *De la colonisation chez les peuples modernes*, 4th edition (1891).
Lignereux, Aurélien, *L'Empire des Français 1799–1814* (2012).
Linton, Marisa. *Choosing Terror: Virtue, Friendship and Authenticity in the French Revolution* (2013).
Linton, Marisa. 'The power of emotions: New light on the *Conventionnels* and the process of the Terror', *H-France Salon*, 11, 2019.
Lusebrink, H.J. and Reichardt, R. *The Bastille: A History of a Symbol of Despotism and Freedom* (trs N. Schurer, 1997).
McPhee, P. *The Politics of Rural Life: Political Mobilization in the French Countryside 1846–52* (1992).
McPhee, P. *The French Revolution 1789–1799* (2002).
McPhee, P. *Liberty or Death: The French Revolution* (2016).
Margadant, T.W. *French Peasants in Revolt: The Insurrection of 1851* (1979).
Marrinan, M. *Romantic Paris. Histories of a Cultural Landscape 1800–1850* (2009).
Marshall, B. *The French Atlantic: Travels in Culture and History* (2009).
Marx, K. *Class Struggles in France*, in K. Marx and F. Engels, *Selected Works* (1968).
Marx, K 'The civil war in France', in *Karl Marx: The First International and After – Political Writings*, Vol. 3 (ed. D. Fernbach).
Mazauric, C. *Babeuf* (1988).
Michel, L. *The Red Virgin: Memoirs* (1891) (ed. and trans. by Bullitt Lowry and Elizabeth Ellington Gunter, 1981).
Michelet, J. *The People* (1846; trs. J.P. McKay, 1973).
Napoleon-Louis, *Napoleonic Ideas* (1840).
Nora, P. and Kritzman, Lawrence D. *Realms of Memory: Rethinking the French Past* (1996).
O'Brien, L. *The Republican Line: Caricature and French Republican Identity 1830–52* (2015).

Pilbeam, P.M. 'The insurrectionary tradition in France 1835–48', *Modern and Contemporary France*, 3, 1993, 253–264.
Pilbeam, P.M. *Republicanism in Nineteenth-Century France* (1995).
Pilbeam, P.M. *French Socialists Before Marx: Workers, Women and the Social Question in France* (2000).
Pilbeam, P.M. 'Jeanne Deroin, feminist, socialist exile', in S. Freitag (ed.), *Exiles from European Revolutions: Refugees in Mid-Victorian England* (2003).
Pilbeam, P.M. *Saint-Simonians in Nineteenth-Century France* (2014).
Pilbeam, P.M. (ed.). *The 1830 Revolution in France* (2014).
Price, M. *The Perilous Crown. France between Revolutions 1814–1848* (2007).
Price, Roger (ed.). *Documents on the Second French Empire, 1852–1870* (2015).
Reddy, William. *The Navigation of Feeling: A Framework for the History of the Emotions* (2001).
Ross, K. *Fast Cars, Clean Bodies: Decolonization and the Reordering of French Culture* (1995).
Serna, Pierre. 'La révolution des droits des êtres vivants 1789–1802, Université Paris 1 – Panthéon-Sorbonne, Institut Universitaire de France. La proposition de débat se construit
autour de trois dates, 1789–1794–1802'. *H-France Salon*, 11, 2019.
Sessions, J.E. *By Sword and Plow: France and the Conquest of Algeria* (2011).
Sewell, William. *Work and Revolution in France. The Language of Labor from the Old Regime to 1848* (1980, with numerous reprints).
Shafer, David. *The Paris Commune* (2005).
Sieyès, E.J. *Political Writings* (ed. and trs Michael Sonenscher, 2003).
Smyth, J. *Robespierre and the Festival of the Supreme Being: The Search for a Republican Morality* (2016).
Spang, Rebecca L. *Stuff and Money in the Time of the French Revolution* (2015).
Sutherland, D.M.G. *The French Revolution and Empire* (2003).
Sutherland, D.M.G. *Murder in Aubagne: Lynching, Law, and Justice during the French Revolution* (2009).
Tackett, Timothy. 'Conspiracy obsession in a time of revolution: French elites and the origins of the Terror, 1789–1792', *American Historical Review*, 105, 2000, 691–713.
Tackett, Timothy. *When the King Took Flight* (2003).
Tackett, Timothy. 'Collective panics in the early French Revolution, 1789–1791: A comparative perspective', *French History*, 17, 2003, 149–171.
Tackett, Timothy. *The Coming of the Terror in the French Revolution* (2015).
Tackett, Timothy. *The Glory and the Sorrow: A Parisian and His World in the Age of the French Revolution* (2021).
Tilly, C. and Lees, L. 'Le peuple de Juin 1848', *Annales: Economies, Sociétés, Civilisations*, 1974, 1061–1091.
Tindall, Gillian. *The Journey of Martin Nadaud* (1999).
Tocqueville, A. de. *Souvenirs* (trs. G. Lawrence, 1971).
Tocqueville, A. de, *Travail sur l'Algérie*, in *Œuvres complètes* (1991).
Todd, D. *A Velvet Empire: French Informal Imperialism in the Nineteenth Century* (2021).
Tombs, R. *The Paris Commune 1871* (1999).
Traugott, M. *Armies of the Poor: Determinants of Working Class Participation in the Parisian Insurrection, June 1848* (1985).

Traugott, M. *The Insurgent Barricade* (2010).
Traugott, M. 'The crowd in the February Revolution 1848', *American Historical Review*, 93, 1988, 683–652.
Varley, K. *Under the Shadow of Defeat: The War of 1870–71 in French Memory* (2008).
Wahnich, Sophie. *La liberté ou la mort, essai sur la Terreur et le terrorisme* (2003).
Walloon, H.A. *Tribunal révolutionnaire* (1880).

Index

Printed in Great Britain
by Amazon